11-19-99

Inside Relational Databases
with examples in Access

Springer
London
Berlin
Heidelberg
New York
Barcelona
Budapest
Hong Kong
Milan
Paris
Santa Clara
Singapore
Tokyo

Mark Whitehorn and Bill Marklyn

Inside
Relational
Databases

with examples in Access

Springer

Mark Whitehorn
Information Technology Services, University of Dundee,
Dundee DD1 4HN, UK

Bill Marklyn
Ocean Park Software Corporation
2332 E Aloha Street, Seattle, WA 98112, USA

ISBN 3-540-76092-X Springer-Verlag Berlin Heidelberg New York

British Library Cataloguing in Publication Data
Whitehorn, Mark
  Inside relational databases : with examples in Access
  1.Access (Computer file)   2.Relational databases
  I.Title   II. Marklyn, Bill
  005.7'56
ISBN 354076092X

Library of Congress Cataloging-in-Publication Data
Whitehorn, Mark
    Inside relational databases : with examples in Access / Mark
  Whitehorn and Bill Marklyn.
      p.   cm.
    Includes index.
    ISBN 3-540-76092-X   (pbk. : alk. paper)
      1. Relational databases.   2.Access (Computer file)   I. Marklyn,
  Bill, 1960-   .
  QA76.9.D3W484   1997   97-29241
  005.75'6- -dc21   CIP

© Springer-Verlag London Limited 1998
Printed in Great Britain
2nd printing 1998
3rd printing 1998

Typesetting: Ian Kingston Editorial Services, Nottingham
Printed and bound at the Athenæum Press Ltd., Gateshead, Tyne and Wear

34/3830-5432 Printed on acid-free paper

Contents

Part 3 Multi-Table Multi-User Databases 129

Part 4 Related Database Topics 139

Preface

This book has two authors: me (Mark Whitehorn) and Bill Marklyn. I (Mark) penned most of the words, and whenever the pronoun 'I' appears in the text, I accept full responsibility. So what is Bill doing there on the front cover? Well, writing down the words in a book is only one component. Books also need ideas and enthusiasm. I may have written the words, but Bill, more than anyone else, fired my enthusiasm for databases, provided his own inexhaustible enthusiasm and many of the ideas. I couldn't have written it without him, and he would probably not have found the time to write it himself, so it is truly a joint venture.

We were undeservedly lucky in our choice of reviewers and proofreaders; friends whom we managed to coerce into reading and correcting the manuscript.

Top of the list has to be Mary Whitehorn, a talented writer in her own right and not unrelated to one of the authors; she put in so much work she nearly qualified as another author. The rest, in alphabetical order, are:

- ◆ Helen Arthan
- ◆ Mark Burton
- ◆ Stephen Elwell-Sutton
- ◆ Adrian Larner

They deserve praise, not just because they were so helpful and amiable, but because their comments were often humorous and always cogent and helpful. (Some of the better ones are included in the text.)

I (Mark) also acknowledge a huge debt to Professor John Parker. He was my PhD supervisor many years ago and is currently the Director of the Cambridge Botanic Gardens. Whatever communication skills I have acquired came directly from sitting at the feet of a master of the art.

1

Introduction

Chapter 1 of Sir Henry Birkin's autobiography 'Full Throttle', published in 1932, ends with the following: 'I can waste no more time on this matter; for the end is reached of what I now confess to have been 24 pages of deceit. I have disguised under the designation of Chapter One what was really nothing more than an introduction; but I know quite well, that had I been honest and called it an introduction, nobody would have read it'.

If Henry Birkin wasn't my hero for racing two-ton motor cars on appalling road surfaces at speeds well in excess of 100 m.p.h., he would be my hero for sheer literary nerve.

In current nineties style, I'll be less disingenuous. This chapter *is* an introduction. It defines the very basic terms that you may need like 'database', 'relational', 'DBMS' and 'RDBMS'. It tells you why the book was written, at whom it is aimed, and how it is organized.

If you know all of this already, or it sounds tedious and you really want to get down to the nitty gritty, please don't bother reading this chapter; dive straight into the book at Chapter 2 or wherever you fancy. As far as I'm concerned, anyone who has paid me the considerable compliment of actually exchanging money for my words is entitled to read them as they please.

1.1 What Is a Database?

A database is simply a collection of data. Nowadays the term tends to be used about computerized systems, but the old cards which were used to classify and locate books in a library are a good example of a non-computerized database. The difference that computers have made to databases is deceptively simple: computers make access to the data faster. That means, on a trivial level, that instead of hunting through 50,000 pieces of cardboard in a dusty room for three days, a computer will do the same job in under a second. However, there is more to this speed than meets the eye.

Suppose I asked you to find me the names and addresses of all male hospital patients in the country who are over 60 years old, have a history of diabetes in the family, and have two children. Given a local, paper-based system, the question is unanswerable in any meaningful way. By the time you have traveled around the country and searched all the available records, most of said patients would be dead. With centralized, computerized patient records, this question should be answerable in minutes, or at worst a few hours. So computerizing databases hasn't simply speeded them up, it has opened up whole new ways of looking at data that simply weren't possible before.

And databases are becoming ever more pervasive. If you book a seat on a plane or train then someone, somewhere, is using a database. A bank account is nothing more than a complex database; credit cards, your appointment with the doctor – all are likely to be entered into a database.

1.2 Databases vs. Database Management Systems

One important distinction which should be made early on in this book is the difference between a database and the software which is used to control and manipulate that database. A database is a collection of data – perhaps a list of your customers, their addresses, fax numbers and so on. In order to keep the data in your database under control, you need software known as a DBMS (DataBase Management System). The DBMS is to a database what a word processor is to a letter. The former is the controlling software, the latter the data that it manipulates.

1.3 Relational Database Management Systems

There are several fundamentally different ways in which data can be handled or modeled – Hierarchical, Network and Relational are three such models. Without doubt the most widely used is the relational model, the brainchild of Dr Edgar Codd.

Codd is often described as 'the Father of the Relational Database' (with obligatory upper-case letters), and this is perfectly fair since he came up with the original idea and spent many happy years refining it. However, Codd has a truly wicked way with words. As a sampler, try to make sense of this:

> Note that a view is theoretically updatable if there exists a time-independent algorithm for unambiguously determining a single series of changes to the base relations that will have as their effect precisely the requested changes in the view.

I have the very greatest respect for Dr Codd, but I have to work very hard to understand anything he writes.

Chris Date was at one time a co-worker of Codd's and has, in my opinion, done far more to explain, popularize and generally advance the use and understanding of the relational model. He ranks along with Henry Birkin as another of my heroes.

So, why do you need to know anything about Codd and Date? Well, the world of databases is crowded with people who will try to impress you with their knowledge (which makes it exactly the same as every other branch of life). If you don't know these two names you can be seriously out-bluffed.

For example, in 1985 Codd published a set of rules which defined the concept of a relational DBMS at that time. These rules have subsequently become enshrined in database lore and are constantly referred to in conversation – for example, 'You can't do that, it contravenes Codd's 7th rule!'. Experience suggests that very few people have actually gone back to the source material (*Computerworld*, 14–21 October 1985) and read them, so simply knowing who Ted Codd is and that he has a set of rules somewhere should be enough information to allow you to argue on even terms. However, if you want to know more about these rules, read Chapter 21, which lists and defines them all in (hopefully) understandable terms.

As an aside, there is nothing to stop you from playing the same game. If you find that you are being out-bluffed, you can try 'Well, of course, when Chris contacted me about this last week he said that... [fill in appropriate supporting statement]'. It will be up to you to decide if you can get away with this one and also whether you dare substitute 'Ted' for 'Chris'.

Whatever the personalities involved, any DBMSs you use are likely to based on the relational model. Such DBMSs are, perfectly sensibly, known as RDBMSs (Relational DataBase Management Systems).

1.4 Why This Book?

One of the main aims of this book is to demystify the relational database model. I have come to believe that it is an excellent way of handling information, but I am unhappy about the way it is often presented. This book attempts to introduce the concepts and ideas behind the relational model without the usual jargon. By doing so, I hope to make the relational model accessible to more people.

A fair question at this point is 'Why should anyone want to know about the relational model?'. The answer to that lies in a major sea-change that has taken place among the people who are building databases.

In the dim and distant past (say, about ten years ago) computerized databases were so difficult to construct that they were only worth building for complex projects, and the only people who could build them were 'database professionals'. These people were usually well trained so they had a good grounding in relational database theory and they also knew how to use the particular RDBMS on their system. This was just as well because the RDBMS software of ten years ago was about as user-friendly as a pit of pythons.

This rather sorry state of affairs has been transformed in the interim by the arrival of RDBMSs such as Access, which make databases almost infinitely easier to construct.

The release of such tools has, in turn, made a dramatic difference to the threshold at which it becomes worth computerizing a database. It is now not only possible, but perfectly sensible, to use a database to store relatively simple data, such as customer lists, product lists or even the birthdays of your friends.

Equally importantly, the type of person who is called upon (or who volunteers) to build a database has changed out of all recognition. Since the tools necessary to construct databases are now being bundled with the so-called 'Office' suites for personal computers, databases are being built by, if you'll pardon the expression, 'normal' people rather than database professionals. The number of normal people constructing databases now, in my estimation, far exceeds the number of professionals engaged in the same work.

This has become clear from the feedback I get from readers of *Personal Computer World* (*PCW*). I've been writing about databases for the last ten years and have been writing the database column in *PCW* for the past four. Over that time I have seen a remarkable change in the feedback I receive from the readers. In the early days, most questions came from database professionals who asked relatively detailed questions about how to perform a particular task. For example, there is a feature peculiar to databases called 'referential integrity'. The database professional would know that it was necessary to enforce this referential integrity and would ask how it could be enforced given a particular RDBMS.

Nowadays the questions are almost exclusively from people who are not employed directly to develop databases; such work has simply become a part of their job. They often ask deceptively simple questions. For example, they might discover that their databases are not giving the correct answers and ask 'Why doesn't my database work?'. In any given case the answer might be 'Because you haven't enforced referential integrity', which is a very unhelpful answer to someone who hasn't heard of referential integrity. So the answer has to contain a large element of background information to be of any use. The good news is that products like Access have made the process of actually enforcing referential integrity so easy that this part of the answer is now trivial.

But there you have the sea-change mentioned earlier. Database users rarely ask *how* to do something (because doing things has become easier), but they do need to know *why* they should be doing them.

Hence this book about the relational model, because it is that model which explains why you should work in a particular way.

1.5 Who Should Read This Book?

You should read this book if:

♦ You have created databases, but they don't seem to work very well. Perhaps you:
  - can't retrieve the information that you want
  - have to type in the same information over and over again
  - type in data and it appears to go missing
  - ask questions and get answers that you know are wrong
♦ You can use Access, but you don't know exactly what to do with it.
♦ You know that a relational database lets you create multiple tables in the database but you are uncertain why this is to your advantage.

- There are lots of features that sound interesting, but you have no idea what you are supposed to do with them.
- You hear words in connection with databases like:
  - normalization
  - functional dependency
  - inner join
  - union
  - redundant data
  - data dictionary
  - meta-data

  You haven't got the faintest idea what they mean but there is no one you can ask.
- You want to know about some aspect of databases in more detail, such as SQL or normalization.

You *shouldn't* read this book if you are looking for a 'How to use Access' book. This book is about the relational model which underlies Access and all RDBMSs. It doesn't tell you in a step-by-step manner how to perform a particular operation, except in a few rare cases. Instead of telling you how to do something, it tells you why you would want to do it and what advantage you would gain from doing so.

1.6 Organization of the Book

Within a database itself, the data is stored in tables. A simple database will contain a single table, while more complex ones can contain many tables. For example, if you want to keep your address book in a database (as I do on a small pocket computer), then a single table is perfect. However, if you want to store all of the business transactions of a company, you will find that it is more efficient to store the data in multiple tables – one for the customers, another for the goods you sell and so on.

This book is divided into four parts.

Part 1 concentrates on databases which contain only single tables because this should make some of the basic principles easier to understand. It describes the components which make up a typical database:

- tables
- forms
- queries
- reports

Part 2 explains that when most people start building databases they tend to try and put all of the data into one table. The part illustrates why this is a bad idea in practice, and then outlines how you can use multiple tables to overcome the problems inherent in single-table databases. Part 2 is a seriously chunky part, since much of the relational model is explained in there.

Part 3 is amazingly short – so short in fact that you may wonder why it is a part in its own right. However, it outlines a very important, and fundamental, decision that you have to make about your database. That decision concerns where you store the data for your database. In turn that affects who can access the data.

Part 4 is very different from the other three. The first three are lovingly hand-crafted so that each chapter builds on the information in the previous one (or, at least, that was the idea). The chapters in Part 4 can be read in any order because the information in each one is essentially unconnected to that in the others. Much of the information in any given chapter in Part 4 assumes that you do understand the information in Parts 1–3, but there is essentially no cross-requirement between chapters in Part 4. Thus, if you understand the information in Parts 1–3 and want to know about SQL, go straight to Chapter 25 and read it. If someone is bugging you with terms like 'third normal form' or 'functional dependency' then read the chapter on normalization.

1.7 Some Ground Rules

As an aside, almost all of the tables, forms etc. which are used in this book are available on the CD-ROM. This is so that, if you want to, you can have them open on screen while you are reading the book.

The files were all created in Access 2.0, and Access 97 was used for the screen shots. However, Access can only read files from its current or earlier versions. So, if I provided the files in Access 97 format, anyone with Access 95 or earlier wouldn't be able to read them. For this reason the files are provided in Access 2.0 format. If you have a later version it will be able to read them.

Each Access file is tied to its chapter by name; so, for example, the Access file associated with Chapter 2 is called CHAP2.MDB. Occasionally a chapter warranted more than one database file, so sometimes you will find names like CHAP25A.MDB and CHAP25B.MDB.

This book assumes that the reader will be interested in relational databases. There are several other models for organizing data but the relational is the most common. Thus, in the text which follows, in order to avoid continually having to prefix the word 'database' with the word 'relational', you can assume that I mean relational unless it is explicitly stated otherwise.

I am all too aware of the fact (having been corrected many times) that 'datum' is the singular form of 'data', and so I should write 'every datum' rather than 'every piece of data'. The trouble is that using 'data' as both the singular and plural forms is now so widespread that to do otherwise smacks of pedantry and obscures rather than clarifies. I've been swayed by the common usage argument and have used just 'data'.

In fact, now is a good time to point out that this entire book fails to use exact terminology. I know that a table isn't a table, it is a 'relation'. Or to be precise, a table isn't *exactly* a relation it's... and so on. I happily acknowledge that I shouldn't talk about the number of rows (or, slightly more accurately, the number of 'tuples'); what I really mean is the cardinality.

Relational databases have their origins in the precise world of mathematics, and that particular world has a very precise language. The trouble is that I also live and work in the real world, and in it real people talk about tables, rows and columns. So, at the expense of a small degree of accuracy and the gain (I hope) of a great deal of clarity, I have elected to use less formal terminology whenever possible. Apologies are proffered in advance to those who are terminally offended. However, there is a glossary where the mathematical-world equivalents of these words are given, so that you can look them up when other people use them.

So, that's the end of the introduction. I'd love to know how many people actually read it; perhaps Sir Henry is right. Either way, I hope that you get as much pleasure from the elegance of the relational model as I have done, and I will be delighted if this book illuminates even a small section of it for you.

Copying Files From the CD-ROM

To copy all the files from the CD-ROM, changing the file attributes from read-only, use the following procedure.

The files must be copied at the MS-DOS prompt. Exit Windows to go to the C:\> prompt.

Change drive to the D:\> prompt (or whichever drive letter is allocated to the CD-ROM), type the following:

```
COPY
```

and press Return. This will create a directory on the C: drive called INSIDERD which will contain two further directories, ACCESS2 and ACCESS97, in which the different versions of the Access database files are located.

Part 1

A Simple, Single-Table Database

2

Introduction to Part 1

The first database you build is likely to do something relatively simple, such as keeping a list of your customers or friends and is likely to be constructed on a standalone PC. Happily, constructing a simple database like this can be used to introduce the four most important components of a database, namely:

♦ tables

♦ forms

♦ queries

♦ reports

It is difficult to overstress the importance of these four components, and we will start with a quick look at each.

2.1 Tables

Tables are the basic structures in which data is stored within a database. Think of a table as the container in which the data sits and the other three components as devices which manipulate the data contained in the table. A table that contains information about your employees might look like the one shown in Figure 2.1.

Almost all of the tables, forms etc. used to illustrate this book are provided on the CD-ROM as Access MDB files. There is usually one appropriately named MDB file per chapter, so the one for this chapter is CHAP2.MDB. The table name shown, in this case EMPLOYEES, is the name of the table in the appropriate MDB file.

EMPLOYEES

EmployeeNo	FirstName	LastName	DateOfBirth	DateEmployed
1	Manny	Tomanny	12 Apr 1956	01 May 1989
2	Rosanne	Kolumn	21 Mar 1967	01 Jan 1990
3	Cas	Kade	01 May 1967	01 Apr 1992
4	Norma	Lyzation	03 Apr 1956	01 Apr 1992
5	Juan	Tomani	12 Apr 1956	01 Apr 1992

Figure 2.1 *A table of data about employees. The name of the table (EMPLOYEES) is shown in UPPER-CASE.*

2.2 Forms

The answer tables that I use to illustrate this book are usually shown with names; for example, in this case, it is EmployeesBornAfter1960. This is simply the name of the query which generated the answer tables. The query can be found in the appropriate MDB file, in this case called CHAP2.MDB.

A form (Figure 2.2) is a device which allows you to look at and edit the data in a table. In fact, you can usually go directly to a table itself and perform both of these actions, but typically they are accomplished via a form. A good question at this point is 'Why use a form?', and a simple (but true) answer is that forms can be made more attractive and easier to use than tables. For more compelling reasons to use forms, see Chapter 4 – Forms.

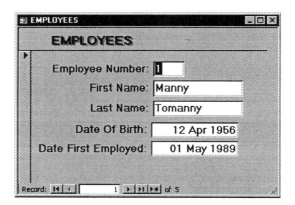

Figure 2.2 *A form showing information from the table of data about customers.*

2.3 Queries

Queries are questions that you can ask of the data in a table. If you wanted to find all of your employees who were born after, say, 1960, you would use a query. Queries are used frequently within databases because typically the tables hold very large amounts of data, and we often want to deal with, or look at, just a subset of that data.

EmployeesBornAfter1960

EmployeeNo	FirstName	LastName	DateOfBirth	DateEmployed
2	Rosanne	Kolumn	21 Mar 1967	01 Jan 1990
3	Cas	Kade	01 May 1967	01 Apr 1992

Figure 2.3 *The result of a query to find the employees who were born after 1960.*

2.4 Reports

Reports (Figure 2.4) are used to produce printed output from the table. If you want a list of all of your customers' names and addresses, you would use a report to roll out just such a list from the printer.

Simple, isn't it? And if you can get to grips with these four fundamental components – tables, forms, queries and reports – you will have acquired a very good handle on databases in general. Of course, there is more to them than just their definitions, so in the next four chapters we'll have at look at each in more detail.

EMPLOYEES

20-Jul-97

EmployeeNo	Name	DateOfBirth
3	Cas Kade	01 May 1967
2	Rosanne Kolumn	21 Mar 1967
4	Norma Lyzation	03 Apr 1956
5	Juan Tomani	12 Apr 1956
1	Manny Tomanny	12 Apr 1956

Figure 2.4 *An example of a report – in this case a printed list of information about employees, sorted by last name.*

3

Tables

Tables are containers for holding data which is similar in layout. If you collected information about your employees, the data about each would be similar and would therefore make the contents of a perfectly satisfactory table (Figure 3.1).

EMPLOYEES

EmployeeNo	FirstName	LastName	DateOfBirth	DateEmployed
1	Manny	Tomanny	12 Apr 1956	01 May 1989
2	Rosanne	Kolumn	21 Mar 1967	01 Jan 1990
3	Cas	Kade	01 May 1967	01 Apr 1992
4	Norma	Lyzation	03 Apr 1956	01 Apr 1992
5	Juan	Tomani	12 Apr 1956	01 Apr 1992

Figure 3.1 *A sensible table containing suitable, sensible data.*

This part is all about databases made up of a single table, so it may come as a bit of a shock to find that CHAP3.MDB (the Access file which holds the sample files used for this chapter) has more than one table. However, this is simply because I use different tables to illustrate different points.

On the other hand, you cannot put one or more carefully spotted train numbers and a list of your favourite books into the same table. To do so would entirely miss the point that tables should contain data with similar structure (Figure 3.2).

3.1 Rows and Columns – Records and Fields

Tables consist of rows (horizontal) and columns (vertical).

NON-SENSIBLE

EmployeeNo	FirstName	LastName	DateOfBirth	DateEmployed
1	Manny	Tomanny	12 Apr 1956	01 May 1989
2	Rosanne	Kolumn	21 Mar 1967	01 Jan 1990
3	Cas	Kade	01 May 1967	01 Apr 1992
4	Norma	Lyzation	03 Apr 1956	01 Apr 1992
5	Juan	Tomani	12 Apr 1956	01 Apr 1992
6	2312234	Steam Train	Red and Black	3.45 to Bedford
7	The Egg-Shaped Thing	$1.20	Christopher Hodder-Williams	Hard Back
8	34223	Diesel	Black and Soot	2.17 to Seattle
9	The Mullenthorpe Thing	$2.50	Christopher Hood	Hard Back

Figure 3.2 *This table is sensible, but contains some unsuitable data, so the result is non-sensible.*

In the sample table shown in Figure 3.1 (the sensible one), each row contains the data about one employee, and the data contained in one row is known as a record. Thus it is perfectly correct to say 'I've added a row to the table' and equally correct to say 'I've added a record to the table'. In many cases the terms row and record can be used interchangeably; the difference is that 'row' refers explicitly to the table, 'record' refers more to the data that is contained in a row. In most databases, each table can be considered to be infinitely expandable in terms of the number of rows it can contain and no limit is set on the number of (in this example) employees which can be accommodated in the table.

The same is not true for the number of columns which is typically limited to 255. This is, in practice, more than enough for most purposes. The terms 'column' and 'field' are, again, mainly interchangeable, although pedantically 'column' refers explicitly to the table, 'field' refers more to the data that is contained in a column. It is a characteristic of all tables that each column must have a name (called the 'field name') and that each field name, within a given table, must be unique. This is not unreasonable, since two fields in the EMPLOYEES table, both called FirstName, would be bound to cause confusion.

It should be clear that the EMPLOYEES table is designed to hold information about employees. For a start, the name of the table (EMPLOYEES) tends to give the game away, but also the names on the top of the columns (the field names – FirstName, LastName, DateOfBirth etc.) clearly indicate that this is a table for storing information about people rather than, say items offered for sale.

In a perfect world, the RDBMS would provide an infinite number of empty tables, each one designed to hold a different category of information – one for employees, one for customers, one for orders and so on. However, even if this were possible, it still wouldn't be much help, because different databases will require different information to be stored about the same category of information. Suppose that you and I are both setting up databases for our businesses and that we both need a Customer table. Clearly we would have some columns in common (PhoneNumber), but you might, for example, be interested in providing your customers with financial services and

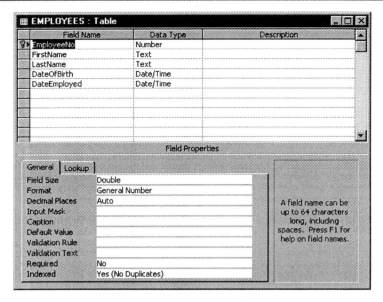

Figure 3.3 *Designing a table in Access.*

would need detailed information about credit rating and so on. I, on the other hand, might want to sell antique books for cash but provide a discount for members of the ABC (Antique Book Club) and therefore need to store information about each customer's membership status.

The later versions of Access (from 2.0 onwards) provide a set of 'Wizards' which let you choose the general class of table that you want (say, EMPLOYEES) and then step you through the process of making it. These are very helpful, but because it is impossible for the wizard to provide every possible variation of EMPLOYEES table that everyone will need, Access also provides a means by which we can build our own tables from scratch or modify the ones produced by the wizard (Figure 3.3). As a rule, once the structure of a table (in terms of the columns) is complete, it is rarely changed. This certainly isn't an absolute rule: I just make the point to highlight the difference between rows and columns. The former will inevitably change as new information is added to, and subtracted from, the table; the latter are generally fixed for any given table.

Your first task in setting up a database is to design a table to hold your data. In doing so you will have to specify the names of the fields that you think you will need.

All tables and all fields have names. Access allows the use of UPPER-CASE and lower-case characters in both table and field names. It also allows the use of spaces in these names. Thus it is possible to call a table Part time Employees and a field Rate Of Pay.

I have elected never to use spaces in field names for two reasons. The first is that I feel it will make the text in the book clearer. Spaces in object names produce problems peculiar to writing about databases. For example, given the text '...a reference to the field called TEST.Save it clarifies...'. The field name in this case might be 'Save' or 'Save it'. The meaning might become clear if we saw more of the context but it is intuitively clearer if both table and field names are always a single word.

Secondly, while Access allows spaces in field names, other RDBMSs do not. If you use them, you might be storing up problem for yourself in the future. Suppose, for example, that you build an Access application for your company that turns out to be wildly successful. Promotion quickly follows, with a place on the board and stock options; the world is your oyster. Then you are asked to upgrade the database to a client–server system (see Part 3). No client–server RDBMS of my acquaintance will support spaces in field names and you suddenly have a major headache. Take my advice and avoid spaces in field names.

I have also elected always to use UPPER-CASE for table names and the delightfully named CamelCaps for field names. Finally, if I need to refer to a specific field in a specific table, I will always do so by separating the two names with a dot or point(.). Thus:

`EMPLOYEES.EmployeeNo`

refers to the `EmployeeNo` column (or field) of the table called `EMPLOYEES`.

Incidentally, one of the reviewers of the book commented 'CamelCaps are more accurately known as BiCapitalization, but "CamelCaps" is much more fun! Purely, for information, did you know that random CaPitaLization is known as StudlyCaps?'

That finishes with the aside. Now, back to the records. (As another aside, this expression 'Now, back to the records' is a rare example of a database pun. We need to treasure it because there are so few of them.)

3.2 Building a Table

The actual mechanism for designing a table in Access is straightforward. You supply the names of the fields that you require in any given table and it takes care of the tedious details like constructing the table. However, if you elect to use the 'Design View' you will find that you are asked for more than just the field names. For each field you will be asked to choose the 'type' of data which the field will hold (known as the 'data type') and the size of the data which will be placed therein. We'll have a look at what each of these terms means and why it is usually to your advantage to choose wisely.

3.2.1 Types of Data

The most commonly used data types (Figure 3.4) are:

Text	Most characters found on the keyboard, including numbers; usually limited to 255 characters.
Memo	Large blocks of text.
Number (or numeric)	Numbers only, no text characters.
Date/Time	As the name suggests; dates, times or both.

Currency	Essentially numeric with four decimal places and a currency symbol.
AutoNumber	A number that is automatically incremented for each new record.
Yes/No	For discrete information that falls neatly into two categories; like True/False, Yes/No, Up/Down.
OLE Object	An object such as a Microsoft Excel spreadsheet, a Microsoft Word document or graphical information.

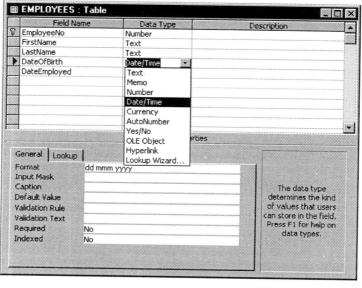

Figure 3.4 *Choosing data types during the design of a table in Access.*

Choosing the correct data type for a given field is usually easy. If you create a field called FirstName, then Text is clearly likely to be the correct data type; Currency would be a good choice for a field called Salary and so on. But *why* do we have to tell the RDBMS what type of data is going into the table? Why can't it just store whatever we choose to put in it, as, indeed, some very simple DBMSs will do? The answer is that defining the data type has four advantages (in no particular order of importance). It can:

♦ allow more 'meaningful' operations to be performed upon the data
♦ exclude certain types of error
♦ make the storage of the data more efficient in terms of size
♦ make data recovery more rapid.

Meaningful Operations
Suppose you want your EMPLOYEE table to store the date upon which each employee started to work for your company (perhaps you want to send

them an anniversary card). You decide to declare a field called `DateEmployed` to store it. What data type would you choose? Date/Time seems like a good choice, but experience suggests that it is not uncommon to find that people new to databases will choose the default data type, which happens to be Text. Even more surprisingly, this appears to work (at least initially) because a text field will accept any alphanumeric character that you can find on the keyboard. The following are all acceptable in a text field:

- ♦ Penguin
- ♦ ROSS
- ♦ Sophie
- ♦ 45
- ♦ Salt & Pepper
- ♦ 12+45%
- ♦ 12/5/67

Note that the last one looks like a date. Since text fields will accept data which looks like a date, why bother declaring the field type to be anything else? The answer is that dates, as you have probably noticed, are horrendously complex:

30 days hath September,
April, June and November,
All the rest hathn't

(or words to that effect).

The good news is that if you declare this field to be of type Date/Time, the RDBMS will be able to perform what is known as 'date arithmetic'. For example, it should be able to tell you how long each employee has been with you simply by subtracting the date stored in `DateEmployed` from the current date. In addition, it should be able to give you the answer in days, months or years, whichever temporal currency you happen to prefer.

You can see this in action in Figure 3.5, where the calculation even allows for leap years. Incidentally, note that we are using a form here to look at the data in the table. It serves as an excellent illustration of exactly why forms are so useful. Tables cannot manipulate the data that they contain; they are simply storage vessels. Forms, on the other hand, were designed for precisely this type of manipulation.

Clearly this is only possible because the RDBMS 'understands' that a date like '12 April 1956' is actually the twelfth day of the fourth month in 1956. It can only assume that this is so because we have effectively told it by declaring the field called `DateEmployed` to be of type Date/Time.

As another example, consider telephone numbers. What sort of field type should be used to store them? (Be warned: this is a trick question.) The obvious answer is to store them in a number field, but that happens to be the wrong answer. Number data types treat the data they contain as numbers, so they remove leading zeros, which catastrophically changes country codes like 001 to 1. In addition, they won't tolerate spaces or parentheses in numbers, which is also unfortunate. The net result is that you want to store, say:

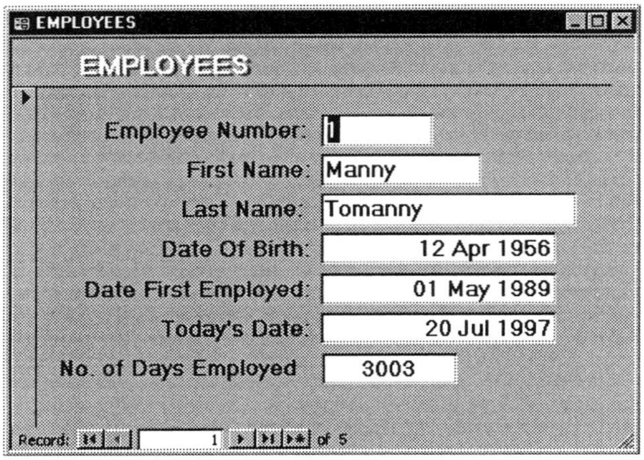

Figure 3.5 *Access calculating the number of days for which an employee has been with the company.*

001 206 123 4567

or

(001) 206 123 4567

but all you can store is:

12061234567

which isn't the same thing at all.

The correct answer is to store telephone numbers in a text field where leading zeros, spaces and parentheses are happily tolerated. This use of text fields for telephone numbers isn't as counter-intuitive as it might appear. Numbers are values that we manipulate mathematically; telephone numbers aren't numbers in that sense at all. When did you last calculate the average of your friends' phone numbers? Telephone numbers are actually non-mathematical identifiers which happen to be numeric; in practice they could equally well be a string of text characters.

Excluding Certain Errors
Given that the RDBMS will expect only dates to be entered into a Date/Time type field, it will reject dates like:

34th April 1978
29th February 1993

Incidentally, you don't have to type dates into the database as a mixture of text and numbers such as '21 Feb 1993'. You can type them in as numbers and you can set the expected format to be US or UK. Thus, if Access is set for UK format dates, then typing in 7/4/96 means the seventh of April. If it is set for US format, then it is the fourth of July (and time for a party!).

There has been a lot of talk about problems which will appear in the year 2000 because computers don't handle dates properly. More specifically, some computer systems have stored dates as, for example, 1/1/67. In other words, they don't store the '19' part of 1967. Come the year 2000 there is a major problem. If, for example, the date of an order is typed in as 1/1/00, the computer may assume that it is 1/1/1900 and that the order is now 100 years out of date. The good news for Access users is that, right from version 1.0 of the product, it has stored dates in full form, even if they don't appear so on screen, so you shouldn't have problems come the year 2000.

Making Storage More Efficient

Suppose you want a field to hold the number of offspring of each employee. The obvious choice is to make the data type 'Number'. However, there are several different sub-types of 'Number'. You *do not* need to learn these off by heart, but just to give you an idea of the range, the most commonly used are given in Table 3.1.

A byte can be thought of as a single unit of storage in a computer. Disk space is usually measured in megabytes (1 Mbyte = approximately 1 million bytes) or gigabytes (1 Gbyte = approximately 1,000 megabytes).]

Table 3.1 *Sub-types of the Number data type*

Sub type of Numeric	Storage capacity and size
Byte	Stores numbers from 0 to 255 (no decimals). Each occupies 1 byte.
Integer	Stores numbers from −32,768 to 32,767 (no decimals). Each occupies 2 bytes.
Long Integer	Stores numbers from −2,147,483,648 to 2,147,483,647 (no decimals). Each occupies 4 bytes.
Single	Big numbers. Numbers well into the billions and beyond.
	For the technically minded, numbers with six digits of precision, from approx. −3.4E38 to +3.4E38. Each occupies 4 bytes.
Double	Stores really huge numbers, I mean really monstrous. In a double data type you can store a number which is far greater than the number of atoms in the entire observable universe. Since this number must, by definition, exceed the number of employees or customers you have, it should be big enough!
	For the technically minded, numbers are stored with 10 digits of precision and range from approx. −1.8E308 to +1.8E308 complete with decimals. Each occupies 8 bytes.

One of the reviewers of this book wrote 'Is this really true?' next to the bit about 'you can store a number which is far greater than the number of atoms in the entire observable universe'. 'Yes' is the short answer. Last time I looked into this (which was a while ago) the estimate was 1×10^{73} atoms (1 with 73 zeros after it). Even if that estimate has risen ten million-fold, that would still only be 1×10^{80}, and a 'double' will store 1×10^{308}. Of course, these numbers are stored without much precision, but they are still mind-stretchingly huge.

Now, for a start, offspring are integers. Given a particularly obnoxious offspring you might attempt to claim responsibility for only a small part of it but we don't normally describe someone as having 0.1835 children. Secondly, how many people do you know with more than 255 children? How many people do you know with negative children? (This is not the same as asking, 'How many people do you know who are negative *about* their children?') So the correct numeric sub-type in this case will be Byte, which stores positive integers between 0 and 255, or Integer if Byte is not available.

So, what major catastrophe occurs if you get it wrong and accept the default Number data type, which isn't Byte or Integer? (Double was the default in Access 2.0, but it changed to Long Integer in Access 7.) The answer is 'Nothing too drastic really, unless you start to collects lots of data' (see Field size below). However, since you are often unsure of exactly how much data you will collect, it is always a good idea to try to take the long-term view.

Making Data Recall More Rapid

As a general rule, if you make a field a Long Integer and then fill it with positive integers between 1 and 20, you are wasting space. A digit between 1 and 20 would fit in a Byte field and therefore take up only one byte of disk space. However, the same number stored in a Long Integer field takes up four times as much disk space. This has the effect of making the table larger than it needs to be, which has the knock-on effect of slowing the database down when it is queried, because there is more of it to be processed. However, it is important to keep a sense of proportion here.

Suppose you are building a table to hold a list of your friends. Popular as you are, you never expect the table to contain more than 300 records. In this case, it really doesn't matter if you use a Byte or Double data type for storing how many children each friend has, because neither size nor speed will ever be a noticeable problem. Having said that, of course, there is always the little matter of pride. There is a certain satisfaction in getting it right. In addition, many databases I have seen built for small companies *have* expanded beyond the designer's wildest dreams. So, on balance, even given a healthy sense of proportion, I would always try to get it right first time.

First time? Yes, because Access will allow you to change a data type, even after you have added data to the table. Exactly what happens to the data will depend upon the change you make, and sometimes a loss of information is inevitable. For example, if you store data in a Double field, you can include numbers with decimal components. If you subsequently change it to an Integer type, Access will keep the whole numbers and will round them depending upon the decimal component. Thus 4.4 becomes 4 while 5.5 becomes 6.

3.2.2 Field Size

If you declare a field called LastName to be of type Text, you will also need to tell Access how many characters that field can hold. This can be a bit of a guessing game; what's the longest last name you can think of? Marklyn? Whitehorn? Weatherbottom? Zimmer Van Kyllon? Most RDBMSs need to know this sort of information because the size of the field will affect storage space and retrieval speed. Suppose you decide to make the field 50 characters long; this means that for every record added to the table, 50 bytes are set aside to hold the person's last name. If the longest last name you ever store is 26 characters long (Zimmermann der Grossenamen), then you are wasting 24 bytes per record. Since tables are stored on disk, you are now wasting 24 bytes of disk space per record. Given that you want to store records for, say the population of Scotland (approximately 5 million souls), you will waste 120 Mbyte of disk space by simply accepting a default value. If you make similar mistakes for 10 fields, that multiplies up to over a gigabyte.

Surprisingly, this waste of disk space isn't *too* big a crime nowadays because disk space has become so cheap. But there is another problem; the bigger a table gets, the longer it takes to search. Choosing the wrong field size can contribute to a database which runs like congealed porridge. Such databases are generally unpopular with their users.

The excellent news for Access users is that, ever since version 1.0, Access has been intelligent enough to store only the actual characters that you enter into each text field. Thus if you declare the text field to be 50 characters wide, but store 'Penguin' in the first record, this will only take up 7 bytes of disk space. In fact, Access only asks you to decide how many characters that field can hold so that you have control over the maximum number of characters which are entered. However, most RDBMSs are less forgiving with text fields and will waste space if you declare the size of the field unwisely.

3.2.3 General Notes on Table Design

Think First

If you want a new table you shouldn't really sit down at the computer without doing some thinking first. Creating a table (and indeed a database) requires two fundamentally different stages, which we can call 'Structure Definition' and 'Implementation'. (These are not formally recognized terms, they just happen to be useful here.)

Structure definition essentially means deciding which fields will be required, what information will go into them and how large each one should be. This is not a process which involves a computer; indeed it should be carried out as far away from a computer as possible.

Implementation means constructing a computer representation of the design.

It could be imagined that the first stage just takes common sense and is therefore a matter of little consequence. On the other hand, because the second step involves a computer and an RDBMS, it could be seen as more difficult.

In fact the converse is true; design is difficult and implementation is easy. Having said that, design *is* mostly common sense (it just depends on how sensible you are). One golden rule of design is *not* to ask the question:

What information do I want to *put into* the table?

Instead you should ask:

What information do I want to *get out* of the table?

You are, after all, only building the database so that information can be extracted. Having decided what questions you are likely to ask of your table, you can then work backwards and decide what information needs to be put in, and from that you can deduce the structure.

Again, an example helps make this clear. You need to be able to send mail to certain target groups of Influential People (IPs). (Make a note: you will need fields for names and others for addresses.) IPs are often fussy about their titles (note: separate field for title). You will need to target them based on their income group (field for income), number of children (integer field) and political party (text field). You want to include a direct reference to their spouse in the letter (text field for spouse's name) and so on.

If all this sounds far too obvious, believe me it isn't. I have seen several tables which have been stuffed with useless information; so well stuffed that the entire database was running like treacle, which was why I had been asked to take a look. The information wasn't there because anyone was going to use it but was there because it had been easy to collect. In two cases, the information had been available electronically so it didn't even have to be typed in. Ease of collection is not, on its own, a good reason for storing data.

Context

Another good rule is to think about the data that you will collect in the particular context in which it will be collected. The size of a field needed to hold people's last names will depend upon the ethnic group to which they belong.

PC or not PC? That Is the Question

Try to avoid field names like `ChristianName`; not everyone has one because not everyone is a Christian. I would hate this to sound like a sop to the great god 'Political Correctness' but why offend people when it is easy, with a little thought, to avoid doing so?

Hard-line political correctness makes table design a minefield in which even the wariest database designer can be caught. As one of the reviewers of an early draft of this book pointed out:

Fine to abandon 'Christian' names because of cultural diversity, but not then to say 'First' or 'Last' name. 'Tsiao Ping' is not Mr Deng's Christian name, but it is not his first name either; it is his *given name* (and 'Deng' is his *surname* or *family name*). Actually, you can't win: 'Magnusson' isn't Magnus's family name; it's his *patronymic*.

I suppose that we can take comfort in the fact that whatever we choose will be wrong, so at least we know where we are from the start.

Controlling Data Entry

Access allows you to set up filters which control the input of data into fields. It is worth mentioning here because you can use field types to help ensure that valid data ends up in the table.

Suppose you wish to collect information relating to a person's gender. You could set up a text field and expect the users of the database to type in 'Male' or 'Female' in response to the question 'Sex?'

Experience suggests that if male students are allowed to enter the data for themselves, about 5% will answer 'Yes' and a further 10% will respond 'Yes please!' While this data tells you that about two-thirds of the students with a sense of humour are also polite, it doesn't help you to collect the information you want.

There are several alternatives. You could set up the field to be of type Yes/No and entitle the field 'Female?' (or 'Male?' if you like). The system would then only allow the response 'Yes' or 'No'. By doing this you are making use of the data type to control data entry.

Another (and possibly better) way is to make use of a more specific control mechanism that Access allows during the construction of a table. You can choose a data type, such as text, set it to a specific length, say 6, and then specify that only the input 'Male' or 'Female' is acceptable for that field.

Of course, neither system will prevent any individual student from claiming to be the wrong sex (either from perversity or feeble-mindedness) but controlling such factors lies outside the remit of even the most advanced database.

Access allows the control of data input to the table to be set up in a very versatile manner. You can, for example, set up a numeric field which will accept values only between 1.34233 and 6.4453. As another example, you can set a field called `Title` to accept only the input 'Mr', 'Mrs', 'Miss', 'Ms', 'Dr' or 'Prof'.

One of the reviewers added 'I wouldn't, though. I once tried to enumerate them all ('Sir', 'Lord' etc.) Ouch!'

True, there must be hundreds. However, have a look at the validation rule in the lower part of the screen shown in Figure 3.6 to see how it can be done.

You can also use forms as a further level of control. This issue is discussed further in Chapter 4 and in considerably more detail in Chapter 16.

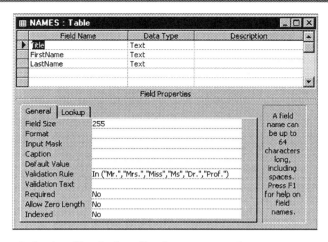

Figure 3.6 *A table which will only accept specific input into its fields.*

Field Names

Most of the early RDBMSs put significant restrictions on the size of field names and the characters they could contain (such as eight letters or fewer, no lower-case letters and no spaces). In turn this has given rise to field names like `FNAME`, `LNAME`, `CUST#` and so on. I hate these because they are a barrier to understanding, and happily many of the modern RDBMSs remove these restrictions. Access allows field names with longer names like `Customer Number`. For reasons discussed above I would avoid spaces, but using more than eight characters can often make for more readable field names. Throughout this book I have carefully ignored my own advice, using as few letters as I can while still retaining some readability. In my defense, I'll claim that when building databases for the 'real world' I *do* use longer field names. However, the databases used here are examples for a book. The printed page is an all too narrow medium for displaying tables, so I have tried to work as best I can within that rather odd restriction.

Splitting Names, Addresses etc.

It is tempting, but usually inadvisable, to store data which can be logically subdivided. For example, if you store names as in Figure 3.7, all will be well until someone asks you to list all of the people in the table alphabetically by surname. In fact, with much effort and gnashing of teeth, it is possible to do this, but why make life difficult for yourself? If you store the same data in three fields, as in Figure 3.8, you can then simply sort on the contents of the third field (Figure 3.9).

Subdividing data like this also makes it much easier to, say extract all the Professors from the list.

The rule for subdividing data is quite simple. If you have data which can be logically split into sections, give serious consideration to doing so. If you can see any future need at all to manipulate the data via one of its possible subdivisions, it is almost essential to split it up into different fields.

Name
Prof. John Parker
Dr. Brian Featherstone
Miss Julie Arberlington
Mr. Mike Barham

Figure 3.7 *Some badly stored names.*

Title	FirstName	LastName
Prof.	John	Parker
Dr.	Brian	Featherstone
Miss	Julie	Arberlington
Mr.	Mike	Barham

Figure 3.8 *Some correctly stored names.*

Title	FirstName	LastName
Miss	Julie	Arberlington
Mr.	Mike	Barham
Dr.	Brian	Featherstone
Prof.	John	Parker

Figure 3.9 *Figure 3.8 sorted alphabetically by* LastName.

Addresses are another good case in point. It is possible to argue that an address is usually used as a single unit. However, once the data is in a database, you are likely to be asked to perform operations such as finding all of the customers in Boston. This will be much easier if the address is split into separate fields, one of which is called something like City/Town. And, of course, postcodes and zip codes contain a plethora of information as long as you can get at it. Always store them in their own field.

Don't Store Redundant Information

If, in an order table, you store CostOfItem and NumberOfItems, don't store the total cost, since this is already indirectly stored as the product of the other two fields. If we ever need the information we can calculate it as CostOfItem * NoOfItems (see Chapter 4). Storing the product of these two in the table not only wastes space, it produces updating problems. Suppose you enter a record and complete the three fields – CostOfItem, NumberOfItems and TotalCost. Then your customer alters the order, doubling the number of items. You might update the number of items but forget to alter the value in the TotalCost field as has happened in the sample table shown below (Figure 3.10). (To save you working it out, the record for Mark buying shrimps is incorrect. He originally ordered 75 which gives the price of $242.25 but later altered the order to 100. Since the TotalCost field wasn't updated to $323.00, he got a bargain, which means our company lost money.)

ORDERS

OrderID	Customer	Item	CostOfItem	NoOfItems	TotalCost
1	Holly	Haddock	$3.45	23	$79.35
2	Bill	Herring	$2.56	45	$115.20
3	Jane	Haddock	$3.45	43	$148.35
4	Henry	Salmon	$5.67	34	$192.78
5	Mark	Shrimps	$3.23	100	$242.25
6	Mary	Prawns	$3.45	34	$117.30
7	Bill	Herring	$2.56	56	$143.36
8	Holly	Haddock	$3.75	45	$168.75

Figure 3.10 *The potential update problems of storing derivable data in a table.*

I have assumed that the price of fish is variable with time, so it is perfectly reasonable for haddock to vary in price from one order to another.

In theory there are solutions to this problem which still allow you to store the redundant data. You could, for example, get the RDBMS to automatically recalculate the TotalCost whenever the values in either of the other two fields are altered. Actually ensuring that the recalculation takes place under all conditions takes time and effort. Experience has shown that in most cases it is far simpler and safer not to store redundant information.

3.3 Base Tables – Not Defined Here

Since this chapter is about tables, it feels instinctively like the right place to define a concept that you will probably need, that of a 'base' table. The problem is that base tables only really make sense when compared and contrasted with, well, tables which *aren't* base tables. All of the tables we have covered so far *are* base tables, so the definition is going to be cumbersome until we reach the other sort of table (which happens to appear in Chapter 5 – Queries). So I'll salve my conscience by defining a base table as exactly the sort of table that you have met so far, namely those which you create and within which you store the data for your database. We can improve on that definition later.

4

Forms

Data resides in the tables, but a database is more than simply data. It also includes components that are used as tools to look at, enter, delete and manipulate that data. Those components are called forms.

Once you have defined a table, you can start putting data into it. Tables are usually represented on screen in a manner similar to that shown in Figure 4.1, one row for each record and one column for each field. However, it is important not to lose sight of the fact that this 'table view' of the data is simply one way of representing the data. Your data is actually stored in a highly abstract way as a series of magnetic impressions on a disk and can be represented on screen in a whole variety of ways. In practice, data isn't usually entered directly into the table via the view as shown in Figure 4.1, although this is possible. Almost all data entry, editing and deleting operations are carried out via forms. You can think of forms as being screens or filters which sit between the tables of data and the users of the database.

EMPLOYEES

EmployeeNo	FirstName	LastName	DateOfBirth	DateEmployed
1	Manny	Tomanny	12 Apr 1956	01 May 1989
2	Rosanne	Kolumn	21 Mar 1967	01 Jan 1990
3	Cas	Kade	01 May 1967	01 Apr 1992
4	Norma	Lyzation	03 Apr 1956	01 Apr 1992
5	Juan	Tomani	12 Apr 1956	01 Apr 1992

Figure 4.1 *A table of data.*

There is nothing intrinsically wicked about entering data directly into a table, but forms are usually used simply because human beings often prefer to be able to see each record in isolation rather than occupying a row on the screen alongside many other records. The type of presentation shown in Figure 4.2 is known as a form view of the data. Access has a form designing section where you can build forms (Figure 4.3), and it also has a Form Wizard that will design and build a form for you; all you have to give it is the table. In fact, the form shown in Figure 4.2 was constructed by the wizard.

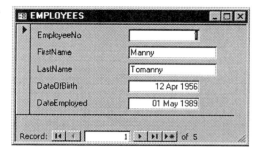

Figure 4.2 *A form view of the same table.*

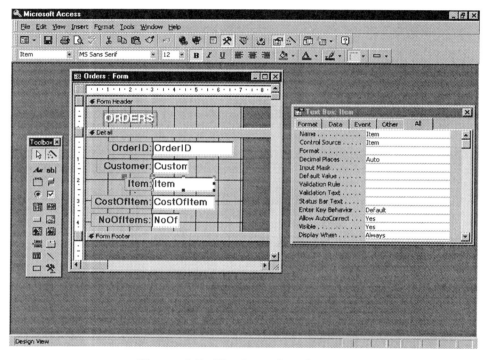

Figure 4.3 *The Access form designer.*

As shown in Figure 4.2, a basic form has one area for every field in the table. It is worth noting at this point that these areas on the form are not the fields themselves; rather, they are areas which allow you to view and (usually) edit the data in a field. In Access these areas on forms are known as 'text boxes'.

Typically a form shows one record on screen at a time and allows you to move between the text boxes by using the Tab key and to move between records with the PgUp and PgDn keys.

At their most basic, forms are simply devices for making it easier for people to interact with the table. After all, as discussed in the previous chapter, the restrictions of some RDBMSs can force field names to be rather cryptic.

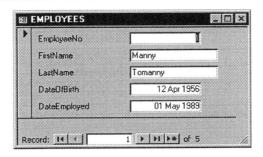

Figure 4.4 *The basic relationship between a form and a table view.*

Care to guess what should be placed in a field called PatAge? A form allows you to place descriptive text beside a text box, so instead of having to enter data into field called PatAge, you can enter it into a text box labelled 'Patient's Age.'

Even used in this very simple way, forms justify their existence by humanizing the database, and the importance of this cannot be overemphasized: people still find computers intimidating, let alone databases. The easier the process of interacting with either or both can be made (or even, dare we hope, more pleasurable), the more effectively the database can be used. For example, it is often possible to use forms to make the interface to the database resemble the existing paper-based systems that the database is replacing.

Forms have many features which help towards this end. Perhaps the best way to understand how these help is to look at several in isolation and then see how they can be used together.

4.1 Multiple Forms per Table

The table is the repository of the actual data and the form is simply a 'window' onto that data. There is therefore nothing to stop you from creating more than one form based on a single table; each form can be used to give a different view of the same data (Figure 4.5).

4.2 Text Boxes Can Be Made Read-only

Remembering that text boxes are not the fields themselves, it is possible to alter the properties of a text box so that, for example, they become read-only; this means they will show the data in a given field but will not allow

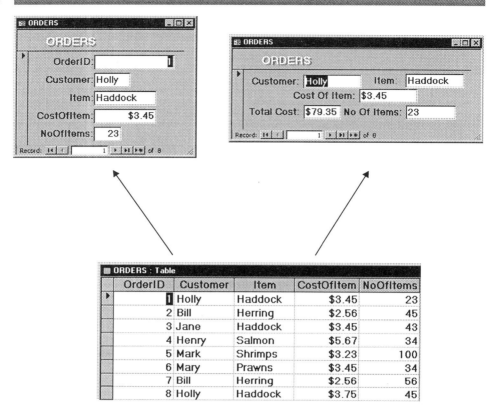

Figure 4.5 *Multiple forms can be based on a single table.*

the user to change it. Combine this with the idea that you can have multiple forms per table and it becomes possible to have two very different forms. One could be for data entry, the other for simply viewing a subset of the information in the table.

4.3 Text Boxes Don't Have to Present Data from Just One Field

As discussed in the previous chapter, it is excellent practice to ensure that you don't store several discrete pieces of data in the same field. For example, suppose you store names in two (or more) fields, as in Figure 4.6.

Given this table and a form for data *entry*, you would have to present the user with two different text boxes, appropriately labelled so that the correct information was placed in the correct place. If you didn't, users might start entering the last name into the FirstName field.

EMPLOYEES

EmployeeNo	FirstName	LastName	DateOfBirth	DateEmployed
1	Manny	Tomanny	12 Apr 1956	01 May 1989
2	Rosanne	Kolumn	21 Mar 1967	01 Jan 1990
3	Cas	Kade	01 May 1967	01 Apr 1992
4	Norma	Lyzation	03 Apr 1956	01 Apr 1992
5	Juan	Tomani	12 Apr 1956	01 Apr 1992

Figure 4.6 *A table of data which stores names in two parts.*

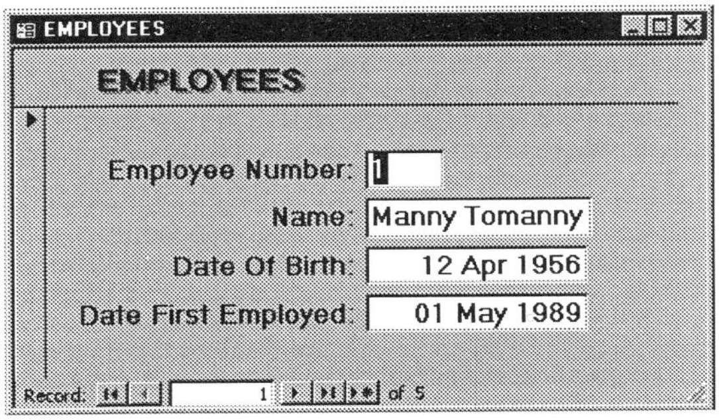

Figure 4.7 *Data from two fields joined together in a single text box for use in a form for viewing the data in a table.*

However, suppose that you are using a form solely for *viewing* the data. There is then no need to treat these items of data as separate entities and they can be joined in one text box, as in Figure 4.7.

Note that this kind of manipulation doesn't affect the integrity of the data in any way and is worth doing because it makes life easier for the user of the database.

The example above is simply 'adding' (or concatenating) two text fields. It is equally easy to perform more complex mathematical manipulations on numerical fields. Again, as discussed in the previous chapter, it is not desirable to store information which can be calculated from data in existing fields. Clearly, since forms are the preferred way of looking at the data, they are also places for synthesizing the more complex form of the data. You can have a text box which is labelled 'Total Cost' and which displays the result of multiplying the values in CostOfItem and NumberOfItems. Unlike in the last chapter, there is no corresponding field called TotalCost in the ORDERS table (Figures 4.8 and 4.9).

The text box simply provides additional useful information for users of the form. If, as implied earlier, users of the database always interact with the table via a form, as far as they are concerned the Total Cost of the invoice is always visible. And if they alter either of the original values, the Total Cost text box will automatically update, precisely because it is solely dependent upon the other two.

ORDERS

OrderID	Customer	Item	CostOfItem	NoOfItems
1	Holly	Haddock	$3.45	23
2	Bill	Herring	$2.56	45
3	Jane	Haddock	$3.45	43
4	Henry	Salmon	$5.67	34
5	Mark	Shrimps	$3.23	100
6	Mary	Prawns	$3.45	34
7	Bill	Herring	$2.56	56
8	Holly	Haddock	$3.75	45

Figure 4.8 *A table of orders placed with a company.*

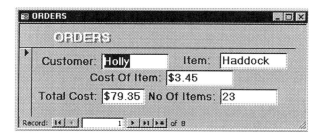

Figure 4.9 *In this form the Total Cost is calculated from the original data each time the record appears in the form. Thus it will automatically update as the other data in the record is altered.*

4.4 It Isn't Necessary for Each Field in a Table to Appear on the Form

Since a form is just a view of the data in the table, it isn't necessary for every field in the table to appear on a given form. This is more significant than it first appears; see the summary at the end of this chapter.

4.5 Controlling Data Entry

As outlined in the previous chapter, choosing the correct data type for a field can help to ensure that the correct data is placed therein. In addition, it is possible to control data entry more closely at the table level, again described in the previous chapter. It is also possible to apply the same sort of control at the form level but as a *general* rule it should be applied at the table level. Why? Well, as has just been discussed, you can have multiple forms which are based on a single table. If you have a data entry rule that is crucial and you apply it at the form level, what will happen if you create a new form and forget to apply the rule there? Or what happens if you pass the database on to someone else and *they* don't know about the rule and create a new form? In both cases, there is now a strong possibility that corrupt/incorrect data will be allowed into your table. Imagine the shame! Imagine the mortification! Corrupt data in your table! If you have a good reason for applying control at the form level, then clearly that is the best place. Otherwise, apply it at the table level. See Chapter 16 for more details.

4.6 Use of Forms Can Be Controlled

RDBMSs like Access allow you to control, via passwords if necessary, the access that any particular user has to the components of the database (tables, forms, queries, reports etc.). In databases of any complexity it is common to forbid users direct access to the tables and to restrict their access to specific forms. Thus one group of users may be given access to one set of forms and another group may have access to a different set.

4.7 Summary

♦ Forms are filters which allow users to see the data in a table, and it is possible to create one or more forms per table.

♦ Text boxes can be placed on a form which show the data from one field, or which combine and manipulate the data from more than one field.

♦ Not all fields have to be represented on a form and text boxes can be made read-only.

♦ Finally, the access that a user has to the set of forms can be controlled.

Given this level of flexibility, forms become quite remarkable tools. Imagine that you have a table which stores information about your employees. It contains some data that is generally available (name, address, phone number etc.) and some which is confidential (salary, medical history, criminal record). Clearly it is unacceptable to give all of your employees direct access to this table. Nevertheless different people in different departments need access to different subsets of the data that it contains.

Three of the forms that you might consider building are:

♦ a read-only form designed to help the employees locate and contact each other; this form is freely accessible. It shows only the individual's name (concatenated into a single text box), department, extension number and email address.

♦ one which is only available to the medical department and shows the name (again concatenated), department and medical history. Only the last field is editable and access to the form is controlled using a password known only to the medical department.

♦ one which shows the name (as two separate fields), address, home phone number, department and extension in editable text boxes. It is available to the personnel department.

The manner in which you set up these forms and the access that you allow different people to the data in the table is a matter for discussion within your company. The important point is that forms are the tools which can control access in this way.

5

Queries

Creating a database and then entering all the data takes time and effort. Simply creating a database is not an end in itself; unless you are one of those sad people who actually enjoys that sort of thing, there has to be some gain for the pain. That gain lies in the easy access to the data that an electronic database provides.

5.1 Queries Usually Find Subsets of the Data

By far the most common operation performed on the data in a table (Figure 5.1) is to subset it.

This operation can be done by field (Figure 5.2), by record (Figure 5.3) or both (Figure 5.4).

EMPLOYEES

EmployeeNo	FirstName	LastName	DateOfBirth	DateEmployed
1	Manny	Tomanny	12 Apr 1956	01 May 1989
2	Rosanne	Kolumn	21 Mar 1967	01 Jan 1990
3	Cas	Kade	01 May 1967	01 Apr 1992
4	Norma	Lyzation	03 Apr 1956	01 Apr 1992
5	Juan	Tomani	12 Apr 1956	01 Apr 1992

Figure 5.1 *A typical, if very small, table of data.*

JustNames

FirstName	LastName
Manny	Tomanny
Rosanne	Kolumn
Cas	Kade
Norma	Lyzation
Juan	Tomani

Figure 5.2 *Subsetting the data by field.*

JustNorma

EmployeeNo	FirstName	LastName	DateOfBirth	DateEmployed
4	Norma	Lyzation	03 Apr 1956	01 Apr 1992

Figure 5.3 *Subsetting data by record.*

JustNorma'sName

FirstName	LastName
Norma	Lyzation

Figure 5.4 *Subsetting the data by field and record.*

Operations which extract data from a table in this way are called queries. Given a table of five fields and five records, there is no need to use a query; you can find the required information by eye. Given 50 fields and 100,000 records your eye may need a little help. These subsetting operations rarely stem from a desire to play with the data *per se*; instead they arise because people ask questions. Figure 5.2, for example, answers a question which might be 'What are the names of my employees?'. In Figure 5.3 the question might be 'What information is available about my employees called Norma?'. Figure 5.4 might have been produced to answer the question, 'What are the full names of all of my employees called Norma?'.

5.2 Queries, Answer Tables and Base Tables Finally Defined Properly and Closure Mentioned Briefly

It is important not to become confused between a query and the answer that it produces.

A query is simply a question which can be asked of the data in a table. This query can be expressed in several ways (see Sections 5.5 and 5.6) and it can even be expressed in human language. In this context, the method of expression is immaterial; a query is a question which you ask about the data in a table. Having asked that question, you expect an answer and the answer appears in a tabular layout called an answer table. An answer table will have columns and rows and it will look and feel like a table. Note that the last sentence sounds dictatorial 'It *will* have columns and rows, it *will* look and feel like a table'; this is because one of the central tenets of relational database theory, known as *closure*, is that the result of a query will always be a table (see, for example, Figures 5.2, 5.3 and 5.4). This principle is very important, but it is easier to explain why it is so important when we are dealing with multiple tables, so I'll leave more detailed discussions until Part 2.

Answer tables are such an important part of a database that it becomes important to be able to distinguish them from the original tables. These original tables can be, and often are, referred to as *base tables* (Figure 5.5).

As we have seen above, base tables have certain characteristics, not the least of which is that the data they contain can be edited. The same should be true of the answer tables which arise from a query; the data you see in the

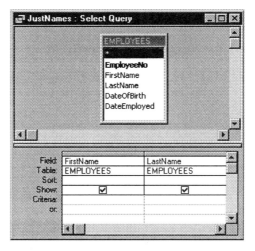

Figure 5.5 *The relationship between a base table, a query and an answer table.*

answer table should be editable. This means you should be able to look at an answer table on-screen and edit the data you see there. Those edits should pass 'through' the answer table and actually alter the data in the base table from which the data originally came.

I say 'should be' editable, because they often are. However, there are two main reasons why you may come across answer tables which are not editable.

The first is that not every PC-based RDBMS implements this highly useful feature, a failure which, incidentally, excludes them from being true relational DBMSs (see Chapter 21). Access, you will be delighted to learn, supports this facility.

The second reason is that, under certain circumstances, allowing you to edit the data displayed in an answer table is, as we database professionals say, 'incompatible with preserving the integrity of the data'.

AgeWhenEmployed

FirstName	LastName	DateOfBirth	DateEmployed	AgeWhenEmployed
Manny	Tomanny	12 Apr 1956	01 May 1989	33
Rosanne	Kolumn	21 Mar 1967	01 Jan 1990	22
Cas	Kade	01 May 1967	01 Apr 1992	24
Norma	Lyzation	03 Apr 1956	01 Apr 1992	35
Juan	Tomani	12 Apr 1956	01 Apr 1992	35

Figure 5.6 *This answer table summarizes data and therefore parts should not be editable.*

This situation can arise, for example, when certain types of query draw data from multiple tables or when a query summarizes data. Under these circumstances the RDBMS should *not* allow you to edit the data in an answer table. For example, we have already seen a table of information about employees. It stores the employees' dates of birth and the dates upon which they were employed. From these two pieces of information, it is clearly possible to work out how old each person was (in years) when employed and we can build a query to do this.

AgeWhenEmployed is being calculated as the integer value of the number of days between the dates divided by 365.25. I know this will very occasionally give the wrong answer, but then dates are notoriously tricky anyway...

The answer table looks like Figure 5.6. The data in the first four fields comes directly from the base table EMPLOYEES and can be edited in the answer table above. The data in the fifth field, AgeWhenEmployed, is calculated and therefore cannot be edited. If this seems strange, ask yourself this question: 'If we alter the value in the first record to read 35 instead of 33, which of the two date fields in the underlying base table should be altered to make the calculation yield 35?'. The RDBMS cannot make this sort of decision, so the field is uneditable.

However, assuming that a given query *is* editable (both in theory and practice), I stress again that the actual changes you make to the data will be fed back to the underlying base tables (see Figure 5.7). In other words, despite the fact that answer tables look like distinct entities on screen, in practice it is perhaps more accurate to think of them as windows onto the original base table.

There is another reason for stressing the fundamental difference between a query (which is, in essence, a question) and the answer table that a given query generates. Suppose you create a query, store it and use it on more than one occasion. Would you expect it to produce the same answer table every time it is run?

If the data in the base table is the same, the answer table will be identical. But if the data in the base table has changed, the data in the answer table may also have changed. A little thought shows that we can use this very much to our advantage.

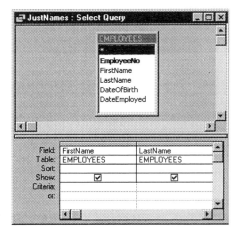

EMPLOYEES : Table				
EmployeeNo	FirstName	LastName	DateOfBirth	DateEmployed
1 Manny		Tomanny	12 Apr 1956	01 May 1989
2 Rosanne		Kolumn	21 Mar 1967	01 Jan 1990
3 Cas		Kade	01 May 1967	01 Apr 1992
4 Norma		Lyzation	03 Apr 1956	01 Apr 1992
5 Juan		Tomani	12 Apr 1956	01 Apr 1992

Figure 5.7 *How the edits made to an answer table are actually editing the data in the underlying base table.*

Suppose you build a query which looks at the data in the table shown in Figure 5.8 and summarizes the total amount spent on each product (see Figure 5.9). Time passes and more orders arrive (Figure 5.10). When the same query is run again, it generates a different answer table (Figure 5.11) which contains the up-to-date information.

ORDERSFEW

OrderID	Customer	Item	CostOfItem	NoOfItems
1	Holly	Haddock	$3.45	23
2	Bill	Herring	$2.56	45
3	Jane	Haddock	$3.45	43

Figure 5.8 *A table of data.*

TotalSalesForEachProduct-ORDERSFEW

Item	Total
Haddock	$227.70
Herring	$115.20

Figure 5.9 *The answer table from a query which shows the total sales for each product.*

ORDERSMANY

OrderID	Customer	Item	CostOfItem	NoOfItems
1	Holly	Haddock	$3.45	23
2	Bill	Herring	$2.56	45
3	Jane	Haddock	$3.45	43
4	Henry	Salmon	$5.67	34
5	Mark	Shrimps	$3.23	100
6	Mary	Prawns	$3.45	34
7	Bill	Herring	$2.56	56
8	Holly	Haddock	$3.75	45

Figure 5.10 *More data is added to the table....*

TotalSalesForEachProduct-ORDERSMANY

Item	Total
Haddock	$396.45
Herring	$258.56
Prawns	$117.30
Salmon	$192.78
Shrimps	$323.00

Figure 5.11 *The answer table from the same query, showing that the answer has changed.*

In the sample database supplied on the CD-ROM, these answer tables are actually produced by two queries. In fact, the two queries are effectively identical; they are just looking at two separate tables. This is to save you the effort of typing in the extra records. If you want to be sure I'm not fooling you, just type the extra records into the table called ORDERSFEW and re-run the appropriate query.

This separation of the query from the answer is wonderfully useful and many queries are used over and over again at different times. And if you ever need to take a snapshot of the data at a particular time, you can always get the query to generate a separate, new table which is written to disk under a different name (making it, in effect, a base table), thus preserving the data for future reference.

One of the reviewers added 'It might be worth saying that the table will no longer be an answer table in the sense that you can't update through it. However, you can still update the data it contains – including the fields that you couldn't update before'.

5.3 Summarizing Data

At their most basic, queries extract a subset of the data in a table, but they can do much more. It is perfectly possible to use a query not only to extract a subset of the data but also to perform some mathematical manipulation upon it. In the case of Figure 5.6 the manipulation involves dates, but given numerical data many other mathematical operations are possible (averages, standard deviations, variances, minimum and/or maximum values etc.).

5.4 Other Useful Queries

And it just gets better and better. Not only can queries be used to summarize data, they can be used to perform lots of other manipulations. For example:

♦ *Update*

Queries can be used to update the existing data in a table. For example, if you have a table of items for sale and you want to increase all of the prices by 10%, you can use an update query to do the job. You can also be more selective and update the price by 10% only if the item costs more than $2.45.

♦ *Append*

Queries can be created which will locate specific data in one table (find the names of the salespeople who have exceeded this year's sales quotas) and add that data to another table (one which holds the names of everyone who is going on the company outing).

♦ *Delete*

Queries can also be created which will locate specific records in one table (find the names of the salespeople who have *not* exceeded this year's sales quotas) and delete those records from the table.

5.5 Graphical Querying Tools

A query is a question you ask of a table and that question can be expressed in a variety of ways. It can be asked in a human language, such as English: 'Give me the phone numbers of all the customers who live in Dundee' or mangled French 'Donnez-moi le phone number de tout les customers qui restent en Dundee'. Sadly, no one has yet built an RDBMS which is capable of understanding the rich variety of ways in which humans can express questions, so we use more formal ways of expressing questions to an RDBMS.

In order to make the process of querying a database more accessible to the majority of users, RDBMSs typically have graphical querying tools (Figure 5.12).

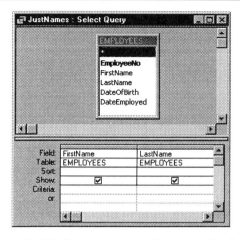

Figure 5.12 *A query expressed in a graphical way.*

5.6 SQL

Graphical querying tools are excellent, yet in the world of databases you will constantly hear people talking about SQL (Structured Query Language). SQL is a text-based querying system (see the example below) which takes slightly longer to learn and is less intuitive to use than a GUI-based querying system.

```
SELECT DISTINCTROW EMPLOYEES.FirstName, EMPLOYEES.LastName
FROM EMPLOYEES;
```

So why would anyone bother with SQL? Well, SQL is a standard, meaning that many RDBMSs use it. In addition, it is more versatile than graphical querying tools; some complex queries which can be expressed in SQL cannot be expressed using a graphical tool.

If you are new to databases, I'd give SQL a miss for the moment. However, once you begin to get used to querying data, SQL is a subject which well repays some study. Those who feel the need are directed to Chapter 25.

6

Reports

Reports are rather like queries in that they can be used to summarize the information in a database. One difference is that reports usually produce printed output. Suppose that, at the end of every month, you need to produce a list of all invoices issued in that month, together with their individual values and a total. The best method is to use a report.

You need the invoices grouped by product with subtotals? Hey, no problem, use a report.

Customer	No Of Items	% of Total
Bill		
	45	
	56	
	101	27%
Henry		
	34	
	34	9%
Holly		
	23	
	45	
	68	18%
Jane		
	43	
	43	11%
Mark		
	100	
	100	26%
Mary		
	34	
	34	9%
Grand Total:	**380**	

Figure 6.1 *A simple report.*

The sad truth is that the full power of reports cannot be demonstrated when they are used with single tables of data. Fear not: they will make more sense when we get on to using multiple tables. However, just to give you an idea of a simple one, Figure 6.1 shows a report which totals the numbers of items ordered by different customers. This report is based on the data in Figure 5.10.

7

Summary of
Part 1

To summarize the basic components of a database:

♦ A base table is a repository for data.
♦ Forms are devices for viewing and entering data into the table.
♦ Queries are used to extract, subset and summarize data from the table, and to update the table.
♦ Reports are used to print out some or all of the data in the table.

Tables, forms, reports and queries are the core components of a database. So far I have described each in isolation. However, when they are used together, they display a wonderful synergy. For example, as described above, queries are storable questions, the output from which are tables. Forms are based on tables; thus a form can be based on a query. This is a really important point, so it is worth repeating. Forms can be based upon queries.

Suppose you have a table that stores all of the orders that have come in from your customers. If you create a query that extracts only those orders which remain unpaid, you can then base a form on that query. Whenever you tell the software that you want to use the form, it will automatically run the query, extract the relevant information and display it in the form. Figure 7.1 shows a simple database constructed in this way.

Part of the reason for building databases is to simplify the interface that the user encounters. Forms can be easy to use and understand, so they can be made into the sole way in which the user interacts with the data. To add a new order they choose the NewOrders form; to see how much money is currently outstanding, they select the form which displays this information and so on. Indeed, forms can be constructed whose sole function is to allow access to other forms. The one shown in Figure 7.2 simply provides a series

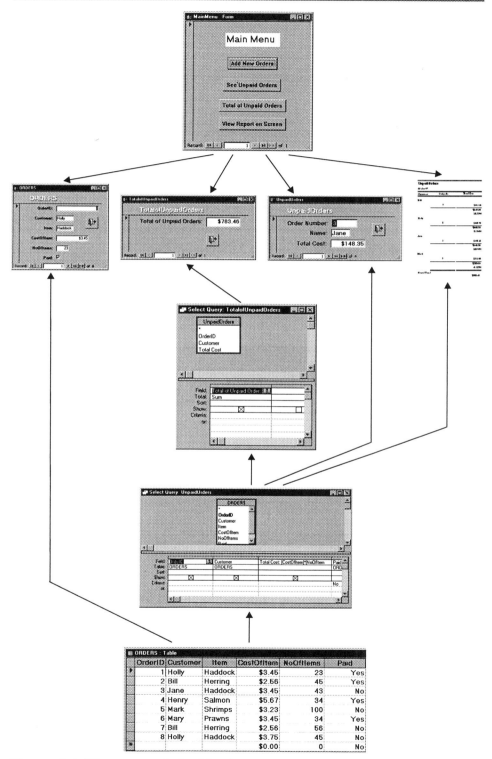

Figure 7.1 *The ways in which tables, forms, queries and reports can be used together.*

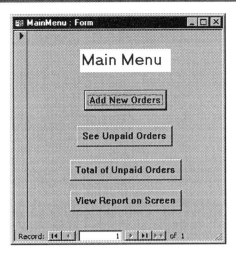

Figure 7.2 *A main menu form which gives access to the components of the database.*

of buttons which, when pressed, lead to other forms, or cause reports to print the required information.

This part has looked at databases that are built around single tables of data. In practice, databases are often best built around multiple tables. The next part explains why multiple tables are such a good idea and describes the mechanisms that are used to make their use as painless as possible.

Part 2

A Multi-Table, Single-User Database

8

Introduction to Part 2

So far we have confined ourselves to databases based upon a single table of data. Such databases are great for learning about databases and occasionally the data you meet in the real world will actually fit neatly into just one table. For example, I once built a single-table database for SHARP (Scottish Heart and Arterial disease Risk Prevention: http://www.scotland.net/business/sharp).

Distressingly, Scotland remains one of the world leaders in the league table of premature deaths from cardiovascular disease. SHARP is a charity that aims to make people aware of both the problem and possible remedies. From a base in a traveling bus, SHARP staff used to visit sites (factories, schools etc.) and assess individuals from the community for their risk of heart disease. The data collected consisted of 109 different pieces of information about each person. Since the data collected for each patient was unique, there was no advantage in using multiple tables. I built SHARP's database and it was a rare case; the only time I have ever used over 100 fields in a table and the only time I have built a single-table database (apart from simple address lists). So single-table databases do exist but experience suggests that almost all databases actually need multiple tables of data.

A perfectly reasonable question at this point is 'Why?'. After all, single tables are easy to manage and often feel intuitively right. We have lots of orders and we want to store information about each order; why can't we just use a single ORDERS table? The Victorian clerks beloved of Dickens' novels put such orders into a ledger book which was essentially a single table of data.

What I have to do now is to convince you that single tables produce problems in computerized databases. Then I have to convince you that the extra effort involved in learning how to construct and maintain multiple-table databases is worthwhile. To put that more simply, I have to convince you that the gain is worth the pain. The next two chapters are designed to do just that.

After absorbing those two chapters, hopefully, you'll be convinced and will be prepared to read the rest of the part which tells you what you need to know in order to make multiple tables work together effectively.

9

Serious Problems with Single Tables

Suppose we decide to use a single table to store information for our company. In that table we store the details of the orders that we process. These details include item sold, price, customer information, date of sale etc. If we ran a bonus incentive scheme, we would also need to include the name of the employee who made the sale. Since this is the only table we are going to use, we also need to include any other information that we store about the employees – name, date of birth, date first employed, salary, address, home telephone number etc. – see Figure 9.1.

SINGLETABLE

OrderNo	FirstName	LastName	DateOfBirth	DateEmployed	Customer	Supplier	Price	Item
1	Manny	Tomanny	12 Apr 1956	01 May 1989	Henderson	Harrison	$235.00	Desk
2	Norma	Lyzation	03 Apr 1956	01 Apr 1992	Thompson	Ford	$234.00	Chair
3	Manny	Tomanny	12 Apr 1956	01 May 1989	McColgan	Harrison	$415.00	Table
4	Rosanne	Kolumns	21 Mar 1967	01 Jan 1990	Wellington	Ford	$350.00	Lamp
5	Cas	Kade	01 May 1967	01 Apr 1992	Henderson	Ford	$234.00	Chair
6	Rosanne	Kolumns	21 Mar 1967	01 Jan 1990	Wellington	Ford	$350.00	Lamp
7	Rosanne	Kolumns	21 Mar 1967	01 Jan 1990	Henderson	Harrison	$235.00	Desk

Figure 9.1 *A single table containing information about orders placed with a company.*

We would also need to store the same sorts of details about the customers, but I have left much of the detail out of the example so that the table doesn't spread right across the page and disappear off the edge.

However, even with its unrealistically small set of fields, this table can technically be described as a 'dog's breakfast' and for several reasons.

9.1 Redundant Data

There is a considerable amount of repeated (or redundant) data in this table. Names, prices and dates are all stored multiple times, simultaneously wasting vast amounts of disk space and potentially slowing down any queries we run against the table. In addition, every time an employee makes another sale, we have to type in their name, date of birth, date first employed etc. Would you want to type in all that data every time? And, since many of our customers (hopefully) will be giving us multiple orders, we will find that their details are also appearing over and over again. In addition, you will notice that we use Harrison as our supplier of desks. This fact is recorded twice already in the table and, if we sell a thousand desks, it will be immortalized 1,000 times; one can't help feeling that once would be enough. And the problems don't end with the amount of work required to input the data.

9.2 Typographical Errors

Each record in this table represents a sale and we would hope that most customers come back for repeat purchases. If you had to type in words like 'Henderson' and 'Thompson' several hundred times (once for each sale to that customer), could you guarantee to do so perfectly every time? What about 'McCollgan' (one 'l' or two)? And even if you were sure you could do it correctly each time, what happens if several different people are entering data into the table? Will they all be consistent? It is all too easy to end up with a table like Figure 9.2.

VERYBADSINGLETABLE

OrderNo	FirstName	LastName	DateOfBirth	DateEmployed	Customer	Supplier	Price	Item
1	Manny	Tomanny	12 Apr 1956	01 May 1989	Henderson	Harrison	$235.00	Desk
2	Norma	Lization	03 Apr 1956	01 Apr 1992	Tompson	Ford	$234.00	Chair
3	Manny	Tomanny	12 Apr 1956	01 May 1989	McCollgan	Harrison	$415.00	Table
4	Rosanne	Kolumns	21 Mar 1967	01 Jan 1990	Wellington	Ford	$350.00	Lamp
5	Cas	Kade	01 May 1967	01 Apr 1992	S. Henderson	Ford	$234.00	Chair
6	Rosanne	Columns	21 Mar 1967	01 Jan 1990	Ms Wellington	Ford	$350.00	Lamp
7	Rosa	Kolum	21 Mar 1967	01 Jan 1990	Henderson	Harrison	$235.00	Desk

Figure 9.2 *A single table containing inaccurate information about employees and their sales.*

If we now search the table to find out how many sales a certain 'Rosanne Kolumns' has made for the company, we will get the answer 'one'. If she works on commission she will not be pleased.

Incidentally, just in case you don't believe that people really make typographical errors, the following (Figure 9.3) is a list of variations of my name that I have received in the post over the past five years or so. Many have been received multiple times and most appear to be in some kind of database or other. For the record, I do have two middle initials – they are A and F – and a Ph.D.

D Whitehorn	Dr Whytehorn
Dr A Whitehorns	Dwhutehorn
Dr M A F Whiteh	Marie Whitehorn
Dr M A T Whitehorn	Marj Whitehorn
Dr M A Whitehord	Mark Whitburn
Dr M F Whitehorn	Mark Whitehall, Esq.,
Dr M Tehorn	Mark Whiteham
Dr M Whiteham	Mark Whitehaven
Dr M Whitethorn	Mark Whitehern
Dr M Whitewhorn	Mark Whiteholn
Dr M Whytehorn	Mark Witehorn
Dr MAF Whitecorn	Mike Whitehorn
Dr Mark Whitehord	Mr D R Whitehorn
Dr Mark Whitekorn	Mr D.A.M. Whitehorn
Dr MHF Whitehorn, BSc, PhD	Mr M Horn
Dr N A F Whitehorn	Mr M Whiteham
Dr N Whitehorn	Mr Mack Horn
Dr Whipehorn	Mr Mark Whitehead
Dr Whitehall	Mr Mark Whitehoarn
Dr Whitehan	Mr Mark Whitehouse
Dr Whitehorne	Mr Mark Whithorn
Dr Whitekor	Whitehorn Dark
Dr Whiteman	

Figure 9.3 *A list of name variants.*

I rather like 'Whitehorn Dark'; it's sophisticated and a little mysterious. 'Dwhutehorn' is not bad either... but I'm not so sure about 'Whipehorn'.

9.3 Updating Data

Suppose that Rosanne Kolumns is a good and loyal employee and manages to broker thousands of sales for the company over a number of years. Then she marries and elects to adopt her husband's last name. If we want to keep our records consistent, someone is going to have to go through all of the records and manually change her name.

9.4 Modifying Data

Given that all of the data is placed in a single table, we have problems when we try to store certain types of information. These problems are called 'modification anomalies' and can be demonstrated with the table shown in Figure 9.1.

Suppose we delete the record for sale number 3 (the record with OrderNo equal to 3). This happens to be the only record which contains the data which tells us that tables are supplied to our company by Harrison and that they cost $415.00. We can't afford to lose this information, but, given a single table, we have nowhere else to store it. And what happens if we want to store information about a new employee who has just started work but hasn't made any sales yet? If we insist on using this single-table structure, we have to wait until the new employee makes his or her first sale before we can record the fact that the new employee was born on 01-May-1957 or we have to use incomplete records to store such information.

The former is known as a 'deletion anomaly' and the latter an 'insertion anomaly'; both can be cured by using an additional pair of tables, one to store information about the items that we sell, the other for information about employees.

9.5 Summary

Single tables suffer from serious problems when they are used to store complex information. Those problems are:

- ◆ Redundant data, which makes the table large, slow and unwieldy.
- ◆ Typographic errors caused by typing the same information multiple times.
- ◆ Difficulties in updating and modifying data

I am aware that some of these problems can be overcome without going to multiple tables. For example, consider the problem of Rosanne Kolumns' name change. We could use an update query to replace her old name with the new. In addition, we might even decide that we want to keep her old name on the old orders. The deletion and insertion anomalies are more difficult to deal with, although we could start storing records which are incomplete.

However, experience has shown that these solutions end up being more complicated than going over to a multi-table database. After all, multi-table databases don't have any virtue in themselves; the only reason that they have been widely adopted is that they solve the problems inherent in single-table databases in the most efficient way possible.

10

Multiple Tables Cure Serious Problems

So, let's have a look at the way in which multiple tables can remove these problems.

The two tables shown in Figure 10.1 hold the same information as the unwieldy one in Figure 9.1, but together they take up less space on the hard disk. (In fact, the reduction in disk space is completely trivial in this example because the initial table was so small. However, as later examples will show, the saving becomes really significant with greater quantities of data.)

EMPLOYEES

EmployeeNo	FirstName	LastName	DateOfBirth	DateEmployed
1	Manny	Tomanny	12 Apr 1956	01 May 1989
2	Rosanne	Kolumns	21 Mar 1967	01 Jan 1990
3	Cas	Kade	01 May 1967	01 Apr 1992
4	Norma	Lyzation	03 Apr 1956	01 Apr 1992

ORDERS

OrderNo	EmployeeNo	Customer	Supplier	Price	Item
1	1	Henderson	Harrison	$235.00	Desk
2	4	Thompson	Ford	$234.00	Chair
3	1	McColgan	Harrison	$415.00	Table
4	2	Wellington	Ford	$350.00	Lamp
5	3	Henderson	Ford	$234.00	Chair
6	2	Wellington	Ford	$350.00	Lamp
7	2	Henderson	Harrison	$235.00	Desk

Figure 10.1 *The same data as in Figure 9.1, but now in two tables.*

What I have done is to move the data relating to employees into a sepa-rate table and to use a 'pointer' to that data in the form of the EmployeeNo field in the ORDERS table. Thus from the ORDERS table we can see that sale number 2 was made by the employee with the EmployeeNo of 4. Referring to the EMPLOYEES table, we can then see that this is Norma Lyzation. (This use of 'pointers' is essentially part of the mechanism used to maintain a rela-tional database and is covered in detail in Chapter 14.)

In fact, it is clear that we could continue this process and separate out the information about customers into a third table and the information about items into a fourth. However, with the very restricted number of fields shown in this cut-down table, that would be rather pointless. In addition, the process involved in creating each of those would be exactly the same as that required for the EMPLOYEES table, so we'll just use these two tables to illustrate the general principle for now.

It is true that, to recover the original information, constant reference must be made to the employee number in both tables, and the process feels horribly unwieldy. In practice the RDBMS will do this for you transpar-ently (meaning that you don't even have to be aware that it is being done). As we will see later, once the database has been set up, you wouldn't nor-mally look at these tables in their 'raw' state like this. Instead, you would in-teract with the data via forms (Figures 10.2 and 10.3) which would show the data in whatever manner you desired.

In the last chapter we looked at four areas that can be problematical if you use single tables, namely:

♦ Redundant data
♦ Typographical errors
♦ Updating data
♦ Modifying data

We'll cover the same four areas again, looking at how the use of multiple tables can reduce or eliminate those problems.

Figure 10.2 *An order-centric view of the data from the tables in Figure 10.1.*

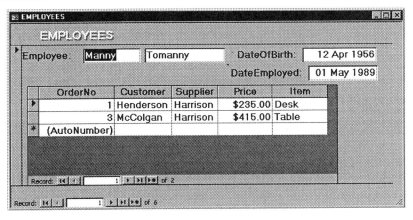

Figure 10.3 *An employee-centric view of the same data.*

10.1 Redundant Data

Given the small examples shown here, the savings in table size produced by splitting tables appear trivial, but more realistic tables have significant savings. For example, suppose you have 1,000 employees and store 1 kbyte of data about each. Your database also stores 2 kbyte of data about each of 100,000 sales. If you elect to use a single-table solution (as in Figure 9.1), each of the 100,000 records will contain an extra 1 kbyte of data about the salesperson. Given a two-table solution, that information is held only once. Thus the sizes are as shown in Table 10.1.

Table 10.1 *The savings in disk space that can be produced by using two tables*

	One Table	Two Tables
No. of records	100,000	100,000 (from the ORDERS table) + 1,000 (EMPLOYEES table) = 101,000
Employee data	100,000 kbyte	1,000 kbyte
Sales data	200,000 kbyte	200,000 kbyte
Total data	300 Mbyte	201 Mbyte
Data saving		99 Mbytes

For information:

1,024 bytes = 1 kbyte
1,024 kbyte = 1,048,576 bytes = 1 Mbyte

The saving is slightly exaggerated, since adding the EmployeeNo fields to the two-table system produces a slight overhead, but you probably get the general idea.

This looks good but it gets better. As the complexity of the data expands, the size problem inherent in using a single table increases catastrophically. Suppose we assume (quite reasonably) that each order can be for more than one item. Since each record in the single-table solution can only hold information about one item in the order, an order for three items will need three records in the table, as shown in Figure 10.4.

MULTIPLEPARTORDERS

Part	OrderNo	FirstName	LastName	DateOfBirth	DateEmployed	Supplier	Item	Customer
1	1	Manny	Tomanny	12 Apr 1956	01 May 1989	Harrison	Table	Henderson
2	1	Manny	Tomanny	12 Apr 1956	01 May 1989	Harrison	Desk	Henderson
3	2	Norma	Lyzation	03 Apr 1956	01 Apr 1992	Ford	Chair	Thompson
4	3	Manny	Tomanny	12 Apr 1956	01 May 1989	Harrison	Table	McColgan
5	3	Manny	Tomanny	12 Apr 1956	01 May 1989	Ford	Chair	McColgan
6	4	Rosanne	Kolumns	21 Mar 1967	01 Jan 1990	Ford	Chair	Wellington
7	4	Rosanne	Kolumns	21 Mar 1967	01 Jan 1990	Ford	Lamp	Wellington
8	4	Rosanne	Kolumns	21 Mar 1967	01 Jan 1990	Harrison	Desk	Wellington
9	5	Cas	Kade	01 May 1967	01 Apr 1992	Ford	Chair	Henderson
10	5	Cas	Kade	01 May 1967	01 Apr 1992	Ford	Lamp	Henderson
11	6	Rosanne	Kolumns	21 Mar 1967	01 Jan 1990	Harrison	Table	Wellington
12	6	Rosanne	Kolumns	21 Mar 1967	01 Jan 1990	Ford	Lamp	Wellington
13	7	Rosanne	Kolumns	21 Mar 1967	01 Jan 1990	Harrison	Desk	Henderson

Figure 10.4 *Showing part of a single-table solution for orders which can contain multiple items.*

We can make the same assumptions as before: 1,000 employees, 1 kbyte of data about each one and 100,000 sales with 2 kbyte about each. We can add the assumption that we can sell any one of 2,000 different items (and hold 1 kbyte on each one) and we will assume that an average order is for five items. The correct way of handling this data is to split it across four tables: one for the employees, one for the orders, one for the items and a fourth one which joins the items to the orders. The need for this fourth table hasn't been explained as yet (it will be in Chapter 14), but if you could take it on trust for the present, it will make my life a lot easier. (Trust me: I'm a database freak.) Each record in this joining table will be tiny, perhaps 8 bytes long (or 0.01 kbyte to be generous).

Again we can compare the efficiency of the single-table and multiple-table solutions in an approximate manner, as shown in Table 10.2.

Table 10.2 *The even greater savings in disk space that can be produced by using four tables.*

	One-table solution	Four-table solution
No. of records	500,000	1,000 (EMPLOYEES) + 100,000 (SALES) + 2,000 (ITEMS) + 500,000 (JOIN) = 603,000
Employee data	500,000 × 1 kbyte = 500,000 kbyte	1,000 × 1 kbyte = 1,000 kbyte
Sales data	500,000 × 2 kbyte = 1,000,000 kbyte	100,000 × 2 kbyte = 200,000 kbyte
Items data	500,000 × 1 kbyte = 500,000 kbyte	2,000 × 1 kbyte = 2,000 kbyte
Joining data	none	500,000 × 0.01 kbyte = 5,000 kbyte
Total	500,000 kbyte + 1,000,000 kbyte + 500,000 kbyte = 2,000,000 kbyte = 2 Gbyte	1,000 kbyte + 200,000 kbyte + 2,000 kbyte + 5,000 kbyte = 207,000 kbyte = 207 Mbyte
Saving		Approximately 1,800 Mbyte = 1.8 Gbyte

For information:

1,024 Mbyte = 1 Gbyte

While this waste of disk space is horribly inelegant, an even greater problem is that all of this repeated data will really slow the database down.

> This example doesn't use a separate table for Customers. As an exercise, if you feel so inclined, you can calculate the additional savings if we assume that we have 2,000 customers and store 2 kbyte of data about each one.

10.2 Typographical Errors

You are, of course, still at liberty to misspell poor Rosanne's last name. However, if you do, the error is likely to be much more obvious because every time her name appears it will be incorrect. In addition, since her name only has to be typed in once, we might hope that data entry boredom would be less of a factor.

10.3 Updating Data

Obviously, changing employee data has only to be done once if an error is made or an employee changes his or her name.

10.4 Modifying Data

The modification anomalies described in the previous chapter disappear as soon as we move to a multi-table solution, assuming that the data is split up into an acceptable set of tables. As you can see from Figure 10.5, we have been able to accommodate a couple of new employees without generating an incomplete record.

EMPLOYEES

EmployeeNo	FirstName	LastName	DateOfBirth	DateEmployed
1	Manny	Tomanny	12 Apr 1956	01 May 1989
2	Rosanne	Kolumns	21 Mar 1967	01 Jan 1990
3	Cas	Kade	01 May 1967	01 Apr 1992
4	Norma	Lyzation	03 Apr 1956	01 Apr 1992
5	Juan	Tomani	12 Apr 1956	01 Apr 1992
6	Del	Eats	01 May 1957	01 May 1994

Figure 10.5 *The EMPLOYEES table with a couple of new employees.*

11

Making Multiple
Tables Work
Together

 You may wonder about the use of the word 'object' in this and subsequent chapters. You may have noticed a great deal of interest in so-called 'object-oriented programming' and you might wonder if there is any connection. In fact, I am using the word 'object' here simply to mean 'thing' or 'entity'. The only reason I don't use the word 'thing' is that it looks thoroughly unprofessional to do so in a book about a serious subject like databases. There is, however, no hidden complex meaning in 'object' as the word is used here, and if you want to mentally substitute the word 'thing', that's fine by me.

The only added complexity is that occasionally I will need to distinguish between an object itself and the class (or type) to which it belongs. For example, Norma Lyzation is an object and she happens to belong to the class of objects called Employees and information about her is therefore stored in the EMPLOYEES table. In practice, people often fail to distinguish between these in conversation. They will say, for example, 'Employees and customers are clearly different objects'; in fact they mean 'Employees and customers are clearly different *classes* of object'.

Worrying about the distinction between an object and the class to which it belongs shouldn't keep you awake at night and I will follow common practice by not bothering to make the distinction unless I think it makes the text clearer to do so.

The last chapter should have convinced you that multiple tables are the only way in which to store complex data efficiently. Now we need to look at how they can be managed in a relational database. This in turn brings us to a consideration of what we want a database to do for us.

Databases Are Designed to Model the Real World

The real world is full of objects – employees, orders, customers, items for sale etc. In the real world, these objects have relationships with each other – one employee will deal with multiple customers, one customer can buy multiple items and so on.

Databases, therefore, have to store information about these different objects and also about the relationships that exist between them.

What do you have to think about before you can build a database? There are five key areas which need to be considered:

1. How is information about the different objects stored in the database? In other words, how do we 'map' our real world objects onto our tables and ensure that we get the right data into the right tables?
2. What relationships can exist between real world objects?
3. How are these relationships modeled and maintained in a database?
4. How can we make the tables, forms, queries and reports work together in a database?
5. How do we maintain integrity within the data that we store in the database?

I suspect that it will come as no great surprise that these five topics make up the next five chapters.

12

Getting the Data into the Correct Tables

How do you ensure that you split your data up into an acceptable set of tables? For example, if I store all of the information about employees in one table, how did I know that one table for employees was a good idea? What made me choose a separate table for the items that we sell? Again, if we sell mostly furniture and then start selling ice-cream, should the information relating to ice-cream sales go in the same table as that for furniture sales or a different one? How are you supposed to make these decisions?

Well, there's some good news and some bad news. The bad news is that this *can* develop into a complex question, with equally complex answers. The good news is that it usually doesn't. If, for example, you are trying to build a multi-table database for a small to medium-sized business, it is usually fairly obvious which tables you need, and there is an excellent 'rule of thumb' to help you, which is as follows:

> Provide a separate table for each class of 'real world' object about which you are trying to store information in the database.

That's it. Thus an employee is one such class of object, a customer is another and an order is a third. (Chapter 14 discusses an 'extension' to this rule but I'd ignore it until you get there, unless, of course, I have inflamed your curiosity by mentioning it.) The tables then take only the fields which contain information which is unique to the object that the table represents. So the name of the customer goes into the CUSTOMERS table, the name of the employee into the EMPLOYEES table and so on.

Which bring us rather neatly to the problem that I posed above. If we sell mostly furniture and then start selling ice-cream, should the information relating to ice-cream sales go in the same table as that for furniture sales or a different one?

I can't give a 'Yes/No' answer here because it will depend on the information that we need to store. Think of it this way. Suppose we sell furniture and want to store the following information about each piece that we stock:

Stock no.
Purchase date
Purchase price
Sale date
Sale price
Color

Then we start selling ice-cream and it so happens that we want to store the following information about ice-cream:

Stock no.
Purchase date
Purchase price
Sale date
Sale price
Color

Since we happen to be interested in exactly the same characteristics (or properties) for these two classes of object (furniture and ice-cream), then as far as the database is concerned, we actually have only one class of object here. In other words, we can happily store furniture and ice-cream in the same table.

If, on the other hand, the information we wanted to store about ice-cream was characterized like this:

Stock no.
Flavour
Melting point
Shelf life
Viscosity

then it would clearly be foolish to try to store the information about ice-cream in the same table as the information about furniture.

Rather neatly, the act of considering this sort of problem gives us another mechanism for identifying classes of object in the database. This doesn't mean that we have to alter the rule of thumb given above, it simply means that we now have an additional way of identifying and classifying objects.

Objects can be distinguished by the properties (characteristics, attributes – call them what you will) that we want to store about them in the database. Suppose you are evaluating two apparently different object types, say full-time and part-time employees. Simply list the properties (fields) that you need to store about each one. If the list is the same, then they are actually one type of object and you only need one table. If the list is different, you have two classes of object and need two tables.

12.1 Not Normalization (and Not ER Modeling Either)

So, the rule of thumb is simple; give each 'real world' object class a table of its own.

However, I would be failing in my duty if I didn't tell you that there are times, particularly if you are working on large complex databases, where this rule of thumb (even in the modified form discussed in Chapter 14) fails to ensure that you have chosen the correct tables and fields. This failing was noticed early in the history of relational databases and quite a long series of papers was published which addressed this problem. From these papers, a process called normalization emerged, and there is a large chapter dedicated to normalization in Part 4. The reason that it isn't covered here is simply that, under most circumstances with simple databases, the rule of thumb is sufficient.

Personally, if this was my first attempt to understand relational databases, I'd ignore normalization for now and concentrate on all the other concepts that have to be absorbed. Then, once I'd got a good grasp of those, I'd read the chapter on normalization. This isn't meant to imply that normalization is a particularly difficult concept, simply that you probably don't need it now.

While we are on the subject of 'nots', there is another process called ER (Entity Relationship) modeling which is worth mentioning (but not covering) here. ER modeling started as a way of representing the design of a database on paper. It is a formalized way of showing the overall design of the database without including so much detail that the complete picture is difficult or impossible to understand. Not surprisingly, computerized packages have subsequently been developed which allow you to lay out these designs on-screen. ER modeling is wonderful, but, just like normalization, I don't think it is worth covering here. True, ER modeling makes the process of database design easier, but only when the database is relatively complex. When you are starting to design databases, it simply represents yet another layer of complexity. I haven't even included a chapter about the subject, since there is no definitive ER standard. However, if and when you start designing large complex databases, the process of ER modeling is likely to repay further study.

Anyway, that's enough about what we are *not* going to cover....

We are going to need an example to demonstrate how you can get the right data into the right tables, so let's rough out an example database now and try to identify the obvious objects that make up the data. I'll try to keep an eye on the size. It needs to be large enough to illustrate all of the principles we need, but not so large that it becomes unwieldy.

12.2 Object Identification

Imagine that you run a small business which exists to sell items to customers. Immediately we can see at least three object classes – Customers, Items and Orders (which records the transactions).

♦ You employ people who work for you (object class – Employee).

- ◆ Certain of your employees are allocated rooms in the head office in which to work (object class – Rooms).
- ◆ You also rent buildings, such as warehouses (object class – Buildings).

We can go on for a while longer (an object class like Suppliers springs instantly to mind) but these six objects are all we need to illustrate the principles.

So, we have six clearly defined object classes:

Customers
Items
Orders
Employees
Rooms
Buildings

Following the rule of thumb, we need six tables:

CUSTOMERS – information about customers.
ITEMS – information about the items that we offer for sale.
ORDERS – information about orders placed.
EMPLOYEES – information about employees.
ROOMS – information about the individual rooms that we have in our head office.
BUILDINGS – information concerning the rents that the company pays for its buildings.

What fields will go into each table? Only those which are unique to that table. Consider into which table you would place the following potential pieces of information:

Date of birth of employee
Order number
Customer name
Employee name
Item name
Customer address
Next of kin of employee
Room numbers
Rent

The answers:

Date of birth of employee – EMPLOYEES
Order number – ORDERS
Customer name – CUSTOMERS
Employee name – EMPLOYEES
Item name – ITEMS
Customer address – CUSTOMER
Next of kin of employee – EMPLOYEE
Room numbers – ROOMS
Rent – BUILDINGS

To stop this all sounding too abstract, here are a couple of the tables (Figure 12.1), each with a small quantity of data. Again I have tried to keep these as small as possible.

EMPLOYEES

EmployeeNo	FirstName	LastName	DateOfBirth	DateEmployed
1	Manny	Tomanny	12 Apr 1956	01 May 1989
2	Rosanne	Kolumns	21 Mar 1967	01 Jan 1990
3	Cas	Kade	01 May 1967	01 Apr 1992
4	Norma	Lyzation	03 Apr 1956	01 Apr 1992
5	Juan	Tomani	12 Apr 1956	01 Apr 1992
6	Del	Eats	01 May 1957	01 May 1994

CUSTOMERS

CustomerNo	FirstName	LastName
1	Brian	Thompson
2	Sally	Henderson
3	Harry	McColgan
4	Sandra	Wellington

Figure 12.1 *Sample tables from the database.*

13

Relationships in the Real World

It is worth remembering that each table represents a type of object in the real world. If this were a real (rather than a demonstration) database, each record in the CUSTOMERS table would refer to a real customer and each entry in the EMPLOYEES table would represent a real employee. The first step in deciding what relationships we need to set up between the tables is to ask the question, 'What types of relationships can exist between these real world objects?'.

The term 'relationship' as used here has nothing to do with the use of the word 'relational' in 'relational database' (see Chapter 20). It is used here simply to imply an association and/or interdependency.

It turns out that there are four possible kinds of relationship between any given pair of objects, as follows:

♦ one-to-many
♦ one-to-one
♦ many-to-many
♦ none

13.1 One-to-Many

The relationship between customers and the orders that they can place with our mythical company is a one-to-many relationship. Saying this simply means that each customer can place none, one or more orders with the company. The relationship is asymmetrical in that any given order is placed by one and only one customer. Note that there is no implication that any one customer *has* to have placed an order before we can store that customer's details in the database. Nor does the word 'many' imply that a customer must place lots of orders; only that we are allowing for that possibility.

One-to-many relationships happen to be very common; they appear over and over again in the business world.

13.2 One-to-One

Suppose that, for whatever reason, it is essential that each of our employees is allocated their own room in the company, perhaps because the company buys and sells bearer bonds and customers prefer to carry out these transactions in private. We therefore decide that it is a rule within the company that each employee must be allocated to one room, but that, owing to cost considerations, no employee is ever allocated more than one room.

The relationship that exists between rooms and employees is a one-to-one relationship. Note that, in this case, we might well have rooms that aren't allocated to employees, so again the relationship isn't symmetrical.

One-to-one relationships are uncommon.

13.3 Many-to-Many

Consider the relationship between customers and employees. Over a period of time, would you expect a customer to be served by one or more than one employee and would you expect an employee to serve multiple customers? The answer to both of these questions is typically 'Yes', at least in most companies. Thus the relationship between customers and employees is a many-to-many relationship. In this case the relationship is symmetrical. Once again, there is no implication that a given customer *has* to be served by multiple employees; indeed, after their *initial* contact with our company they will presumably have dealt with only one employee. However, the potential exists for each customer to interact with multiple employees, and vice versa.

Many-to-many relationships are very common in business situations.

13.4 None

Some of the objects under consideration here do not have any relationship with each other. For example, the information about building rents has no relationship with the information about customers. We can ignore this class of relationship (or lack of it!); it is only included in this list for the sake of completeness.

13.5 Mapping Real World Relationships to Tables

So, there are three possible kinds of relationship which we need to actively consider between the objects represented in a database:

- ♦ one-to-many
- ♦ one-to-one
- ♦ many-to-many

of which only the first and third are common.

I have taken the trouble to consider and enumerate these because we can map the relationships between the objects in the real world (customers, employees, etc.) onto the tables which hold information about those objects. For example, the one-to-many relationship between customers and orders maps directly onto the CUSTOMERS and ORDERS tables, as we shall see in the next chapter.

As an exercise, you might like to consider the six object classes in the database and decide upon the obvious relationships that exist. Unless you are a masochist, don't bother with the less obscure ones. I know it sounds unlikely, but if we explicitly declare the obvious ones, the more obscure ones tend to take care of themselves. In addition, given six object classes there are $5+4+3+2+1=15$ possible relationships, so it will be a slightly tedious exercise if pursued to its conclusion.

14

How Are Relationships Modeled?

OK, so we've got our objects – employees, customers, orders etc. – nicely represented as tables in the database. We now understand the relationships that can exist between these objects. The next step is to see how we can model the relationships in the database.

The tools we use to perform this wizardry are:

♦ keys (both primary and foreign)
♦ joins

These two can be considered to be separate entities, but in practice their use tends to be interwoven. For example, you need to create one or more primary keys before you can create a join, but it is the act of creating a join which essentially completes the creation of a foreign key. In case this makes these tools sound horribly complicated, they aren't at all. In fact, once you understand them, they have a wonderful elegance and simplicity which makes you wonder how you ever lived without knowing about them. Me, I lie in bed at night just dreaming about them.

The easiest way to discuss these two tools is to see them in action. A very common form of relationship is the one-to-many relationship already discussed in the previous chapter. This is exemplified by the relationship which exists between customers and the orders that they place with a company, so we'll use that as the first example.

Remember the naming convention discussed in Chapter 3. I have elected always to use UPPER-CASE for table names and CamelCaps for field names. If I need to refer to a specific field in a specific table, I will always do so by separating the two names with a dot or point (.). Thus:

CUSTOMERS.CustomerNo

refers to the CustomerNo column (or field) of the table called CUSTOMERS.

In Figure 14.1 I have extended the simplified version of the ORDERS table that we used earlier; it now has pointers to the CUSTOMERS table as well as the EMPLOYEES table.

This version of the ORDERS table is not perfect, since it still stores redundant information about the items which would really be in the ITEMS table. However, this is as complex a structure as we need for now, and the ORDERS table will be improved later on in the chapter.

If you have a look at the CUSTOMERS and ORDERS tables in Figure 14.1 you can see that the data which ties them together is contained in the two fields

CUSTOMERS

CustomerNo	FirstName	LastName
1	Brian	Thompson
2	Sally	Henderson
3	Harry	McColgan
4	Sandra	Wellington

ORDERS

OrderNo	EmployeeNo	CustomerNo	Supplier	Price	Item
1	1	2	Harrison	$235.00	Desk
2	4	1	Ford	$234.00	Chair
3	1	3	Harrison	$415.00	Table
4	2	4	Ford	$350.00	Lamp
5	3	2	Ford	$234.00	Chair
6	2	4	Ford	$350.00	Lamp
7	2	2	Harrison	$235.00	Desk

EMPLOYEES

EmployeeNo	FirstName	LastName	DateOfBirth	DateEmployed
1	Manny	Tomanny	12 Apr 1956	01 May 1989
2	Rosanne	Kolumns	21 Mar 1967	01 Jan 1990
3	Cas	Kade	01 May 1967	01 Apr 1992
4	Norma	Lyzation	03 Apr 1956	01 Apr 1992
5	Juan	Tomani	12 Apr 1956	01 Apr 1992
6	Del	Eats	01 May 1957	01 May 1994

Figure 14.1 *Three tables from the sample database (CHAP14A.MDB) with their primary keys emboldened and the foreign keys italicized.*

(one in each table) which are both called CustomerNo. It should be reasonably clear that the number 2 in the first record of ORDERS.CustomerNo means that Sally Henderson bought the desk. We are using the value 2 here as a pointer to the record in CUSTOMERS which refers to Sally. You can use the same logical process to deduce that Manny Tomanny was the employee who clinched the deal.

We could use either the relationship between CUSTOMERS and ORDERS or the relationship between EMPLOYEES and ORDERS to illustrate the use of keys because both are built and managed in exactly the same way. In an entirely arbitrary manner, I'll elect to use CUSTOMERS and ORDERS, so you can forget about the EMPLOYEES table for a while (but it will return in due course).

In order for two CustomerNo fields to be able to tie the tables together in a sane and meaningful way, each field must display certain characteristics. These characteristics can be summed up by saying that CUSTOMERS.CustomerNo must be a *primary* key and that ORDERS.CustomerNo must be a *foreign* key.

So, to create a one-to-many relationship between two tables, you need a primary key in one table and a foreign key in the other. The primary key models the 'one' end of the relationship and the foreign key models the 'many' end. We are using these fields and numbers to represent the relationship that exists in real life between customers and the orders they place, namely that one individual customer can place multiple orders with the company.

Clearly, primary and foreign keys are important, so we'll have a look at their characteristics in more detail now.

14.1 Primary Keys

The exact requirements for a primary key are simple. I could list them for you now, but it is considerably more fun (and hopefully more memorable) to derive them. So much of relational theory is actually common sense that you can derive many of the rules for yourself.

Remember that the CustomerNo field in CUSTOMERS is the primary key of that particular table. Consider this field CUSTOMERS.CustomerNo then. It contains a number which identifies each customer; 1 is Brian Thompson, 2 is Sally Henderson and so on. What would happen if both of these customers were given the same number, say 1? The tables would look like Figure 14.2.

It is now impossible to determine who should be sent the bill for order number 2; it could have been either Brian or Sally who bought the chair. (In addition, order numbers 1, 5 and 7 are also problematical, but we'll deal with that class of problem in the section on foreign keys.) So, the first rule we can derive about primary keys is that the values placed in primary key fields must be unique for each record; no duplicates can be tolerated.

Next, what happens if a value in a primary key field isn't entered (Figure 14.3)?

Harry hasn't got a value for CUSTOMERS.CustomerNo. Does he have to pay for that third order, or not? Even if the tables looked like Figure 14.4 the answer would not be clear. The easiest way to avoid this kind of ambiguity is to insist that all primary keys have a value. A missing value in a database is called a *null* value, and the problems (sorry, challenges) associated with

CUSTOMERS

CustomerNo	FirstName	LastName
1	Brian	Thompson
1	Sally	Henderson
3	Harry	McColgan
4	Sandra	Wellington

ORDERS

OrderNo	EmployeeNo	CustomerNo	Supplier	Price	Item
1	1	2	Harrison	$235.00	Desk
2	4	1	Ford	$234.00	Chair
3	1	3	Harrison	$415.00	Table
4	2	4	Ford	$350.00	Lamp
5	3	2	Ford	$234.00	Chair
6	2	4	Ford	$350.00	Lamp
7	2	2	Harrison	$235.00	Desk

Figure 14.2 *A primary key flawed by duplication.*

CUSTOMERS

CustomerNo	FirstName	LastName
1	Brian	Thompson
2	Sally	Henderson
	Harry	McColgan
4	Sandra	Wellington

ORDERS

OrderNo	EmployeeNo	CustomerNo	Supplier	Price	Item
1	1	2	Harrison	$235.00	Desk
2	4	1	Ford	$234.00	Chair
3	1	3	Harrison	$415.00	Table
4	2	4	Ford	$350.00	Lamp
5	3	2	Ford	$234.00	Chair
6	2	4	Ford	$350.00	Lamp
7	2	2	Harrison	$235.00	Desk

Figure 14.3 *A primary key flawed by a null value.*

nulls make them worthy of their own small chapter (Chapter 23) in Part 4. See that chapter for more details.

That's it. We have just derived the important characteristics of a primary key – namely that the information it contains for each record must be unique and must not be a null value. It's easy really. RDBMSs like Access, of course, 'understand' these rules. All we have to do is to tell Access which fields are primary keys and it will ensure that we are never allowed to create a record which breaks either of these rules. 'Hmm', you're probably thinking. 'Does he really mean that, if a table contains, say 100,000 customers, Access will check each and every new one that I add against all of the others

CUSTOMERS

CustomerNo	FirstName	LastName
1	Brian	Thompson
2	Sally	Henderson
	Harry	McColgan
4	Sandra	Wellington

ORDERS

OrderNo	EmployeeNo	CustomerNo	Supplier	Price	Item
1	1	2	Harrison	$235.00	Desk
2	4	1	Ford	$234.00	Chair
3	1		Harrison	$415.00	Table
4	2	4	Ford	$350.00	Lamp
5	3	2	Ford	$234.00	Chair
6	2	4	Ford	$350.00	Lamp
7	2	2	Harrison	$235.00	Desk

Figure 14.4 *A suspicious pair of null values caught in the act of adding ambiguity to a relationship between a pair of tables.*

to ensure that the rule about "no duplicates" is obeyed and none of the values in CustomerNo is duplicated?'. Yes, that's what I mean. In fact, Access (and any good RDBMS) can do this so quickly and with so little effort that you won't even notice it happening.

14.1.1 Using Multiple Fields as Primary Keys

Although it may not immediately be apparent, these two requirements (unique values and no nulls) don't limit a primary key to a single field.

There is nothing to stop you from declaring two fields, say FirstName and LastName, to be the primary key. If you do that, then the contents of both fields in both records have to be identical before the uniqueness of the data is compromised. So you would be able to have 'John Smith' and 'John Smyth' in your table but not two people called 'John Smith'. Despite the fact that it is possible to create a primary key from more than one field, as a rule it is usually a bad idea, unless there is a clear reason to do so. However, there are some cases where it is *essential*. We'll have a look at an example later in this chapter, in the section on many-to-many joins.

14.1.2 What Makes a Good Primary Key?

So, having told you that it is possible to use one or more fields as a primary key, how do you decide which fields (and how many) to choose?

Well, as outlined above, there are times when it is advisable or essential to use multiple fields. However, if you cannot see an immediate reason to use two or more fields, then use one. This isn't an absolute rule – it is simply advice. However, primary keys made up of single fields are generally easier to maintain and faster in operation. By that I mean that if you query the database, you will usually get the answer back faster if the tables have single field primary keys.

Next question – which field should you pick? Well, the value in the chosen field must uniquely identify the record in which it appears. In a table of employees, clearly any field like `FirstName` is a poor, choice since you would only be able to have one employee called 'Bill'.

There is a story which I have heard several times. It says that Bill Gates is so paranoid that, in the early days of the company, he wouldn't employ anyone else at Microsoft called Bill. The usual figure quoted (see *Accidental Empires* by Robert X. Cringely) is that the company had to get to well over 500 employees before another Bill was hired. It's a great story; it just happens to be untrue. Bill Marklyn, the co-author of this book, was hired well before that. Clearly, Microsoft doesn't use `FirstName` as the primary key in its EMPLOYEE table.

The easiest way to choose a field as a primary key (and a method that is commonly employed) is to get the database itself to automatically allocate a unique number to each record. Access has a field type (Counter in Access 1.0 to 2.0, AutoNumber in later versions) which will do this for you. It is excellent for objects like orders, employees and so on. However, you might find that you are already storing a unique identifier in the table. In the UK for example, you might well want to record your employee's National Insurance number, and in the USA there is the Social Security number. These are guaranteed to be unique, so you might well use the appropriate one as a primary key.

Finding truly unique identifiers is not as easy as it first appears. See Chapter 24 for more details.

14.1.3 How Do I Create a Primary Key?

Creating primary keys is an important process and, although this isn't a book about 'how to use Access', illustrating how it is done at each step helps to illustrate the differences that exist between primary and foreign keys. For example, creating a primary key is done during table design, whereas creating a foreign key is not done explicitly; rather, it is done as part of the process of creating a join.

So to answer the question about how you create a primary key: during table design, you simply click on the field you want to be the primary key and then click on the 'Set Primary Key' button in the toolbar. By convention, the primary key field is placed as the first one in the table, although it doesn't have to be. If you want to set two fields to be the primary key, simply select both at the same time before clicking the 'Set Primary Key' button. That's it.

14.2 Foreign Keys

Since we've been using CUSTOMERS and ORDERS as an example, we'll stay with them and demonstrate the characteristics of a foreign key in a one-to-many

CUSTOMERS

CustomerNo	FirstName	LastName
1	Brian	Thompson
2	Sally	Henderson
3	Harry	McColgan
4	Sandra	Wellington

ORDERS

OrderNo	EmployeeNo	CustomerNo	Supplier	Price	Item
1	1	2	Harrison	$235.00	Desk
2	4	1	Ford	$234.00	Chair
3	1	3	Harrison	$415.00	Table
4	2	4	Ford	$350.00	Lamp
5	3	2	Ford	$234.00	Chair
6	2	4	Ford	$350.00	Lamp
7	2	5	Harrison	$235.00	Desk

Figure 14.5 *A flawed foreign key.*

relationship. A foreign key is simply one which references a primary key; in this case the foreign key is the field ORDERS.CustomerNo.

Once again we can derive the most important 'rules' about foreign keys intuitively. Consider the values in the tables of Figure 14.5. (Hint: the last record in ORDERS is worth examining).

The last record in ORDERS contains the value 5 in CustomerNo, which is a little odd because we don't have a customer with the number 5. So, given this particular set of data, we have no idea who should be sent the bill for order number 7. You will be way ahead of me by this point, and you will have worked out that we cannot tolerate this sort of inexact information in the database, so a foreign key must only contain values which are represented in the primary key.

14.2.1 How Do I Create a Foreign Key?

Foreign keys are created/defined during the process of creating a join, so we'll cover it when that process is described.

14.3 Summary So Far

A couple of quick, slightly more formal, definitions before we move on to joins. Refer to Figure 14.6 as needed.

14.3.1 Primary Key

Every table in a relational database must have a primary key. A primary key consists of one or more fields. No value in a primary key can be a null value (that is to say, no entry in a primary key may be left blank). Each record in a table must be uniquely identified by the value contained within its primary key, which is simply another way of saying that each value that appears in the primary key must be unique. Primary keys are defined as part of the table structure.

CUSTOMERS

CustomerNo	FirstName	LastName
1	Brian	Thompson
2	Sally	Henderson
3	Harry	McColgan
4	Sandra	Wellington

ORDERS

OrderNo	EmployeeNo	CustomerNo	Supplier	Price	Item
1	1	2	Harrison	$235.00	Desk
2	4	1	Ford	$234.00	Chair
3	1	3	Harrison	$415.00	Table
4	2	4	Ford	$350.00	Lamp
5	3	2	Ford	$234.00	Chair
6	2	4	Ford	$350.00	Lamp
7	2	2	Harrison	$235.00	Desk

Figure 14.6 *Two tables from the sample database with their primary keys emboldened and the foreign keys italicized.*

14.3.2 Foreign Key

Foreign keys are not essential requirements for each table. In other words, although each table must have a primary key, each one doesn't have to have a foreign key. However, if a relationship exists between two tables, one of those tables will have a foreign key, in which the values are drawn from the primary key of the other table. In practice, most tables do have foreign keys and it is perfectly possible for a table to have more than one. If it has more than one, the table must be involved in more than one relationship. Foreign keys are defined when a join is made, a process that has so far been glossed over but will now be described.

14.4 Joins

In this chapter we are looking at how we model relationships in a database. I said at the start that the tools we use are:

♦ keys (both primary and foreign)
♦ Joins

We've covered keys, so let's turn our attention to joins. In the previous chapter we said that there are three possible types of relationship that can be modeled in a database:

♦ one-to-many
♦ many-to-many
♦ one-to-one

We'll start with the most common, which is one-to-many.

14.4.1 One-to-Many

Suppose that we have two tables like those in Figure 14.6. Can we, *just by looking at these tables*, deduce what relationships exist between them? The answer (like all good answers) is 'Well, yes and no'. We can't be absolutely sure about any relationships that exist, but we could have a good guess.

We could guess that ORDERS.OrderNo is a primary key; the field name sounds promising and the values in the field uniquely identify the records. We could also guess that CUSTOMERS.CustomerNo is also a primary key for the same reasons.

We could notice that the values in ORDERS.CustomerNo are all drawn from the values in CUSTOMERS.CustomerNo which would lead us to suspect that ORDERS.CustomerNo is a foreign key.

Why am I telling you this? Do I expect you to go around looking at tables and guessing what relationships exist? No. What this exercise does is to highlight the important bits which go into creating and maintaining a relationship between two tables.

With those firmly recalled, we can look at the entire process of modeling a one-to-many join, which tends to go like this:

♦ We decide that the database needs to contain information about two objects – customers and orders.

♦ The relationship between these objects is a one-to-many relationship. That is, one customer can have many orders.

♦ We will create one table for each class of object – CUSTOMERS and ORDERS.

♦ Each table will have a primary key for the simple reason that all tables must have primary keys. These primary keys will be called CUSTOMERS.CustomerNo and ORDERS.OrderNo.

♦ Since we want the database to mimic real life, we want a one-to-many relationship to exist between the two tables.

♦ In order to make this relationship possible, we will need a foreign key in the table which is at the 'many' end of the relationship – in this case, the table ORDERS.

♦ This foreign key field can have any name, but it is often given the same name as the primary key it references. It must, however, be of the same field *type* as the primary key it references.

♦ So we add a field called CustomerNo to the table ORDERS.

♦ Finally (the moment you have all been waiting for) we tell Access that a one-to-many join exists between these tables.

In practical terms, this simply means that you open up the relationship editor (Figure 14.7), add the two tables to the editor, drag CUSTOMERS.CustomerNo onto ORDERS.CustomerNo and let go. When the dialog box appears, you select 'Enforce Referential Integrity', accept the default one-to-many option and click on OK. (In case you are wondering what referential integrity does, see Chapter 16.)

This process tells Access that a join now exists. In addition, creating the join has made ORDERS.CustomerNo a foreign key. You can play around, trying

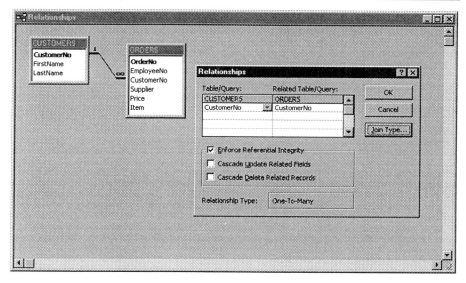

Figure 14.7 *How a one-to-many join is represented in the Access relationship editor.*

to put a number into ORDERS.CustomerNo that doesn't exist in CUSTOMERS.CustomerNo. Every time you do, Access will refuse to accept it.

You can probably see now why joins and keys are so intimately tied together. In order to put a join like this in place you need a primary key and a field which is *set up* to be a foreign key. However, it is the act of creating the join which actually confirms the field *as* a foreign key.

There are a few points that are worth noting here in passing. The join (with referential integrity) will fail to be established if:

♦ the field used at the 'one' end of the relationship isn't a primary key

♦ the data types of the two fields used in the join are not identical

♦ data already exists in the table at the 'many' end which is not found in the 'one' end

On the subject of similar data types, I have said that it is common to use a Counter (Access 1.0–2.0) or AutoNumber – Long Integer (Access 7–97) field as a primary key. You cannot use either of these as the data type at the many end of a join. The data type to choose in this case is Number – Long Integer. This isn't as weird as it sounds. Counters and AutoNumbers are simply Long Integer fields that are automatically incremented.

14.4.2 One-to-One

One-to-one joins are uncommon. However, they are easy to understand and create because they are very similar, in terms of construction, to one-to-many joins. As in those, the join goes from a primary key in one table to a foreign key in the other. The only difference is that the foreign key in the second table is not allowed to contain duplicate values. There are two ways of ensuring that the foreign key doesn't contain duplicate values.

One is to ensure that the foreign key of the second table is also its primary key. In other words the join can be between two primary keys, one of which also acts as a foreign key.

The other way is to give the foreign key a unique index, which again ensures that it doesn't contain duplicate values. This is the one I will demonstrate below.

In the sample database outlined in Figure 14.8, each employee must be allocated to one room but, owing to cost considerations, no employee is ever allocated more than one room.

EMPLOYEES

EmployeeNo	FirstName	LastName	DateOfBirth	DateEmployed
1	Manny	Tomanny	12 Apr 1956	01 May 1989
2	Rosanne	Kolumns	21 Mar 1967	01 Jan 1990
3	Cas	Kade	01 May 1967	01 Apr 1992
4	Norma	Lyzation	03 Apr 1956	01 Apr 1992
5	Juan	Tomani	12 Apr 1956	01 Apr 1992

ROOMS

RoomNo	EmployeeNo
1	2
12	4
23	1
24	6

Figure 14.8 *Two tables where primary and foreign keys are used to create a one-to-one join.*

EMPLOYEES.EmployeeNo is a primary key, so no duplicates are allowed. ROOMS.EmployeeNo has been given a unique index (during table design), so no duplicates are allowed. In addition, it is also a foreign key and can only contain values which already exist in EMPLOYEES.EmployeeNo.

Thus Figure 14.9 is not allowed since the value 9 is not found in the primary key EMPLOYEES.EmployeeNo. In addition, Figure 14.10 is not allowed because the value 2 is repeated in ROOMS.EmployeeNo.

ROOMS

RoomNo	EmployeeNo
1	2
12	4
23	1
24	9

Figure 14.9

Creating a one-to-one join simply involves opening up the relationship editor (Figure 14.11), adding the two tables to the editor, dragging EMPLOYEES.EmployeeNo onto ROOMS.EmployeeNo and letting go. When the dialog box appears, you select 'Enforce Referential Integrity', accept the default one-to-one option and click on OK.

Note that although the relationship exists between two primary keys, it is not symmetrical. A value can exist in EMPLOYEES.EmployeeNo which doesn't exist in ROOMS.EmployeeNo, but not vice versa.

ROOMS

RoomNo	EmployeeNo
1	2
12	4
23	1
24	2

Figure 14.10

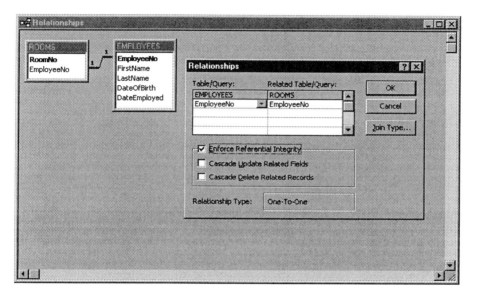

Figure 14.11 *How a one-to-one join is represented in the Access relationship editor. (Note that* ROOMS.EmployeeNo *must have a unique index set before this join can be created.)*

14.4.3 Many-to-Many

Many-to-many joins are common and, once mastered, are incredibly easy to create.

Consider the relationship between customers and employees. One customer can be seen by many different employees; in addition, one employee will typically deal with many customers. Thus the relationship between customers and employees is a many-to-many relationship. The next question to ask is 'What defines an interaction between a customer and an employee?'. Well, while it is true that a customer might interact with an employee without actually buying anything, such interactions are likely to be of no interest, at least in terms of the database. The only time we are interested in a customer/employee interaction is when an item is bought. Whenever an item is bought, an order is generated, so it is the orders that define the interaction between customers and employees.

Now, what relationship exists between customers and orders? Answer – one-to-many. The same kind of relationship exists between employees and orders; see Figure 14.12.

CUSTOMERS

CustomerNo	FirstName	LastName
1	Brian	Thompson
2	Sally	Henderson
3	Harry	McColgan
4	Sandra	Wellington

ORDERS

OrderNo	EmployeeNo	CustomerNo	Supplier	Price	Item
1	1	2	Harrison	$235.00	Desk
2	4	1	Ford	$234.00	Chair
3	1	3	Harrison	$415.00	Table
4	2	4	Ford	$350.00	Lamp
5	3	2	Ford	$234.00	Chair
6	2	4	Ford	$350.00	Lamp
7	2	2	Harrison	$235.00	Desk

EMPLOYEES

EmployeeNo	FirstName	LastName	DateOfBirth	DateEmployed
1	Manny	Tomanny	12 Apr 1956	01 May 1989
2	Rosanne	Kolumns	21 Mar 1967	01 Jan 1990
3	Cas	Kade	01 May 1967	01 Apr 1992
4	Norma	Lyzation	03 Apr 1956	01 Apr 1992
5	Juan	Tomani	12 Apr 1956	01 Apr 1992
6	Del	Eats	01 May 1957	01 May 1994

Figure 14.12 *Sample data in the tables CUSTOMERS, ORDERS and EMPLOYEES.*

Unlikely as it sounds, creating a pair of one-to-many joins like this is all that is required to create a many-to-many relationship between the CUSTOMERS and EMPLOYEES. In fact, there is no special mechanism for making a many-to-many join – you always build them from two one-to-many joins. However, they have to be constructed in the particular orientation shown in Figure 14.13. For example, the two one-to-many joins shown in Figure 14.14 do not create a many-to-many join between the two outer tables.

Often, in my experience, when you identify a many-to-many relationship there is a handy table, like ORDERS in this case, which can act as the required link in the middle. On other occasions this is not so, and it is worth looking at such a case because it will make our sample database slightly more realistic. It also illustrates a case where a two-field primary key is essential (more or less).

When Multiple-Field Primary Keys Are Essential

Consider our sample database from Chapter 12. In it, we identified six object classes:

- ◆ Customers
- ◆ Items
- ◆ Orders
- ◆ Employees
- ◆ Buildings
- ◆ Rooms

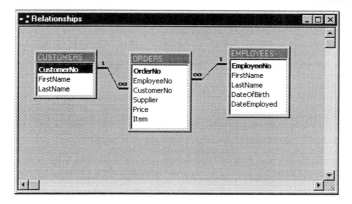

Figure 14.13 *The relationships that exist between CUSTOMERS, ORDERS and EMPLOYEES.*

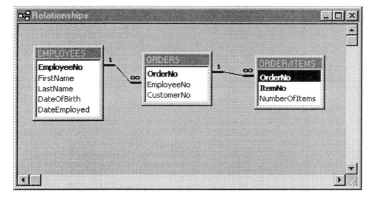

Figure 14.14 *Two one-to-many joins which do not create a many-to-many join between the two outer tables. (These tables are from the Access database CHAP14C which we will shortly be using.)*

We have been concentrating on three of these:

♦ CUSTOMERS
♦ ORDERS
♦ EMPLOYEES

and initially we kept the structure of ORDERS relatively simple because we were using it for demonstration purposes. Now we can look at ORDERS with the structure that it needs in order to fit our initial model properly. I've also included another three tables for easy reference (Figure 14.15). These tables are from the sample database called CHAP14B, which will be used briefly, before we move onto CHAP14C.

As you can see, the ORDERS table is made up of a primary key ORDERS.OrderNo and three foreign keys which reference the other tables.

ORDERS

OrderNo	EmployeeNo	CustomerNo	ItemNo
1	1	2	1
2	4	1	3
3	1	3	4
4	2	4	2
5	3	2	3
6	2	4	2
7	2	2	1

EMPLOYEES

EmployeeNo	FirstName	LastName	DateOfBirth	DateEmployed
1	Manny	Tomanny	12 Apr 1956	01 May 1989
2	Rosanne	Kolumns	21 Mar 1967	01 Jan 1990
3	Cas	Kade	01 May 1967	01 Apr 1992
4	Norma	Lyzation	03 Apr 1956	01 Apr 1992
5	Juan	Tomani	12 Apr 1956	01 Apr 1992
6	Del	Eats	01 May 1957	01 May 1994

CUSTOMERS

CustomerNo	FirstName	LastName
1	Brian	Thompson
2	Sally	Henderson
3	Harry	McColgan
4	Sandra	Wellington

ITEMS

ItemNo	Supplier	Price	Item
1	Harrison	$235.00	Desk
2	Ford	$350.00	Lamp
3	Ford	$234.00	Chair
4	Harrison	$415.00	Table

Figure 14.15 *Four of the tables from the sample database CHAP14B.*

It should be clear (hopefully) that this collection of tables, set up as they are, only allow one item to appear on each order. For example, order number 3 is from Harry McColgan and he ordered item number 4, a table. But what if he wanted a chair (or even four chairs) to go with it? As the tables are currently constructed, there is nowhere to store information about multiple items per order, so each item requires a separate order.

There are several solution to this problem, two of which can appear to be both logical and easy to build; however both can result in serious damage to your database. It seems best to show them to you, if only to poke fun at them and to ensure that you never try to use them.

Figure 14.16 shows the first common (and bad) solution. It looks good doesn't it? Instead of a single column for storing a reference to an item, we have five. Harry now has his four chairs and the others can have additional items on their orders if they so desire.

BAD-ORDERS-TABLE

OrderNo	EmployeeNo	CustomerNo	ItemNo1	ItemNo2	ItemNo3	ItemNo4	ItemNo5
1	1	2	1	4			
2	4	1	3				
3	1	3	4	3	3	3	3
4	2	4	2	1	3		
5	3	2	3			2	
6	2	4	2		4		
7	2	2	1			2	

Figure 14.16 *A bad way of designing an ORDERS table to hold information about multiple items per order.*

It may look good, but it's terrible in practice. For a start, adding four extra fields may be enough for the present, but what happens if a customer orders two tables, a dozen chairs and a lamp? We can, of course, continue to add fields. Suppose that we do this and it turns out that the greatest number of items ever ordered on a single order is 28; so we end up with 28 fields for items. The problem is that the average number of items may be 3 so, on average, 25 of the fields will be wasted per record. This wastes disk space and slows the database down.

In addition, look at the way the data is dispersed in the table. Suppose that we want to find out how many chairs we have sold. It is impossible to be sure which of the fields contain information about chairs, so we have to indulge in complex searches of all the fields. This is a bad solution.

A better (but not great) solution is shown in Figure 14.17. Now the field names provide the information about the nature of the item ordered and the value tells us how many of each item was ordered. Harry can now have his chairs, we know where to find the information about chairs and we no longer have to worry about the number of different items on an order; there's always a column for each item in our range. Great. Sadly, this is still a poor solution. What happens if we add an item to the range that we sell? We have to add another field to the ORDERS table. If we add another, we again have to alter the structure of the table ORDERS. What happens if we run out of fields (most RDBMSs are limited to 255 per table)? We also have exactly the same wasted space problem as before. No, this one looks better, but it is still too bad to consider using.

BAD-ORDERS-TABLE-2

OrderNo	EmployeeNo	CustomerNo	Desk	Lamp	Chair	Table
1	1	2	1			1
2	4	1			1	
3	1	3			4	1
4	2	4	1	1	1	
5	3	2		1	1	
6	2	4		1		1
7	2	2	1			

Figure 14.17 *A better (but still not good enough) solution to the problem.*

So now we come to the right solution (you knew we'd get there in the end). The rest of the tables shown in this chapter are taken from CHAP14C.MDB.

The best way to solve this problem is simple, once your brain is geared to using multiple tables. We have a many-to-many relationship between ORDERS and ITEMS. We construct a many-to-many relationship from two one-to-many joins used back to back. Clearly what we need is a table to put in between ORDERS and ITEMS which allows us to model the relationship. A reasonable name for this table might be ORDER/ITEMS and the three relevant tables would look like Figure 14.18.

ORDERS

OrderNo	EmployeeNo	CustomerNo
1	1	2
2	4	1
3	1	3
4	2	4
5	3	2
6	2	4
7	2	2

ORDER/ITEMS

OrderNo	ItemNo	NumberOfItems
1	1	1
1	4	1
2	3	1
3	3	4
3	4	1
4	1	1
4	2	1
4	3	1
5	2	1
5	3	1
6	2	1
6	4	1
7	1	1

ITEMS

ItemNo	Supplier	Price	Item
1	Harrison	$235.00	Desk
2	Ford	$350.00	Lamp
3	Ford	$234.00	Chair
4	Harrison	$415.00	Table

Figure 14.18 *Finally, an excellent solution to the problem of allowing multiple items on a single order.*

These three tables contain all of the information that is included in the two poor solutions quoted above, so Harry gets his four chairs to go with his table. In addition this solution solves the problems inherent in the other solutions (or rather, it doesn't induce the problems in the first place).

There is no wasted space in the tables: all of the fields in all of the rows are complete. There is no artificial restriction on the number of different items that can appear in a single order. Adding a lamp to an order which held only chairs simply means adding a single record to the ORDER/ITEMS table.

Finally, if we add another item to our product range, we simply add a record to the ITEMS table. We don't have to alter the structure of the ORDERS table or any other table.

So, we have improved the flexibility of our ordering system but what has all of this got to do with multiple fields in primary keys?

It is clear (hopefully) that ORDERS.OrderNo has to be a primary key, ensuring that each order has a unique number. Similarly, ITEMS.ItemNo must be a primary key. However, neither OrderNo nor ItemNo, on its own, can be the primary key in the table ORDER/ITEMS; instead, the primary key must be composed of these two fields used together. If both are used then the table can have identical values in the OrderNo field, as it can in the ItemNo field; see Figure 14.19.

ORDER/ITEMS

OrderNo	ItemNo	NumberOfItems
1	1	1
1	4	1
2	3	1
3	3	4
etc.	etc.	etc.

Figure 14.19 *The value 1 occurs multiple times in OrderNo and the value 3 is repeated in the ItemNo field.*

However, the table shown in Figure 14.20 is forbidden because of the identical values in the second and third records of the primary key.

ORDER/ITEMS

OrderNo	ItemNo	NumberOfItems
1	1	1
1	4	1
1	4	2
2	3	1
3	3	4
etc.	etc.	etc.

Figure 14.20 *The second and third records violate a primary key composed of the two fields OrderNo and ItemNo.*

This actually matches reality very well, since the order should not have the same item appearing more than once. Instead, the NumberOfItems field should be used to record multiple instances of an item on an order.

14.4.4 General Lessons About Joins

The discussion about many-to-many joins has covered quite a lot of ground, so it is probably worth pausing to highlight some general points that have emerged.

Add Flexibility by Adding Records, Not Fields

The solution discussed above for allowing multiple items per order provides a high level of flexibility. You can add items to orders, change the number of a particular item on a given order, or add to the range of items *without* altering the structure of a single table.

I said above that modern RDBMSs like Access allow you to alter the structure of a table reasonably easily. This ability is essential during database development, but once the database is operational, changes of this kind should only be undertaken in extremis. Remember that you will have based forms, queries and reports on those tables. Every time you alter the structure of a table, you will have to check all of these to see if they need to be changed as well. So, as a general principle, any solution to a problem which will require you to constantly change the structure of a table should be regarded with suspicion. Not only is it likely to be troublesome, such a restriction almost certainly means that you have overlooked a more elegant solution somewhere.

GUIs, Not Numbers

These joins constantly deal with numbers in primary keys and foreign keys. We tend to use numbers because they are convenient (although you can use text if you so desire). It is worth stressing that you aren't expected to go to the ORDER/ITEMS table and type these numbers into the table manually.

We use an attractive GUI interface which allows us to pick the customer's name from one combo box, the employee's from another, the item from a third (Figure 14.21) and then to type in the number of items required. The system will look after the tedious job of writing the abstract numbers into the tables for us.

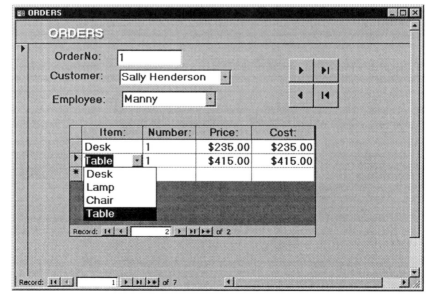

Figure 14.21 *A form which provides a sensible GUI interface to update the tables described.*

How such forms are constructed falls outside the remit of this book, because the book is essentially about the relational model, not about how to build interfaces in Access. However, just to show that it really isn't difficult, have a look at the form called Orders in the sample database CHAP14C, which demonstrates just such a GUI.

There is more on this general subject of using a GUI to 'protect' the user of the database from the rather abstract nature of the tables in the next chapter.

Less Obvious Objects

I told you that you can decide on the tables required in a database just by identifying the real world object classes and giving each a table. Yet I have just added one (ORDER/ITEMS) which isn't an obvious object class. In my defense, what I proposed earlier was simply a rule of thumb. This is about the only major exception to it, and it is pretty easy to remember. If you can identify a many-to-many relationship between two real world objects, and there isn't an obvious object that fits in between those two objects, then you are probably going to need to create a table like ORDER/ITEMS.

A Little Obfuscation

So, joins and keys are easy to use and incredibly useful. However, it is vital to remember that you are slowly but surely entering the world of the database specialist. In that world, it is essential that you are able to describe what you are doing in the obfuscative terms commonly employed by such people, otherwise you won't be treated with the respect that you deserve. Important words here are Parent, Child, Own, Owned, Superior, Subordinate, Dependency and Foreign key.

For example (see Figures 14.22 and 14.23), the ORDERS table is **owned** by the EMPLOYEES table and is therefore its **child**. ORDERS is **subordinate** to EMPLOYEES and also **subordinate** to its other **parent**, CUSTOMERS, which also **owns** ORDERS and is therefore **superior** to it. All **child** tables have at least one **foreign key**, and because ORDERS has two **parent** tables, it has two **foreign keys** – EmployeeNo and CustomerNo. These **foreign keys** establish a **dependency** between the **parent** and **child**; in this case there are two **foreign keys**, so there are two **dependencies**.

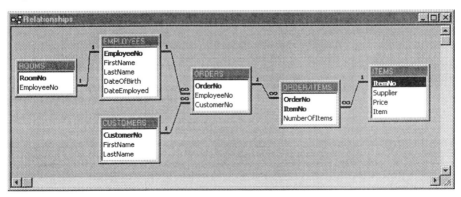

Figure 14.22 *The relationships between all of the tables in the database.*

EMPLOYEES

EmployeeNo	FirstName	LastName	DateOfBirth	DateEmployed
1	Manny	Tomanny	12 Apr 1956	01 May 1989
2	Rosanne	Kolumns	21 Mar 1967	01 Jan 1990
3	Cas	Kade	01 May 1967	01 Apr 1992
4	Norma	Lyzation	03 Apr 1956	01 Apr 1992
5	Juan	Tomani	12 Apr 1956	01 Apr 1992
6	Del	Eats	01 May 1957	01 May 1994

CUSTOMERS

CustomerNo	FirstName	LastName
1	Brian	Thompson
2	Sally	Henderson
3	Harry	McColgan
4	Sandra	Wellington

ORDERS

OrderNo	EmployeeNo	CustomerNo
1	1	2
2	4	1
3	1	3
4	2	4
5	3	2
6	2	4
7	2	2

ORDER/ITEMS

OrderNo	ItemNo	NumberOfItems
1	1	1
1	4	1
2	3	1
3	3	4
3	4	1
4	1	1
4	2	1
4	3	1
5	2	1
5	3	1
6	2	1
6	4	1
7	1	1

Figure 14.23 *The final set of tables in the database (continued on next page).*

There, I think that I managed to get in all of the important words. Note that the foreign keys in ORDERS form relationships with primary key fields in each of the parents. A little reflection should convince you that this is an essential prerequisite, since the parent table is always at the 'one' end of a one-to-many relationship.

ITEMS

ItemNo	Supplier	Price	Item
1	Harrison	$235.00	Desk
2	Ford	$350.00	Lamp
3	Ford	$234.00	Chair
4	Harrison	$415.00	Table

ROOMS

RoomNo	EmployeeNo
1	2
12	4
23	1
24	6

Figure 14.23 *(continued)*

I shouldn't make *too* much fun of the words used in database construction, since all specialist subjects acquire a verbal shorthand which is useful for rapid communication. However this shorthand should be used to speed up communication, not to play a smoke-and-mirrors game of confusing non-initiates and obscuring principles which are essentially simple. The important point is to understand the principles; after that the words make sense and follow naturally.

These tables are still not perfect, since, for example, the ITEMS table still contains repeated data (such as the name of the supplier). I'm leaving them in this slightly imperfect state, since these imperfections will be used in Chapter 15 to illustrate why you should remove redundant data from tables.

15

Revisiting the Big Four – the Synergy Begins

In this part we have been looking at why single tables are bad, why multiple tables are good and latterly at how you actually arrange the data into the separate tables. Now seems like a good time to look at the gains you get from splitting up data in this way. At the same time we can revisit the four basic components of a database that were covered in Part 1, namely:

♦ Tables (briefly)
♦ Queries (extensively)
♦ Forms
♦ Reports

and see how they work with multiple tables of data.

However, just before we do that, there is one more topic that we need to cover – closure.

Closure

Closure is an important part of the relational database model, so much so that it forms one of Ted Codd's rules. You can, of course, go and read Chapter 21, but it's more fun to derive the need for closure logically than just to accept it as a rule. After all, closure isn't important simply because it is a rule; it is important because it fixes an otherwise insoluble problem. So we'll start with the problem and show how closure fixes it. Hopefully by the end you will be one of closure's biggest fans.

For this chapter, I will be using tables from the database in CHAP15.MDB; however, the tables it contains are essentially identical to those in

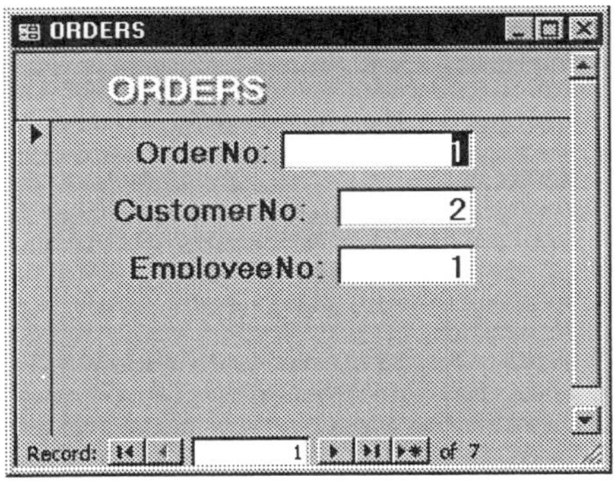

Figure 15.1 *An unsatisfactory form based upon a base table...*

ORDERS

OrderNo	EmployeeNo	CustomerNo
1	1	2
2	4	1
3	1	3
4	2	4
5	3	2
6	2	4
7	2	2

Figure 15.2 *...and the base table upon which it is based.*

CHAP14C.MDB. The data has been split up into several tables and I have spent some considerable time and effort convincing you that this is a good thing to do because it reduces repeated data and has other major benefits.

I have also told you that tables are the containers in which data is stored and that queries, forms and reports can all be based on tables.

However, one major disadvantage arises when we combine this idea of splitting data up between several tables with the idea of basing forms (for example) on base tables. This disadvantage is neatly summed up in the form shown in Figure 15.1 (called BadOrdersForm in CHAP15.MDB), which is based on the table in Figure 15.2. The very act of splitting up the data has left it in a very human-unfriendly state.

The solution is remarkably easy. Queries are perfectly capable of pulling together the information that we need from different tables (see below). Figures 15.3 and 15.4 show the result of a query which pulls data from the three tables – ORDERS, EMPLOYEES and CUSTOMERS.

Suddenly the data is readable again and the problem goes away. But (and it is a big but) notice that the form shown in Figure 15.4 is based not upon a base table but upon the answer table from a query. This is what closure is all about. In a relational database, it is imperative that the answer tables generated by queries must not only *look like* base tables, they must have the same behavior as base tables. That is, they have to allow forms and reports to be based upon them without complaining.

OrdersInformation

OrderNo	Customer	Employee
1	Sally Henderson	Manny Tomanny
2	Brian Thompson	Norma Lyzation
3	Harry McColgan	Manny Tomanny
4	Sandra Wellington	Rosanne Kolumns
5	Sally Henderson	Cas Kade
6	Sandra Wellington	Rosanne Kolumns
7	Sally Henderson	Rosanne Kolumns

Figure 15.3 *The result of a query which pulls together the information that we need...*

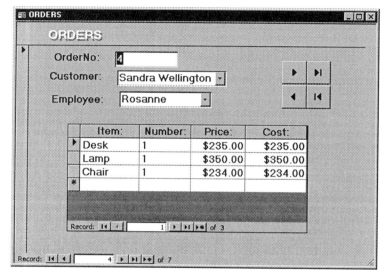

Figure 15.4 *...and a better form based upon it.*

This relational property (that the answer to a query is a full and proper table in its own right) is known as **closure** and it is much more important than it first appears, because it can be used in several ways.

Suppose that you have a table containing the details of 40,000 customers world-wide. You might build a query which lists only those who live in the USA, and you might call that query USCustomers. Now suppose that you want a list of all of the customers based in the USA who have spent more than $10,000 with your company. Instead of querying the main CUSTOMER table, you can query the answer table called USCustomers and look for those who have spent more than $10,000, safe in the knowledge that this will only return US-based customers.

In theory there is no limit to the number of answer tables that you can use in a stack like this. However, in practice I have rarely seen more than about four or five queries stacked on top of each other.

Another example which makes use of closure is the form called Orders in Figure 15.5. This form lets you see the information pertinent to each order.

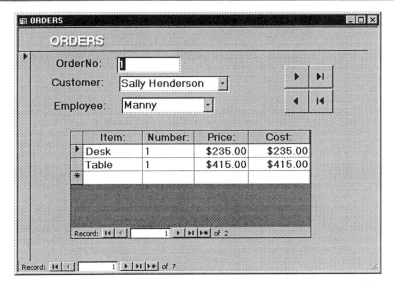

Figure 15.5 *An* Orders *form which is based on several sources of data.*

However, this form is actually drawing information from several sources. One is the table called ORDERS, while another is the query called SubForm, which is providing the details about Item, Price etc. in the lower half of the form. This Orders form is only possible because the query SubForm is producing an answer table which is behaving just like a normal table.

Indeed, closure is such an important part of the relational model that we take it for granted. Often you will hear people talking about a form which is based on a given query, rather than saying that the form is based on the answer table from a query. Closure will appear in the discussions which follow, particularly with regard to queries, forms and reports.

15.1 Tables

Base tables are the repositories of the data that you collect and store in the database. The data stored in these tables should be split up into suitable sets of tables (either formally or by rule of thumb) to reduce/eliminate redundant data and to enhance data integrity. Moving to a multi-table database has (reasonably obviously) the effect of increasing the number of tables in the database, but apart from that there is not much to say about them that hasn't been covered earlier in this part.

15.2 Queries (and a Bit on Forms)

The use of queries, on the other hand, changes substantially in a multi-table database.

In a single-table database, queries are essentially used to subset the data. In addition, they can be used to perform calculations on the data. These can be very simple calculations – for example, the query shown in Figure 15.6 is 'adding together' the data from the First and Last name fields to make the

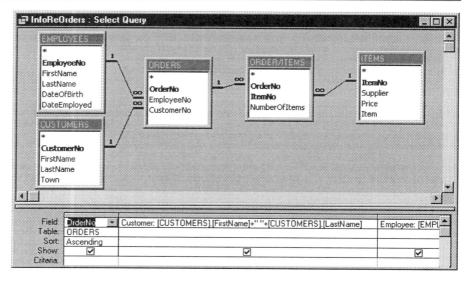

Figure 15.6 *A query which pulls information together from several tables.*

names appear in a more readable way. Calculations can also be much more complex mathematical manipulations (summing, multiplying, performing standard deviation calculations etc.) as discussed in Chapter 5.

In a multi-table database queries can, of course, still be used to do all of this; but they are also used extensively to pull data together from the different tables.

For example, in the sample database in CHAP15.MDB, customer information is stored in one table, employee information in another and order information in a third. While splitting the data up into several tables ensures that this data is stored efficiently, the data is not readily accessible to the average user of the database in this state. Queries can be used to pull the data together with consummate ease, for example the query shown in Figure 15.6 (InfoReOrders) produces the data shown in Figure 15.7, which is much more accessible to the average user.

Note that this query is automatically making use of the information in the primary and foreign keys to produce the data that we see in the answer table. This is one of the major strengths of the relational database model. Once you have set up the joins between the tables, queries can automatically make use of them to provide the correct data.

As mentioned above, the answer tables that queries produce can also have forms and reports based upon them.

So, queries can subset the data in tables, they can perform manipulations on the data, they can draw together data from many tables and they can also have forms and reports based upon the answer tables that they produce; all of which makes them pretty talented. However, the multi-faceted nature of their abilities raises a question. Suppose that you build a database along these lines. The data is stored in the base tables, you use queries to pull the data together and then base the users' forms on the queries. The burning

InfoReOrders

OrderNo	Customer	Employee	Item	NumberOfItems	Supplier	Price
1	Sally Henderson	Manny Tomanny	Table	1	Harrison	$415.00
1	Sally Henderson	Manny Tomanny	Desk	1	Harrison	$235.00
2	Brian Thompson	Norma Lyzation	Chair	1	Ford	$234.00
3	Harry McColgan	Manny Tomanny	Chair	4	Ford	$234.00
3	Harry McColgan	Manny Tomanny	Table	1	Harrison	$415.00
4	Sandra Wellington	Rosanne Kolumns	Chair	1	Ford	$234.00
4	Sandra Wellington	Rosanne Kolumns	Desk	1	Harrison	$235.00
4	Sandra Wellington	Rosanne Kolumns	Lamp	1	Ford	$350.00
5	Sally Henderson	Cas Kade	Lamp	1	Ford	$350.00
5	Sally Henderson	Cas Kade	Chair	1	Ford	$234.00
6	Sandra Wellington	Rosanne Kolumns	Table	1	Harrison	$415.00
6	Sandra Wellington	Rosanne Kolumns	Lamp	1	Ford	$350.00
7	Sally Henderson	Rosanne Kolumns	Desk	1	Harrison	$235.00

Figure 15.7 *The data produced by the query in Figure 15.6.*

question is 'What happens if the users try to edit the data that they see on the form?'. The answer is that, with certain restrictions, it's perfectly possible.

This is quite an important point, because most well-designed databases make extensive use of this facility, so we'll have a look at a series of examples which will gradually increase in complexity.

The customer table in this example has been extended (Figure 15.8) to contain the town in which the customer lives. (We could get into an argument about whether this information represents repeated data in this table, but it is only for an example.)

If we build a query which extracts only the Bostonians, we can then base a form on that query (Figure 15.9). Should we be able to edit the data shown here? Logically there is no reason why not. True, we are only seeing a subset of the data, but those records that the form does show us would look no different if we based the form directly upon the CUSTOMERS base table.

Any RDBMS worthy of the name will allow you to edit the data shown in this form. The edits that you make will be written 'through' the query and will end up in the base table. Thus if we change a customer's name, that change will appear in the CUSTOMERS base table.

CUSTOMERS

CustomerNo	FirstName	LastName	Town
1	Brian	Thompson	Boston
2	Sally	Henderson	Dundee
3	Harry	McColgan	Seattle
...	...	...	...
103	William	Johnston	London
104	Agnes	Keith	Dundee
105	Robert	Edgar	Boston

Figure 15.8 *A sample of the data from the CUSTOMERS table.*

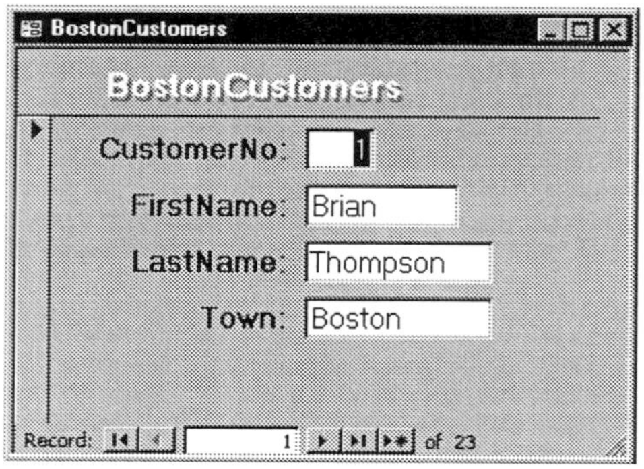

Figure 15.9 *A form based on a query that shows only Bostonians.*

Now, let's make it a little more complicated. Suppose that you sell wood. It comes in all different shapes and sizes, so you sell it by the cubic unit. You don't care if it is in a plank or a block; you simply multiply height by width by depth and sell it by volume.

You store these dimensions in a table (Figure 15.10) but you are smart enough not to store the volume in the table (Chapter 3 tells you why you never store derivable data). Instead, you get a query to work it out for you (Figure 15.11).

WOOD

Item	Length	Breadth	Height
1	6	4	4
2	1	1	4
3	6	6	1
4	3	3	3
5	2	3	4
6	1	2	1
7	5	5	1

Figure 15.10 *A table showing the dimensions of wood stock.*

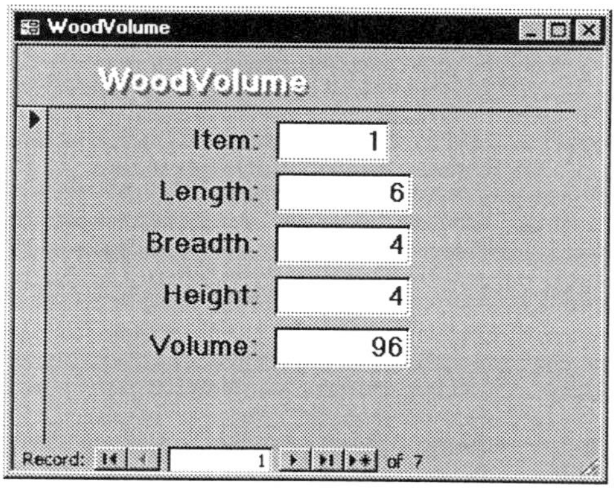

Figure 15.11 *A form based on a query which calculates the volume of the wood.*

Some of the data in this form should be editable, but not the text box which shows the volume. A good RDBMS will allow you to edit any of the dimensions, since those edits can be written back to the underlying table. Indeed, when you do so, it will update the volume information to reflect those changes. However, imagine if you were allowed to edit the data in the volume text box. Which of the dimensions should alter to accommodate that change? One of them or all of them? How is the RDBMS supposed to make decisions like that? The answer is that it can't, so this text box will be uneditable.

Now have a look at the query and answer table shown in Figures 15.6 and 15.7. This query is drawing data from several tables and is manipulating some of the data by 'adding together' the first and last name fields. (Combining text fields in this way is known as 'concatenation'.)

Figure 15.12 shows a form based on the query of Figure 15.6. Should the data shown in this form be editable? The answer, now familiar, is 'Yes and no'. The name fields from the original base tables have been manipulated (by concatenation) so they can't be edited. Most of the data in the other boxes can be edited, sometimes with interesting results. For example, the word 'Desk' appears in several of these orders but it is stored only once in the database (in the ITEMS table). Changing any entry from 'Desk' to, say 'Lectern' will alter the entry in the ITEMS table. Thus all of the other records in the answer table which refer to this entry in ITEMS will show 'Lectern' instead of 'Desk'. If you are using Access and the sample database CHAP15.MDB you can try this for yourself. It can be done from the form, but the effect is more impressive if you make changes to the underlying answer table itself, where multiple records can be seen at the same time. As soon as you change one of the records, a ripple of change runs across the table as the other records update to reflect that change.

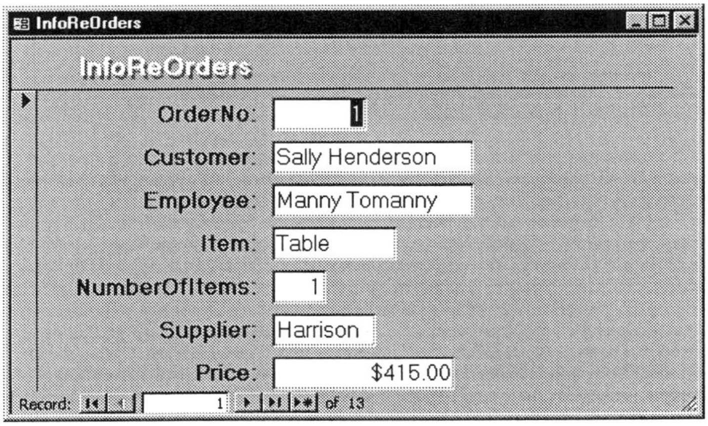

Figure 15.12 *Form based on the query (InfoReOrders) shown in Figure 15.6.*

Intriguingly, if you edit the name of a supplier (e.g. change 'Harrison' to 'Harisson'), some, but not all, of the records will update. If you follow the connections back to the original table, you'll find that the name of the supplier is stored several times in the ITEMS table (Figure 15.13).

ITEMS

ItemNo	Supplier	Price	Item
1	Harrison	$235.00	Desk
2	Ford	$350.00	Lamp
3	Ford	$234.00	Chair
4	Harrison	$415.00	Table

Figure 15.13 *The ITEMS table, showing that the supplier's name is stored multiple times.*

Earlier in the book, I pointed out that there was duplicated data in this sample table, but allowed it to remain. Here it serves as (yet another) excellent illustration of why redundant information in tables is to be avoided.

Finally, the OrderNo isn't editable in this form, but this is simply because it happens to be a counter field in the underlying base table. Counter fields are inherently uneditable, even in the base table, so we wouldn't expect it to suddenly become editable here.

We could go on looking at examples, but the underlying rule should be becoming clear. Queries can be used to pull data together and forms can be based on those queries. Whether the data that appears on such forms is editable or not depends upon the nature of the query (or queries) which have been used. Most RDBMSs provide lists of the different types of queries that you can run and whether or not the resulting answer table can be edited.

There has been some interesting research work done into which classes of answer table are inherently safe to edit and which aren't. It turns out that there are some queries for which a satisfactory 'Yes' or 'No' can never be given! (See Chapter 21.) We don't have to worry about them; RDBMSs generally take a cautious view and if there is any doubt will default to rendering the answer table uneditable.

15.3 Forms

Forms also become more versatile in multi-table databases and some of this increased functionality has been covered during the discussion on queries (see above). However, the main benefits can be see in the Orders form shown in Figure 15.14.

This form draws information from three tables. Several queries are being used to feed data to the sub-form (which shows the items in the order) and to the combo boxes (used for the fields labelled 'Customer' and 'Employee'). New orders can be constructed by moving to a blank record, selecting a customer's name and an employee's name, choosing the items for the order and entering the number purchased. Now, you and I know that underneath all of this, the data is being stored as entries like those of Figure 15.15, but the users simply see a form from which they can make choices.

This form sums up much about, not how the relational model works, but why it has become viable. The model requires that we split the data up into lots of separate tables and use all sorts of unhelpful numbers in primary and foreign keys. We do all of this because it ensures that the data is more difficult to corrupt. In other words, it is a pain, but it keeps the data clean. We

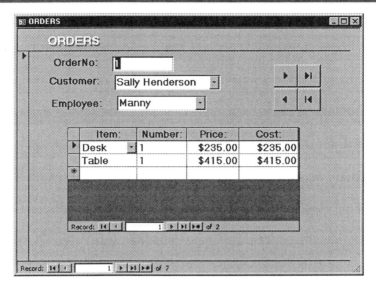

Figure 15.14 *A form which makes good use of a multi-table database.*

OrderNo	EmployeeNo	CustomerNo
4	2	4

OrderNo	ItemNo	NumberOfItems
4	1	1
4	2	1
4	3	1

Figure 15.15 *How orders are stored in the base tables.*

could not expect the average user of a database to cope with all of this complexity, so we use forms like this one to shield the user from that complexity.

15.4 Reports

Not only do reports allow us to print out data, we can use them to summarize and group the information in the database. In a multi-table database, we can base the reports on multiple tables.

For example, given the information in the sample database, we might be interested in which customers bought which items. We can generate a report which draws information from CUSTOMERS and ITEMS. Such a report might look like Figure 15.16. This very simple report lists each item alphabetically, and alongside each is a list of the customers who have bought the item. The customers are sorted alphabetically on surname.

A somewhat more informative report might show the amount each customer has spent and on which items, part of which might look like Figure 15.17. The name of each customer, sorted alphabetically by surname, is

```
┌─────────────────────────────────┐
│ Item Buyers                     │
│ ═══════════════════════════════ │
│                                 │
│  Item        Customer           │
│ ─────────────────────────────── │
│                                 │
│  Chair                          │
│              Sally Henderson    │
│              Harry McColgan      │
│              Brian Thompson     │
│              Sandra Wellington  │
│  Desk                           │
│              Sally Henderson    │
│              Sally Henderson    │
│              Sandra Wellington  │
│  Lamp                           │
│              Sally Henderson    │
│              Sandra Wellington  │
│              Sandra Wellington  │
│  Table                          │
│              Sally Henderson    │
│              Harry McColgan      │
│              Sandra Wellington  │
└─────────────────────────────────┘
```

Figure 15.16 *A report which shows which customers bought which items.*

Customer Totals

Customer	Item	Price	No.	Total Cost
Sally Henderson				
	Chair	$234.00	1	$234.00
	Desk	$235.00	1	$235.00
	Desk	$235.00	1	$235.00
	Lamp	$350.00	1	$350.00
	Table	$415.00	1	$415.00
				$1,469.00
Harry McColgan				
	Chair	$234.00	4	$936.00
	Table	$415.00	1	$415.00
				$1,351.00
Brian Thompson				
	Chair	$234.00	1	$234.00

Figure 15.17 *A report which shows how much each customer has spent.*

shown on the left-hand side, with a list of the items purchased, the price of each item and the number of items purchased. Then the total spent on each type of item is generated, with a total of each customer's purchases at the bottom of the list. A grand total of all customers' purchases (not shown in Figure 15.17) appears at the end of the report.

Reports can be much more complex than these examples, using data drawn from many tables. Subtotals, totals, averages and other summary statistics can be generated from entries in the relevant tables to generate informative reports on the data in your database.

16

Integrity

16.1 Data Integrity – Is It Worth the Effort?

How accurate should the data in a database be? 100% would be good, of course, but what is realistically acceptable in a database of reasonable size? 90%? 95%? The answer is that we need to go much higher than 95%, for one very simple reason.

Imagine we have a database of, say, 10,000 patients in a hospital and that 95% of the data held about each patient is accurate. Further, imagine that the average question we ask of the data is one which spans a number of records – 'How many of the patients are male?'; 'How many are over 40?'; 'How many are on insulin?'. The number of records from which these queries draw data will vary considerably but let's imagine that the average number is a conservative 200.

What is the probability that any one query will return the correct answer?

Since each record that is used in the query has a 95% chance of being correct, then, very simplistically, the chance that 200 be queried and that none contain false data is 0.95 to the power of 200, which equals:

0.000 035

which means that 0.0035% of answers will be correct. To put that another way, well over 99% of the answers will be wrong – very probably only slightly wrong, but incorrect nevertheless.

Before anyone objects, this calculation is badly flawed for a variety of reasons. Not the least is that although the average number of records might be 200, if the distribution of records is very skewed with the majority of queries actually only drawing data from five records (and the odd one from 10,000), then the accuracy of the answers improves dramatically. We can also argue that many inaccuracies don't matter. If the actual number of patients on insulin is 545 and we get an answer of 547, this probably won't alter our plans for ordering insulin.

I agree with these arguments and I would hate anyone to take these figures as definitive or even particularly accurate. What they are intended to show is that, contrary to what many people appear to believe, 95% accurate data does *not* give you 95% accurate answers; the actual figure will be much lower than this. This makes it imperative that you strive to ensure that the data in the database is as accurate as you can possibly make it. In practice, the effort is worth it, because if you can improve the accuracy of the data to 99%, then using the same very simplistic measure, the probability of a correct answer rockets up to 0.13, meaning that 13% of your queries will return correct answers. Get the accuracy up to 99.9% and you get 0.82, so 82% of the answers will be correct.

So data integrity is well worth the effort. Now we'll have a look at the main types of data integrity errors that can arise.

16.2 Types of Data Integrity Error (and Some Cures)

Data integrity is a general term which refers to several processes which keep the data in your database error-free (or as close to error-free as we can get). Very broadly there are four types of integrity error that can occur in a database.

1. Errors in unique data within a single field. You can mis-enter unique data, such as a customer's name, into a single field. For example, you could type 'Smath' instead of 'Smith' into a LastName field. The database cannot realistically be expected to detect or prevent this kind of error.

2. Errors in standard data within a single field. You can mis-enter standard data, such as a customer's title, into a Title field. Suppose that you normally enter 'Prof' as the title for a Professor but for a few of them you happen to use the title 'Prof.' (which has a period after the 'f'). When you search the database for all customers who have the title 'Prof' you will certainly find them all, but you will not be finding all of those customers who are Professors. This differs from the example given above for a last name only because the number of possible titles is small and readily definable. The difference is significant because the database can easily be designed to eliminate this second type of error.

3. Errors between data in different fields. Suppose that you record both the date of birth of your employees and their date of employment. Clearly if the date of birth for a given employee is greater (that is, later) than the date of employment, an error has been made during data entry (or else you have very odd employment rules!). We can use a type of data checking to detect this sort of error at the time of entry and ensure that it never gets into the database. In addition, there is nothing to stop us from making the checking more useful.

    For example, if we assume that you don't employ under-age workers, then any entry which has a date of birth less than 16 years before the date of employment must be an error. If we understand the rules of the business for which the database is designed, we can set up data integrity rules which look for data which contravenes those rules. Such rules are known, perfectly reasonably, as 'business rules'.

    Note that the fields concerned in this type of data integrity check are often in the same table, but don't have to be. For example, you might want to ensure that the value of an order (stored in an ORDERS table) never exceeded a customer's credit rating (stored in a CUSTOMERS table).

4. Errors between keys in different tables – referential integrity. Finally, there is a class of error that occurs between different tables, more specifically between the values that are stored in primary and foreign keys. The system which controls (and prevents) this type of error is known as referential integrity. If a value appears in a foreign key it must also appear in the primary key. This sounds straightforward, and it is, but there are several cases where the designer of the database (that's you!) has several choices, each of which has a different consequence.

Now we'll have a look at the four types of error in more detail.

16.2.1 Errors in Unique Data Within a Single Field

There's not much advice I can give you here except, of course, be *very careful*; sadly, the database can't help when you enter erroneous data of this type. The good news is that it can help with the other three, which are generally more serious anyway.

16.2.2 Errors in Standard Data Within a Single Field

Given data that is essentially drawn from a small pool of possible values (for example Ms., Mrs., Miss, Mr., Dr., Prof.) it is perfectly possible and highly desirable to ensure that no 'rogue' values (such as Professor or Missus) are entered. Most RDBMSs provide mechanisms to ensure this. Such control can also be applied to numerical data. For example, you can specify that a value, such as a height, must be between 1.5 and 2.5 meters.

As an example of, say numerical control, we could specify that the NumberOfItems field in the ORDER/ITEMS table must contain a value between 1 and 100 (Figure 16.1).

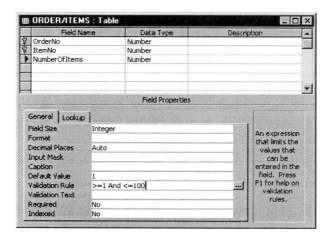

Figure 16.1 *Altering the table structure of ORDER/ITEMS so that the NumberOfItems field will only contain values between 1 and 100.*

We can also specify a set of values for the Title field in CUSTOMERS in much the same way (Figure 16.2).

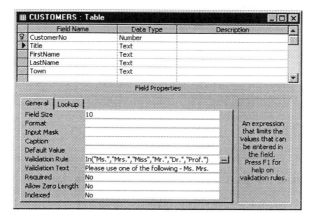

Figure 16.2 *Altering the table structure of CUSTOMERS so that the Title field will only contain certain values.*

The actual validation rule in this case is:

```
In ("Ms.", "Mrs.", "Miss", "Mr.", "Dr.", "Prof.")
```

These figures show the integrity control being applied at the table level. It can also be applied on the form used to enter the data; you (as the database designer) can provide a combo box which only allows the 'acceptable' values to be selected. In Figure 16.3, the combo box can be made to work in conjunction with, or independently of, the control applied at the table level.

The pros and cons of these two approaches (that is, whether control should be applied at the form level or the table level) are discussed below.

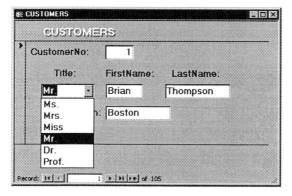

Figure 16.3 *A form which controls the values which can be entered into the Title field of CUSTOMERS.*

16.2.3 Errors Between Data in Different Fields

In Access, as is the case with many RDBMSs, errors between fields can only be controlled at the form level. Within a form it is relatively easy to set up

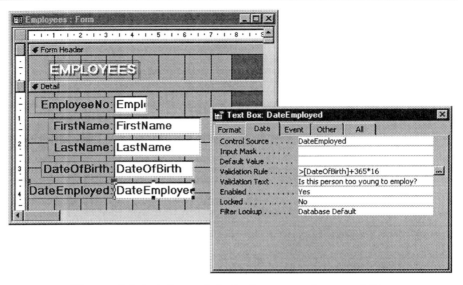

Figure 16.4 *A form which checks integrity between fields.*

quite complex checks which control data entry. As an example, the form in Figure 16.4, shown in the design stage, checks to see if the employment date is approximately 16 years after the person's date of birth.

In practice, you need to be relatively careful setting up checks like this one. For a start, 365.25 * 16 doesn't always check for exactly 16 years difference between two dates. However, an exact check is more complex to set up, and this one is going to be good enough in most cases. More importantly, this check operates only on the employment date, which means that it assumes that the date of birth has been entered and will not be changed after the employment date is entered. In other words, a user of the database can circumvent this check by filling in a date of birth such as 1 Apr 1950, filling in an employment date of 1 Apr 1990 (which is more than 16 years after the date of birth) and finally changing the date of birth to 1 Apr 1980. As the database designer, you are expected to foresee this sort of devious behavior on the part of the user and trap it. Depending upon the complexity of the checking that needs to be done, you may have to use a snippet of code (see Chapter 17).

16.2.4 Errors Between Keys in Different Tables – Referential Integrity

This subject has been discussed in some detail in Chapter 14, but just in case you aren't reading this book sequentially (which I rarely do with books, so I don't see why I should expect you to do it) we'll look at it again briefly.

This is the type of data integrity control which looks after integrity between tables. Why do you need to check integrity between tables? Consider the tables in Figure 16.5. The field EmployeeNo in table EMPLOYEES is a primary key so it only contains unique data. By contrast, the field EmployeeNo in table ORDERS can contain duplicate values. In fact, the more successful your employees are, the more frequently their EmployeeNo appears in the

ORDERS

OrderNo	EmployeeNo	CustomerNo
1	1	2
2	4	1
3	1	3
4	2	4
5	3	2
6	2	4
7	2	2

EMPLOYEES

EmployeeNo	FirstName	LastName	DateOfBirth	DateEmployed
1	Manny	Tomanny	12 Apr 1956	01 May 1989
2	Rosanne	Kolumns	21 Mar 1967	01 Jan 1990
3	Cas	Kade	01 May 1967	01 Apr 1992
4	Norma	Lyzation	03 Apr 1956	01 Apr 1992
5	Juan	Tomani	12 Apr 1956	01 Apr 1992
6	Del	Eats	01 May 1957	01 May 1994

Figure 16.5 *The ORDERS and EMPLOYEES tables.*

ORDERS table. We want a so-called 'one-to-many' relationship to exist between these fields; one number for each employee, but many entries for that employee in the ORDERS table.

In terms of data integrity, it doesn't matter if an employee appears in the EMPLOYEES table but not in the ORDERS table (perhaps they are new to the company and are still undergoing training). However, data integrity is violated if the opposite condition is allowed to arise, as in Figure 16.6, whereby a value (such as 9) appears in ORDERS.EmployeeNo which does not appear in EMPLOYEES.EmployeeNo.

Such a number is clearly nonsense. It seems to suggest that we have an employee who dealt with the order, but we cannot put a name to that employee because there is no corresponding entry in EMPLOYEES.

You can ensure that this problem doesn't arise by the simple expedient of being *very careful* when you enter data, but it is much more sensible to get the software to do the work for you. Most PC-based RDBMSs have facilities which allow you to form relationships between tables, and Access is no exception.

ORDERS

OrderNo	EmployeeNo	CustomerNo
1	1	2
2	4	1
3	1	3
4	2	4
5	3	2
6	2	4
7	9	2

Figure 16.6 *A flawed foreign key.*

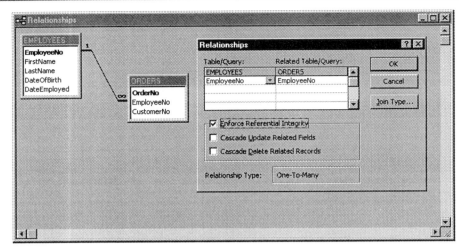

Figure 16.7 *Setting up a relationship which will enforce referential integrity automatically.*

These relationships can then enforce referential integrity for you if you so desire. For example, once the relationship shown in Figure 16.7 has been formed, Access will not allow you to create records like the one shown in Figure 16.6.

The main advantage of referential integrity is that it prevents you from making mistakes, forbidding you, for example, from assigning an order to an employee who doesn't exist. In its basic form, however, it has side-effects which we may or may not care for in any given situation. To overcome these, two 'variants' of referential integrity are provided, cascade delete and cascade update.

Cascade Delete

Suppose that as soon as an order arrives from a customer, it is company policy to enter the order into the database. This will include information such as the number of items required; see Figure 16.8.

Very occasionally, an order is cancelled before it is shipped, in which case we will want to delete any reference to the order from the database. However, referential integrity will forbid us to delete the entry in the ORDERS table because there are entries in the ORDER/ITEMS table which refer to the OrderNo we are trying to delete (Figure 16.9).

The only solution seems to be to delete first all the records which relate to the order in question from the ORDER/ITEMS table by hand, or perhaps with a delete query. Enter (stage left) a facility/concept called cascade delete (Figure 16.10).

If the relationship between these two tables is set to allow cascade deletion, when you delete the record from ORDERS the relevant records will be automatically deleted from ORDER/ITEMS (after the system has warned you first – Figure 16.11). Neat, isn't it?

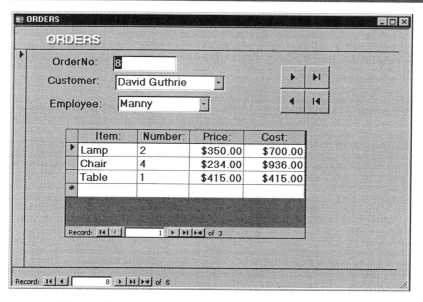

Figure 16.8 *A new order is entered into the database.*

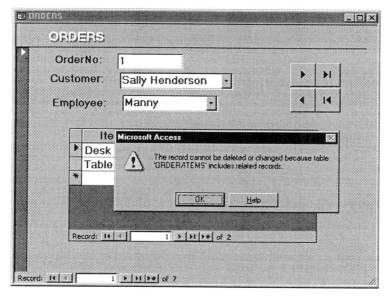

Figure 16.9 *Referential integrity refusing to allow the user to delete a record.*

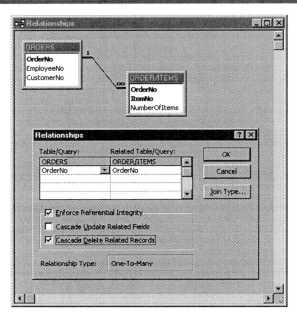

Figure 16.10 *Setting cascade delete between the relevant tables.*

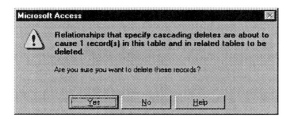

Figure 16.11 *Now the appropriate records in* ORDER/ITEMS *are deleted as well as the record in* ORDERS.

If you are using a counter field in Access to generate ORDERS.OrderNo, then deleting an order in this way will leave a gap in the OrderNo sequence. This may offend humans, since we like neat sequences of numbers, and it might conflict with a company business rule, but it certainly doesn't affect data integrity as far as referential integrity is concerned. All referential integrity cares about is ensuring that all of the entries in a foreign key (such as ORDER/ITEMS.OrderNo) always point to existing values in the primary key (in this case ORDERS.OrderNo).

Cascade Update

Now consider another problem. Suppose that you don't use a counter field for EMPLOYEES.EmployeeNo but use instead some type of government-generated unique identifier. (In the UK it would be a National Insurance number, in the USA it would be a Social Security number.) A new employee arrives who has forgotten this crucial piece of information. This isn't a crime (depending upon the country in which you live) so you insert a temporary number so that the person can get to work. Finally, after several months, the person's paperwork arrives and you can enter their 'proper' unique identifier. But wait. Referential integrity will refuse to allow you to change the temporary number in the EMPLOYEES table if there are entries in the ORDERS table which use that number. Enter (from stage left again) cascade update, which will permit you to make this change. It manages to do this without upsetting referential integrity because it will obligingly locate and change all the records in ORDERS from the temporary to the new number.

Depending upon the RDBMS you are using, you will be allowed to implement either or both of these cascades on any or all of your joins; Access supports both from version 2.0. The next question is should you do so? It's a trick question, of course, because it will depend entirely upon what you want from the database you are building. Given the invoice-type database we have here, you might well want to be able to delete orders as described above. However, if you fire a salesperson, you certainly *don't* want to cascade delete down into the order table (some of those orders may still be unpaid!). Whether, and how, you implement these options is up to you, but they are incredibly useful on occasions, so it is important to know that they are around if you need them.

Cascade in Context

So, where do cascade update and delete fit into the grand scheme of things? They are effectively optional extras; bolt-on goodies which can be added to referential integrity if required. You can have referential integrity without either of them, but you cannot set either of the cascade options without first creating a join between the two tables and setting referential integrity between them.

If this has made sense so far, try this question. Is there any logical reason why you shouldn't be allowed to set both cascade delete and cascade update on the same join?

You have, of course, thought about it carefully and come to the conclusion that the answer is 'No'. That is, no, there is no reason why you can't have both. And you are correct. Perhaps you have an ordering system that uses order numbers generated by a complex interaction of customer name, date etc. You want to be able to delete orders which are cancelled and you might also need, occasionally, to be able to give an order a temporary number if some of the other information is unavailable. Once again, I'm not suggesting that this is a good or bad idea, just that if you come across a situation where both forms of cascade are desirable, there is no data integrity reason why you shouldn't be allowed to set both.

16.3 Other Integrity Issues

It is worth remembering that, in applying data integrity mechanisms, we are usually trying to protect the data from the users of the database. This is not meant to imply that database users are normally malicious or mischievous, it is simply that they will often enter data which seems to them to be reasonable but isn't in terms of the database (the 'Prof.' vs. 'Prof' problem as discussed earlier). Before we discuss where the integrity rules, checks and controls can and should be placed in the database, it is worth pointing out that RDBMSs often provide other security mechanisms which can be used in conjunction with data integrity mechanisms. For example, it is possible and often desirable to limit the access that a user has to a database. We often limit this access to just the forms that have been designed for the users; we deny them access to the base tables and also deny them the ability to create new forms. As discussed below, if we do this, it can have a profound effect on the way in which we then use other types of data integrity enforcement.

16.4 Integrity – Where Should You Set It?

We can consider a database to be composed of layers. At the bottom layer are the base tables, above those are the queries which extract and manipulate the data in the base tables, and then there are the forms which are based on the queries and occasionally directly on the base tables (Figure 16.12). Where, within this model, should integrity checking be applied?

It's a pretty fundamental question. If integrity checks are applied at the base table level then they propagate upwards. That is to say, if you apply a data integrity control at the base table level, then all of the forms which are based on that table (or on queries that are based on that table) will inherit that integrity control. To put that another way, if you apply data integrity at the table level, then that integrity cannot be subverted by, for example, creating a new form. The only way to enter data into that table which disobeys the integrity rule is first to remove the rule from the table.

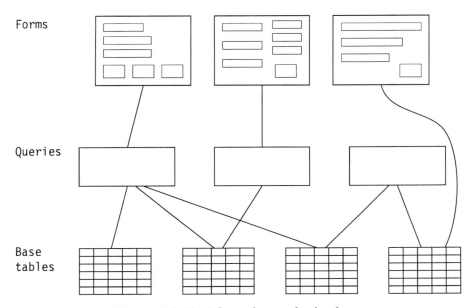

Figure 16.12 *A layered view of a database.*

If, on the other hand, you apply data integrity at the form level, then any new form that is created will not apply the same integrity rules automatically.

In general it is best to apply data integrity rules in such a way as to ensure that:

1. they cannot be subverted;
2. the workload required to maintain the database is kept at a minimum.

In turn, this leads to a more general rule which says that data integrity rules are best applied at the table level whenever possible, because that makes them more difficult to subvert. However, it is only a general rule and there are times when it should be ignored.

Consider a particular company that sells, say computers. The company gives discounts and sales people are allowed to give up to 5% at their discretion. Supervisors can give up to 10% while managers can give up to 50% (in times of dire need to pacify customers already dissatisfied with a previous product). Clearly the upper limit is 50%, but if we simply set that at the table level, a salesperson might accidentally give a discount greater than 5%. The answer is to give each type of employee a different form, each with a different integrity rule.

The bad news is, of course, that this integrity could be subverted if the users of the database were able to access the base tables directly. However, if you know from the start of the design that users will not be allowed to access the base tables directly (see above), then this is no longer a consideration. You are then free to apply data integrity at the form level if it is (as in this case) to your advantage.

As a final general rule, use your common sense. If you can't imagine any reason to allow a rule ever to be subverted, then place it at the base table level if that isn't going to impose a maintenance problem (which it usually doesn't). However, there are times when it is positively an advantage to place a data integrity rule at a higher level, and if you can see such an advantage, then go for it.

17

Building a Database Application

17.1 Building a Database Application

In Part 2 we've looked at all sorts of issues which contribute to the construction of a database. Now seems like a good time to look at the process as a whole and to describe the steps that are often followed in constructing a database.

They are:

1. Identify the real-world objects that exist (employees, orders etc.).
2. Identify the relationships that exist between those objects.
3. Create tables, one for each object.
4. Create joins between the tables which represent the relationships.
5. Decide upon the forms and reports that are required by the users of the database.
6. Create the relevant queries needed to support and service those forms and reports.
7. Create the forms and reports.
8. Add the data integrity constraints.

If you reach this point, you have built a database. Unfortunately, the chances are that the average user would find it very difficult to use. What it needs is the next step:

9. Create a user interface which ties those forms and reports into a single, seamless application.

To me, adding this user interface makes the difference between a 'database' and a 'database application'. Since we are always striving to create databases that people can use with the minimum of effort, a database application is what we typically build, rather than a database.

The problem with any attempt to describe how a database application is constructed, particularly by using a simple recipe as shown above, is that it is bound to be flawed because the process can vary so much. For example, if the database application is large, say a banking system, then it will be much more involved than this.

It will start with a formal design specification which describes in detail exactly what the customer wants. This specification will be bounced back and forth between innumerable committees and consultants, all of whom are likely to alter, amend and, in some rare cases, improve the specification. (If I sound cynical about this process, that's because I am. In my opinion, good design in any field, not just databases, is rarely accomplished by committee.) However, it is part of corporate life that this process must be followed, and it all helps to spread the blame around if the project fails.

What I am trying to say is that the list above is not, under any circumstances, to be taken as definitive: there are many ways of building a database. You might, for example, sketch out the user interface first during your discussions with the users about the objects that they can identify in their database.

In addition, you will almost certainly find that the design changes as you go along (something that the formal design process and all of the committees are designed to eliminate as much as possible). These changes will often be due to the users saying things like 'Oh, we've just remembered. You know we said that there was only ever one salesperson per order. Well, of course, if the order is for more than 50 items, we do allow two salespeople to be credited with the order because junior sales staff have to pass such orders on to a senior member for verification'. Specifications also change, because as the work progresses, the users can begin to develop an understanding of the real power of a database. As they see it beginning to work, they say things like 'Wow! It can produce that report so fast! That used to take us days. Look, we have always wanted to break down the sales by region but it was always too difficult before. Can you make it do that as well?'. Whatever the reason, specifications are very rarely fixed, so you need to expect change and budget for it.

In Part 2 we have covered most of the operations listed above with the exception of the construction of the user interface. This is not part of the relational model, and yet it seems worth covering, at least in passing, for two reasons. The first is simply completeness; the story feels unfinished without it. The second is that the tools you can use to build the user interface are the same as those which are used to construct much of the data integrity described in Chapter 16, so we can kill two birds with one stone.

17.2 GUIs, Macros and Control Languages

Building a user interface and controlling data entry at the form level are typically accomplished in one of three ways:

♦ using the GUI;

♦ using a macro language;

♦ using a programming language.

We'll have a look at all three and examine their pros and cons.

Typically, GUIs are seen as the easiest to use and the least powerful, while programming languages are perceived as the most powerful but the most difficult to learn. Macros sit, like elevator music, slap in the middle of the road (and therefore, in my opinion, deserve most richly to be run over, but more of that later). However, there is often a measure of overlap between these three, so we'll choose a task which can be accomplished by all three to illustrate how they work and how they differ.

It says clearly at the start of this book that it is not about 'How to use Access', but the next few pages are going to read very much like part of a 'How to' book. This is not because I have forgotten the original idea; it is because I want to discuss which of these three ways of building a user interface is the 'best'. In order to compare and contrast them, I have to give some idea of how they are used.

17.2.1 Creating a Very Simple User Interface

Suppose you have a database like that which we have created in the preceding chapters. Customer details are stored in a table called CUSTOMERS and order details in an ORDERS table. You have also created two forms, as in Chapter 15, one showing the customer details and the other, based on a query, which shows the order information for specific orders from particular customers. So far, so good.

But now you want to weld these two forms together to create a tiny part of a cohesive user interface. You want to be able to move directly from the Customers form to the Orders form. This will enable you (or the other users of your database) to enter the details of a new customer and then move directly to the Orders form to enter that customer's first order.

What is required is a button embedded in the Customers form which will open up the Orders form. In addition, we want the Orders form, when opened up in this way, to show us only the orders which relate to the current customer we are looking at with the Customers form. In other words, if we are looking at Sally Henderson's record in the Customers form, when we press the button we want to see only her orders in the Orders form.

17.2.2 Using the GUI

In Access 1.x the GUI could not provide a solution to this problem. Access versions 2.x and later, on the other hand, allow you to do this using a Control Wizard.

If you switch to design mode in the Customers form and call up the toolbox, you will find it has a tool called Control Wizards (top right of the toolbox in Access 97). Turn it on and then use the Button tool to place a button

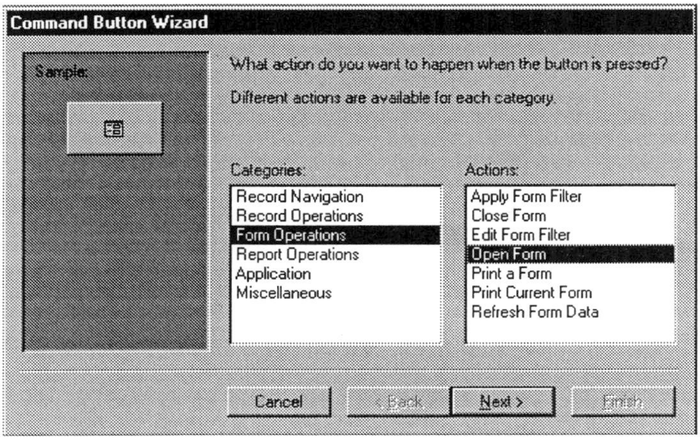

Figure 17.1 *Using the control wizards.*

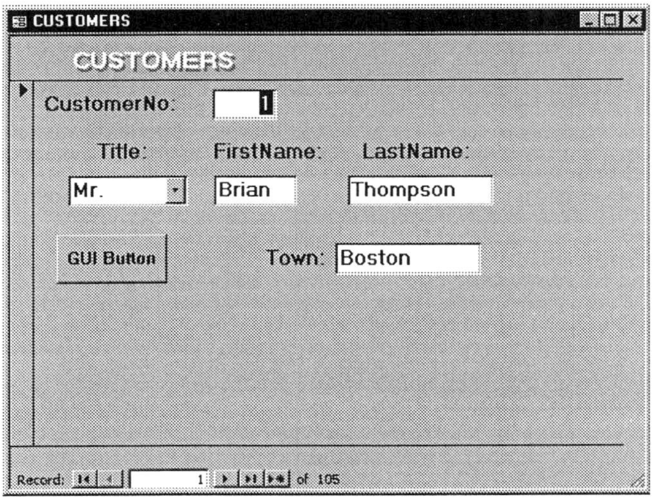

Figure 17.2 *The Customers form complete with its new button.*

on the form. The wizard will come into operation and ask you a series of questions (Figure 17.1).

You need to select Form Operations, Open Form, ORDERS, 'Open the form and find specific data to display', then match the relevant fields, type in some text for the button (perhaps 'Open Orders', although I have used 'GUI Button') and finally give it a name (which can also be 'Open Orders').

This works beautifully. When you press the button, the Orders form opens up (Figure 17.2). You can close the Orders form and the Customers form should still be visible, since it was never closed.

17.2.3 Using a Macro

Go back to the database window, click on the Macro tab and then on the New button. A window opens up which is divided into two sections, Action and Comment. If you click in the first row of the action column a list pops down. Scrolling down this list is fascinating, because it shows all the actions that a macro can perform (and some, like DoMenuItem, are very versatile). We want this macro to open the ORDERS form, so choose the option Open-Form; in fact, typing 'o' will save some scrolling time, because it jumps to the options that start with that letter. A second dialog area appears at the bottom of the macro window (under 'Action Arguments') and it is here that you can enter details such as the name of the form you want to open. Opposite Form Name you can again click to produce a pop-down list from which you can select the form 'Orders'.

One option listed under Action Arguments for Open Form is 'Where Condition'. This essentially means 'Open the form where the following is true'. In this case we want to see only those orders in which the Customer ID field has the same value as that currently showing in the CustomerNo field in the form called Customers. To put that another way, we use the Customers form to flip through the customer records until we find the customer we want. At that point, the relevant name will be showing in the form, as will the CustomerNo number (say, 2). When we switch to looking at the orders, we want to see only those which have a Customer ID number of 2.

Thus we want to see the records in the Orders form where:

the CustomerNo field is equal to the CustomerNo field in the form called Customers.

We can express this more formally as:

Open the form Orders where
[CustomerNo]=[Forms]![Customers]![CustomerNo]

The expression:

[CustomerNo]=[Forms]![Customers]![CustomerNo]

is the statement required in the Where Condition section. In Access 2.x you can use the expression builder (Figure 17.3) to help you to construct this; in Access 1.x you have to type it in yourself.

Close the macro window and give the macro a sensible name like 'Open Orders'.

That's the macro written; all you need to do now is add a button to the form and tell it which macro it should run. Open the form in Design mode, pop down the 'View' menu and choose both Toolbox and Properties. This will cause two modeless (meaning they stay visible on screen until you close them) windows to appear – the Toolbox and the Properties Sheet. Turn off the Control Wizards, then choose the Button tool from the toolbox, click the mouse on the form and a button will appear. Now turn your attention to the Properties Sheet. Find the property called 'On Click' (it is in the list of All Properties and also in the list of Event Properties). Click in the On Click box and you will be able to select your macro from a list (if this is your first macro, you will, of course, get a list of one!); see Figure 17.4.

That's it; when you press the button, the macro should operate in the same way as the GUI-generated one. You can give the button a name like 'Macro Button'.

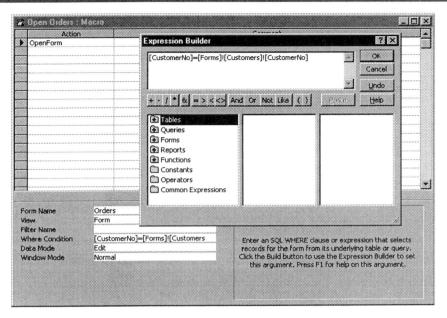

Figure 17.3 *Using the expression builder.*

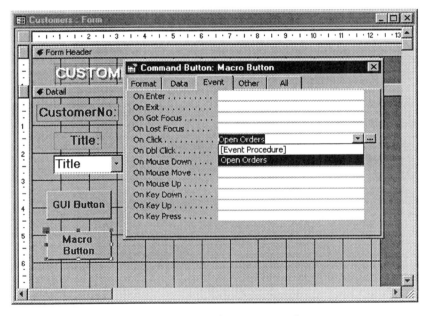

Figure 17.4 *Tying the macro to a button.*

17.2.4 Using the Programming Language

The modern Windows RDBMSs still allow you write very efficient bits of code, but you no longer write them in one huge block. Instead it is normal to use the GUI to create most of the major objects you need (forms, reports etc.) and indeed to populate them with control objects (buttons, combo boxes etc.). The programming language is then used to give these objects a mission in life. For example, you can use the GUI interface to place a button on a form and then to attach a small section of code to it so that it does something when it is clicked by the user. More technically, you supply code which is linked to an event associated with that object.

Every object in the interface has a series of events which are linked to it. For example, a form is an object and has events like 'On Open' tied to it. The events are specified by the designers of Access and reflect the likely uses to which objects will be put. Form objects, for example, do not have events like 'On change color' since, although the color of a form *can* be changed, you are unlikely to want to have a section of code which detects that particularly obscure event and runs when it occurs. On the other hand, forms are continually being opened so we have an event called 'On Open' which will run code every time the form is opened. And buttons have events like 'On Click' which are clearly likely to be useful. In fact, to no one's great surprise, that is the event which we are going to use for code in this case.

Open the `Customers` form in design mode and use the toolbox to place a button upon it. Then use the property sheet to rename the button as 'Press me for Orders' and give it the same caption. Next list the 'Event Properties' and locate the one called 'On Click'. If you click to the right of that event you will find a button with three dots appears. Press it and a dialog box appears which asks whether you want the Expression Builder, Macro Builder or Code Builder: select the third option.

A code window opens up in which you will be able to type the required code.

The code you are going to use is based on the statement:

```
DoCmd.OpenForm
```

The `DoCmd` bit is a commonly used statement in Access Basic which allows you to execute most of the Access 'Actions'. Actions (like the 'actions' described earlier for macros) carry out tasks like opening forms, closing them, opening tables etc. If you search the help system for 'actions: reference' you can find a list of them all.

Opening the form is no problem. We just need to write:

```
DoCmd.OpenForm 'ORDERS'
```

The next question is 'How do we get the form to open up, showing only the `Orders` which refer to the current customer?'. In our case, the `Cus-tomerNo` field in the `CUSTOMERS` table stores an unique identifier for each customer. Each order for that customer also stores that number. Thus Sally Henderson's number is 2 and all of her orders are identified by this number. We can make use of this by looking up her number on the `Customers` form and asking to see only the `Orders` which appertain to that number.

Most actions can be modified by a series of arguments. The `OpenForm` action can have a long string of arguments:

```
DoCmd.OpenForm formname [, view] [, filtername]
[, wherecondition] [, datamode] [, windowmode] [, openargs]
```

Frightening, aren't they? In fact, you can ignore them until you need them. In this case, all we need is the `wherecondition` argument. We can express what we want in English as:

Open the form called `Orders` where the contents of `CustomerNo` field in Orders is equal to the contents of the `CustomerNo` field in the current form `Customers`

This actually translates into:

```
DoCmd.OpenForm "ORDERS", , ,
"[CustomerNo]=[Forms]![Customers]![CustomerNo]"
```

Note that in Access 2.0 this reads slightly differently as:

```
DoCmd OpenForm "ORDERS", , , "[CustomerNo] =
Forms![Customers]![CustomerNo]"
```

The difference is in the lack of a dot between `DoCmd` and `OpenForm`.

Note also that there have to be three commas before the `wherecondition`, which itself must be wrapped up in double quotation marks. Access is pernickety on these points of syntax. If you enter this `DoCmd` statement (Figure 17.5), save it and return to the form, it should work.

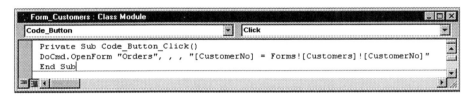

Figure 17.5 *Opening a form using program code.*

17.2.5 Which Is Best?

So what do these three solutions to the same problem tell us about the relative merits of GUIs, macros and programming languages?

As GUIs get better they give us more functionality (as shown by the increased functionality offered by the later versions of Access), but they can never provide all of the versatility that macros and hand-crafted programming can offer. I am all in favour of using the GUI as much as possible; it is faster and easier to use than either of the other two. However, if you develop a moderately complex database application with a reasonable user interface and data integrity checks, you will have to use tools which work at a deeper level.

Macros offer the next level down, extending the functionality of the GUI. Macros are still limited, however, and do not provide anything like the enormous flexibility of a programming language. Both the macro and programming languages take some effort to learn and, surprisingly, often require relatively different skills; in other words, a good working knowledge of macros may not make it much easier to convert to using the programming language. Perhaps even more surprisingly, I do not believe that programming is *fundamentally* more difficult to learn. Macros *are* easier to use, but not by orders of magnitude.

And there is an often overlooked problem here. People who are new to databases tend to assume that their needs are simple. They say things like, 'Oh, I just need to generate some realistic sample data so that I can see how the system works' or 'I just need to change the name "Smith" to "Smyth" in all of these records'. Both sound simple to the uninitiated, but in fact the former is often very complex, while the latter is very simple. The only sensible solution for the former requires code; the latter can be accomplished with an update query created with the GUI.

If you are new to RDBMSs, I suggest (with as much deference as possible) that you may well not be in a position to judge whether you need macros or programming. In that case, my advice is clear. Unless you are sure that your needs really are simple, don't bother learning to use macros. Once you find that you need more than the GUI offers, go straight to the programming language. In this way you avoid the pain of climbing one learning curve only to discover that the view from the top is unsatisfactory and another climb awaits you.

If you need further evidence to convince you, consider the GUI solution that I outlined earlier. When you placed the button on the form, a wizard ran and asked questions about which form you wanted to be opened and under what conditions. Once it had collected all of the answers, the wizard wrote a piece of code (Figure 17.6) for you automatically and attached it to the OnClick event for the button.

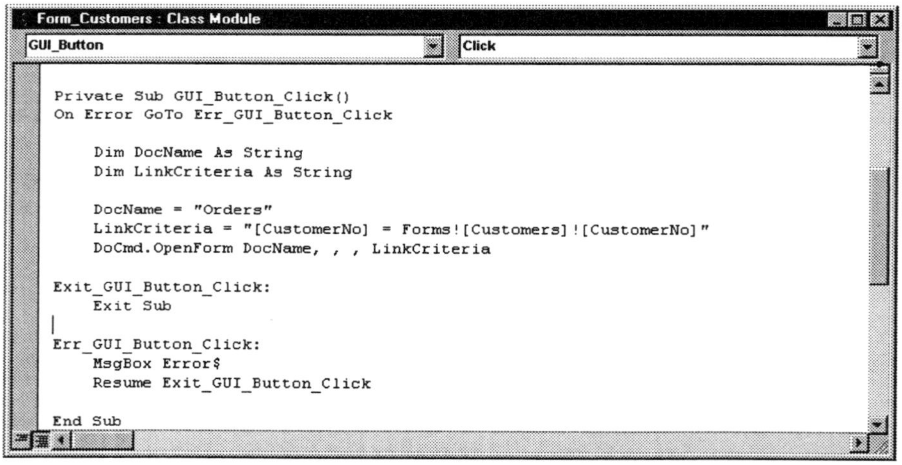

```
Form_Customers : Class Module
GUI_Button                              Click

    Private Sub GUI_Button_Click()
    On Error GoTo Err_GUI_Button_Click

        Dim DocName As String
        Dim LinkCriteria As String

        DocName = "Orders"
        LinkCriteria = "[CustomerNo] = Forms![Customers]![CustomerNo]"
        DoCmd.OpenForm DocName, , , LinkCriteria

    Exit_GUI_Button_Click:
        Exit Sub

    Err_GUI_Button_Click:
        MsgBox Error$
        Resume Exit_GUI_Button_Click

    End Sub
```

Figure 17.6 *The code produced by the Wizard.*

This code appears more complicated than the code I produced, but that is simply because it has some rather elegant built-in error-checking. If you decide to expend the extra effort in learning the programming language, you will then be able to do precisely what I and many other developers do. We use the GUI and its wizards as much as possible, and then simply edit and modify the code they produce to achieve the ends we need.

17.3 Other Languages – SQL

Incidentally, you may well have come across a language called SQL (Structured Query Language) in discussions about RDBMSs. You may be wondering, with all of this talk about control languages, how they relate to SQL. Is SQL an example of the sort of control language which has been discussed here? The simple answer is 'No, it isn't'.

SQL is a standard language which allows a database to be queried (hence the name). It can also be used for other operations, such as creating tables, but it is never used for interface control as described in this chapter. It is often used to pass queries between a front-end RDBMS running on a PC to a database server sitting somewhere on a network. In other words, SQL becomes quite important when the database you are building expands from a single-user database running on a PC to a multi-user database running on a network. This is discussed in more detail in Chapter 19.

SQL is also used internally in Access to describe the queries that you typically create using the graphical query builder. If you build a query and then select View SQL, Access will show you the SQL statement which describes that query.

Chapter 25 covers SQL in some detail for those who want to know more about it, but for the time being, if you are only working on a standalone PC, I would save it for later.

18

Summary of Part 2

This is an exceedingly short chapter, which simply summarizes what Part 2 is all about and points the way to the next part.

I sincerely hope that Part 2 has convinced you that single tables are fine for very simple data, but catastrophic for more complex data; which is the sort of data that most people actually want to store and manipulate.

The relational model gives us the mechanisms we need to store and manipulate complex data in such a way as to ensure that we can query it later and get out the answers that we need. Part 2 outlines most of what you need to know about the relational model to get started building databases.

If you have read and understood Part 2, I reckon that you are more qualified than most people to construct multi-table databases for single users. Ah – you noticed the qualification that slipped in there; that 'for single users' bit. So far, we have only considered databases which run on a standalone PC and can therefore be used by only one person at a time. Part 3 outlines the ways in which a single-user database can be expanded to allow multiple users to access it at the same time.

Part 3

Multi-Table
Multi-User
Databases

19

Multi-Table Multi-User Databases

Where did you put that data,
Where did you put that file?'

So far I have described databases in a partial vacuum: that is, I haven't talked about where the database is running. I have been using Access as an example and, since Access typically runs on a standalone PC, I suppose that such a machine has been the implied location of the database.

There are other places where a database can be located and now seems like a reasonable time to explore the pros and cons of these alternative locations.

There are essentially four 'data location models' that you can employ:

♦ everything on a standalone PC
♦ PC front-end – data on file server
♦ client–server using a database server as the back end
♦ mainframe

A database can be thought of as having four different parts or components (Figure 19.1):

♦ user interface section
♦ data processing engine
♦ conflict resolution section (to deal with conflicts introduced by multiple users accessing the data at the same time)
♦ the data itself

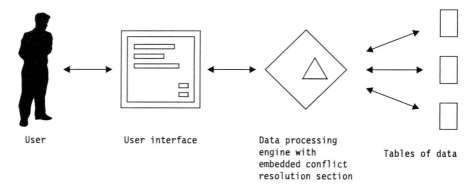

User   User interface   Data processing   Tables of data
                                      engine with
                                      embedded conflict
                                      resolution section

Figure 19.1 *The four major components of a database. Note that in this example the conflict resolution section is embedded in the data processing engine.*

Each of the four 'data location models' involves placing these components in different places.

The fourth data location model, the mainframe, seems inappropriate for discussion in a book which is aimed at PC users, so I'll ignore it. What I will do here is to outline the strengths and weaknesses of each of the other three with approximate performance and size estimates. But first, a few qualifications.

This is a complex area. The decision to choose one of these alternative models will be based upon the interaction of many factors, including:

♦ response time required
♦ number of users
♦ file size
♦ file number
♦ data size
♦ available resources (including hardware, software, expertise and money)
♦ type of data access required (read-only, read–write)

and so on.

These factors interact in complex ways. For example, suppose that your requirements make multi-user access to the data essential: you can instantly rule out a standalone PC. However, if the number of users is guaranteed to be small (say, 3), then, on a given hardware platform, you could allow those users to access a greater volume of data than if there were 50 of them. If the number of users did then increase, the system might still work but the response time would increase. To make matters worse, the interactions between these factors are often non-linear. For example, doubling the number of users on a given system might have very little impact on response time; doubling it again might bring the same system to its knees.

So, the safest thing for me to do is to fail to give any actual figures and instead write useful phrases such as 'If you have lots of users, don't use this data location model'. This is likely to leave you gnashing your teeth and wondering 'So, what exactly counts as "lots"? 3? 25? 500?'. On the other hand, if I do quote hard figures ('You should not consider using a standa-lone PC for more than 1 Gbyte of data'), sure as fate there is someone out there happily using a 300 MHz Pentium with 1,024 Mbyte of RAM to access 1.5 Gbyte.

I *will* quote figures because it seems far more useful to do so, but please just regard them as general figures from which to start discussions. Please don't take them as gospel and please don't build your entire database strategy around them alone.

19.1 Everything on a Standalone PC

The simplest data location model is to install everything on a standalone PC (Figure 19.2). You install an RDBMS like Access, Paradox, dBASE or Fox-Pro on the PC. You design the database, type in the data, query it and so on, all on a single machine. For many people this will be the norm; indeed it may be the only 'data location model' they have ever considered. It has the great advantage of simplicity though it also has a couple of restrictions.

For a start, only one person can use the database at a time. In addition, this data location model is likely to be unsatisfactory for more than about 1 Gbyte of data. Factors which will vary this figure (mostly downwards) are the hardware (less memory = smaller data files) and the manner in which the data is used. For example, if it is rarely updated, then it can be heavily indexed and queries should run against it reasonably rapidly. If the data is constantly updated, the indexes will slow down the updating and yet removing them will slow down the querying! (Indexes are devices for speeding up a database. They are explained in Chapter 27.) In a nutshell, if the data is rarely updated, heavily indexed and you have very impressive hardware,

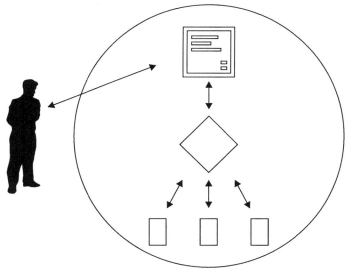

Figure 19.2 *Everything on a standalone PC. Here the workstation is represented by a circle. There is no need for a conflict resolution section as there is only one user on the system.*

you can go above this limit. Given a 286 processor with 640 kbyte of RAM, don't even think about it.

With a standalone PC-based database, there is only one user so the conflict resolution component isn't required and the other three appear as a single, seamless entity to the user. Simple. In fact, it is so simple, why would you ever want to use anything more complex?

One of the major reasons for moving to a more complex data location model is that this one cannot handle multiple users. For one thing there is only one keyboard, so we can expect fist fights if we try for multi-user access. For another, this model doesn't allow for conflicts between the requirements of different users to be resolved. If you need more than one user to access the data at the same time, you need to split up the components described above and partition them between different machines. This leads us to the second data location model.

19.2 PC Front-End – Data on File Server

If you have a need for multiple users to access the same data, it is not beyond the bounds of possibility that you already have a network. Given a network, you have the option of moving to the second data location model (Figure 19.3).

In this model, much continues as before. You would still run Access, Paradox or the RDBMS of your choice on your PC, so the user interface and data processing engine bit of the database stays there. Only two things change. One is that the data files are moved to a file server. The second is that the individual RDBMSs running on the individual PCs need to communicate with each other. They need to do this in order to resolve the multitude of potential conflicts which suddenly arise when more than one

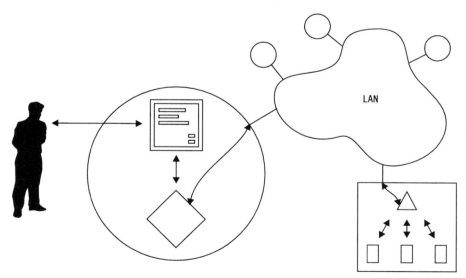

Figure 19.3 *PC front-end with data on a file server. The circles represent workstations, with one enlarged to show detail, attached to a network. Also attached to the network is a file server, shown as a square.*

person accesses the same data at the same time. Consider a simple example. You and I both work for the same company and we are trying to update the company's customer records. I open up the record for A. Smith to increase his credit rating from $2,000 to $3,000. While I am doing so, you delete his record. What happens to his record when I finish editing it and send it back to the file server?

The answer to this question depends upon the RDBMS that you are using. Access, for example, maintains a lock file in the same directory as the data file, and this file is used to store information about who is doing what at any particular time. Thus, if I had opened the record to update it before you tried to delete it, you would receive a message saying that the record was in use by 'Mark' and that you wouldn't be able to update the record until I had finished with it. Other RDBMSs use other mechanisms for dealing with these potential conflicts.

The important point is that, with this data location model, the control of the user interface and the data processing engine remains on the PC, while the data itself and the conflict resolution section are moved to the file server.

The big advantage of this model is that it provides multi-user access to the same data at a relatively low cost. The big disadvantage is that this model is inefficient in two main ways.

First, it tends to load the network. Remember that the data is at one end of the wire (on the file server) but the processing is at the other end (on the PC). Every time you query the data, it has to be moved to the PC, since that is where it is crunched. In a badly designed system, this can mean that every query against a 100 Mbyte table requires the entire table to be shipped to the PC. Intelligent indexing can reduce this considerably (since the indexes can be shipped for searching, and only the relevant records sent out to the client), but how effective this process is in practice will depend upon the RDBMS.

Secondly, the processing is at the PC end, so each PC needs enough resources to cope with the data. If you decide that an increase in the database size warrants an increase in memory of 32 Mbyte, you will need to add that to all of the PCs that access the data. Given 10 such PCs, that's about one third of a gigabyte of RAM that you have to buy and install.

These restrictions mean that the number of simultaneous users and the size of the data are relatively restricted. Think in terms of 10 users and 1 Gbyte.

19.3 Client–Server Model

This model (Figure 19.4) is, again, simply a modification of the previous one. The user interface is the only component that stays on the PC; the data, the processing and the conflict resolution move to a server. This is typically not a file server but a server dedicated to running applications like RDBMSs, hence they are generically known as 'application servers'. Machines which are dedicated to running RDBMSs are often called database servers. Examples of such database servers are IBM's DB2

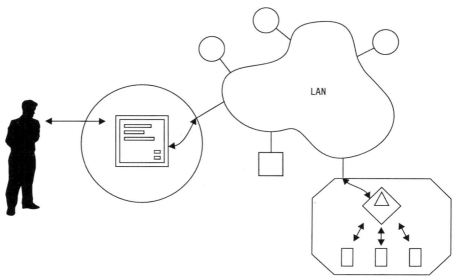

Figure 19.4 *Client–server system. The rectangle with trimmed corners is a database server.*

Universal Database and Microsoft's SQL Server. The PCs are still PCs, but they are often referred to as 'clients'.

But wait. Why go to the expense of a dedicated database server when you have that nice old NetWare 3.x file server already in place? Can't you run a database engine on that as well? The answer is that you can, but you probably don't want to do so.

The reason lies in the network operating system (NOS). NOSs such as NetWare 3.x are optimized for File and Print. Application servers run a NOS which is optimized for running multi-user applications. So a dedicated application server is generally considered to be better. If you really want to run one server for both applications and File and Print, then Windows NT is probably better than NetWare, all things considered.

The client–server model is typically *not* limited by bandwidth. Since the data itself and the data processing are now snuggled together in one place, queries no longer mean that masses of data have to move across the network. Instead, when the GUI running on the client is used to construct a question, only an SQL description of that query is shipped across the network to the server. This SQL will typically be a very short string of ASCII characters.

The database engine on the server processes the query and simply sends the answer (rather than the entire table or collection of tables) to the client. Conflict resolution is also handled centrally with associated benefits in terms of speed and sophistication. In addition, centralizing the data processing means that the whole system is easier and usually cheaper to update. If the database slows down you can throw hardware (in terms of memory and processors) at the server. You don't have to add it to the clients, because they are simply handling the user interface.

On the ticklish subject of size, this model will typically support as many clients and as much data as you can afford. To put that another way, consider this model seriously if you think you will need more than 10 clients or more than 1 Gbyte of data in the foreseeable future.

19.4 Summary

The descriptions given here are necessarily simplified. I haven't touched on such subjects as middleware, data warehousing and the host of other fascinating subjects which have arisen in the database world in recent years. It isn't that I consider these to be unimportant (far from it); they just seem to me to be peripheral to the central subject of this book, which is the relational database model.

Although the joys of Part 4 are still beneath your right thumb, this is essentially the end of this book, at least in terms of the 'story' that we have been following. We started with a single-table database and have ended up with a multi-user, multi-gigabyte database.

The next part contains chapters which can, essentially, be read in isolation. If you want to know more about SQL, read that chapter now. If normalization fascinates you, dip into that chapter over a cup of cocoa this evening.

Part 4

Related Database Topics

20

What Exactly Is a Relational Database?

20.1 Do Multiple Tables a Relational Database Make?

So far I have skated delicately around the definition of a relational database. It is really tempting to believe that the use of multiple tables marks the transition to a relational database. Indeed, I have read several times that a 'relational' database is so called because it allows you to 'relate' information held in different tables. How can I put this politely? This information is not correct. It is wrong. It is horribly wrong. Anyone who tells you this is incorrect. Regard anything that they tell you in the future with the deepest suspicion. If they try to sell you anything, say nothing, smile sweetly and walk carefully away.

So where does the word 'relational' come from? Chris Date says that 'The reason that such systems are called 'relational' is that the term 'relation' is essentially just a mathematical term for a table.' (*An Introduction to Database Systems*, 6th edn, Addison-Wesley, 1995, p. 22).

He then goes on to define a 'Relational Database' as 'a way of looking at data.... More precisely, the relational model is concerned with three aspects of data: data structure, data integrity and data manipulation.' (ibid., p. 98). All three of these are covered in Parts 1 and 2.

In other words, the term 'relational' comes from the rigid mathematical background which underpins the model and the relational database model itself is a relatively complex entity of which only a tiny part is concerned with the 'relationship' between tables. Indeed, the fact that 'relationships' can exist between tables has nothing to do with the naming of the system.

20.2 On Names and Misnames

For the record, a database is a collection of data. The definition is often expanded to include the forms, queries, etc. associated with the data. A DBMS (DataBase Management System) is a system, such·as Access, which can be used to manage a database.

The first DBMSs that appeared on the PC were simple tools only capable of handling one table of data at a time. Rightly or wrongly (wrongly in fact, but let's not get picky) these became known as flat-file DBMSs. Even worse, because many people did and still do confuse DBMSs with databases, they were often known as flat-file databases. Some of these products, particularly Borland's Reflex, were excellent for the job they were designed to do, which was handling single tables of data.

As PCs became faster and more powerful, DBMS products began to appear which were able to handle multiple tables of data simultaneously – the best known of these was dBASE. At about the same time, the relational model of handling data was gaining popularity. While the relational model certainly has the ability to use multiple tables of data, this is but one facet of the model (see Chapter 21 on Codd's rules). In addition, there are other ways of modeling data (hierarchical, network) and these use multiple tables as well.

The multi-table DBMSs (such as dBASE) were certainly not relational DBMSs because they had so few relational features; nevertheless they were very loosely based on the relational model and the companies which sold them had no hesitation in trading on the increasing popularity of the relational model. This is how the products were advertised and sold.

It is tempting to be cynical and say that either the developers of the software were unaware of the failings of their products, or they didn't care. It is more likely that the developers were trying to construct the best products that they could, given the constraints of DOS and the PC. My experience of good software developers is that, as a breed, they are intelligent and honest. In a sense, their craft requires these characteristics; there is nothing so precise and honest as computer code – it brooks no mendacity or imprecision. So, who wrote the word relational on the boxes of these early DBMSs? Well, if the developer's work tends to induce directness and honesty, what of the 'craft' of the advertising executive and salesperson? I know who I blame.

Whoever was responsible, we have inherited a situation where for many people the word relational means 'Able to use multiple tables at the same time'.

Given the complexity of the relational model, many people argue that no DBMS currently offered for sale is actually a true relational database management system, since all fail to implement some aspect of the model or other. However, this argument is essentially immaterial. Whatever the rights and wrongs of the situation, almost all of the DBMSs that you will come across today claim to be 'relational'. Some implement many important aspects of the relational model, some implement lamentably few. (For more details on the relational model, see the next chapter, which is about Codd's Rules). It is still a case of 'buyer beware'. If you are choosing an

RDBMS and you *need* a particular aspect of the relational model for your database, check that the RDBMS you are considering does actually support that feature.

21

Codd's Rules

Relational databases are, by now, so widely accepted that many people are unaware that any other form of database can exist. It is also sad (but true) that many people don't know what particular facets of a DBMS make it relational or not. Since the relational model is the brainchild of Dr. Edgar Codd ('the Father of the Relational Database'), the best place to start is with Ted Codd's rules. These rules have been quoted and misquoted so many times that, in the interests of accuracy, I went back to the original two articles by Codd himself (*Computerworld*, 14th and 21st of October, 1985). In the first of these he writes:

> *In this paper I supply a set of rules with which a DBMS should comply if it is claimed to be fully relational.*

In practice these rules have been modified and extended, and if you want to know more about Codd's ideas try 'The Relational Model for Database Management Version 2', by the man himself.

21.1 Why You Just *Have* to Know About Them

In case you are wondering *why* you would ever want to be familiar with Codd's rules, it is worth knowing that many of the current so-called relational DBMSs really do fail to match the original concept. You have to understand what that original idea was in order to be able to understand why these products are potentially so dangerous. Not that they will explode, but they can destroy the integrity of your data. If your job happens to be looking after data, that can equate to destroying your job.

21.2 Economy vs. Readability

I have the very greatest respect for Dr Codd; after all, he was the one who designed the relational database management system. In his writings, Codd expresses his ideas with admirable accuracy and economy. Sadly this combination leaves them somewhat unintelligible to the average reader, which is a terrible shame, since he is the greatest authority on the subject. What I have tried to do is to render the rules more understandable by expanding them. In the process, inevitably, some of the precision is lost and I apologize in advance for any offence caused. If in doubt, believe Codd's original and not my interpretation.

21.3 A Little Background

Some of the quotes I intend to use from these two papers only make sense if you are aware that by 1985 a great deal had been published about relational databases but few products existed. Several manufacturers were producing systems for mainframes with the word 'relational' on the box (or on the crate in the case of the bigger systems). Most of these products appear to have offended Codd deeply; indeed, the articles are, in places, simply a vehicle for his diatribe against them. This can be seen in the introduction to the first paper:

> *...some vendors of nonrelational DBMS have quickly (and recently) added a few relational features – in some cases, very few features – in order to be able to claim their systems are relational, even though they may not meet the simple requirements for being rated 'minimally relational'. We shall refer to this kind of DBMS as 'born again'. It is a safe bet that these Johnny-come-lately vendors have not taken the time or manpower to investigate optimization techniques needed in relational DBMSs to yield good performance.*

I love those 'born again' and 'Johnny-come-lately' references.

21.4 The Rules Themselves

In excellent propeller-head style, Codd starts numbering the rules at zero rather than one.

> **Rule 0**: For any system that is advertised as, or claimed to be, a relational data base management system, that system must be able to manage data bases entirely through its relational capabilities.

Note that Codd uses a space between the words 'data' and 'base'; this construction has fallen from favour recently.

Rule 0 is reasonably clear. For a DBMS to qualify as relational it must have *all* of the features of the relational model, not just a subset. At the time Codd formulated these rules, many of the DBMSs which were advertised as relational were actually based on a system other than relational (e.g. hierarchical). The manufacturers had just bolted on a few relational 'features' in the hope that everyone would believe the products were fully relational. Surprisingly, this still goes on today; products are marketed as relational when they clearly lack many of the important features of the relational model.

The Information Rule

Rule 1: All information in a relational data base is represented explicitly at the logical level and in exactly one way – by values in tables.

This rule says that all data should be stored in tables and in no other way. The use of tables to store data has become such a fundamental part of modern database systems that it sounds a little odd to explicitly write it down; it's rather like writing that all cars should have wheels. However, when the rules were written it was less accepted and therefore worth saying.

In case anyone is in any doubt about what a table looks like, Figure 21.1 shows one called STUDENTS; it has four fields (or columns) called ID, FirstName, LastName and DOB. It also has five records (or rows).

STUDENTS

ID	FirstName	LastName	DOB
1	MIKE	WELLINGTON	16 May 1975
2	SALLY	JONES	13 July 1976
3	TZANOVICH	SMITH	12 Dec 1976
4	GEOFFREY	PHILLIPS	27 Apr 1967
5	TANIA	NBANGO	12 Sep 1976

Figure 21.1

The Guaranteed Access Rule

Rule 2: Each and every datum (atomic value) in a relational data base is guaranteed to be logically accessible by resorting to a combination of table name, primary key value and column name.

First, some terminology; datum is the singular form of data and a datum is a piece of information. The word does not figure much in everyday usage, since 'data' is now commonly, if inaccurately, used as both the singular and plural form. An atomic value means the information contained in one field of one record. Codd is using the term 'atomic' in the nuclear sense of an item which cannot be subdivided (at least, not without recourse to a particle accelerator).

Rule 2 says that each entry in a table of data must be locatable with no more information than the name of the table, the field name and the value in the primary key. Thus in the table STUDENTS you can find the last name of a given student as long as you know that the table is called STUDENTS, that the relevant field name is LastName and that the student's ID number is, say 4 (Figure 21.2).

STUDENTS

ID	FirstName	LastName	DOB
1	MIKE	WELLINGTON	16 May 1975
2	SALLY	JONES	13 July 1976
3	TZANOVICH	SMITH	12 Dec 1976
4	GEOFFREY	*PHILLIPS*	27 Apr 1967
5	TANIA	NBANGO	12 Sep 1976

Figure 21.2

As Codd says when expanding on this rule '*the primary key concept is an essential part,*' so we can take this rule to say also that each table in a relational database must have a primary key and each data value in that key must be a unique identifier.

Systematic Treatment of Null Values

> **Rule 3**: Null values (distinct from the empty character string or a string of blank characters and distinct from zero or any other number) are supported in fully relational DBMS for representing missing information and inapplicable information in a systematic way, independent of data type.

Codd also says in his commentary on the rules that '*it must be possible to specify "Nulls not allowed" for each primary key column.*'

Null values are very important in databases, much more so than their name implies. A null value is supposed to represent an absence of information; it's not the same as a space or a zero, a dash, a hash or any other representation. A null means that we don't know what information should be entered into this field. It certainly does not imply that we don't care about the content of the field. This may seem like a trivial distinction, but it isn't. In the context of Rule 3, the important point is that nulls should be handled in a logical and consistent manner. Oddly enough, handling them logically isn't too difficult if the problems that they raise are considered in isolation. Ensuring that an RDBMS is entirely consistent in the way it handles nulls is more difficult. It is interesting to note that Codd simply states that the RDBMS must do it; he doesn't suggest a way in which this ideal can be implemented. This reminds me of the instruction given to an aspiring actor who was having trouble with a difficult part. 'Right, I want you to try that again and do it better this time'.

Dynamic On-Line Catalog Based on the Relational Model

> **Rule 4**: The database description is represented at the logical level in the same way as ordinary data, so that authorized users can apply the same relational language to its interrogation as they apply to the regular data.

An implicit assumption in this rule is that every RDBMS will have a 'database description'; Codd apparently believes this to be so fundamental to the whole concept of an RDBMS that he does not actually state it. A database description, more commonly known as a data dictionary (a term which Codd himself uses in his expansion of Rule 4) or system catalog, is an entity which holds a description of the tables in the database, their structure, the relationships between them, the queries and so on. (For more details see Chapter 23, which is about the data dictionary.) This data is often referred to as the 'meta-data'.

The rule says that the structures in which the information in the data dictionary is held should be the same as those for data in the database itself and that there should be no additional complexity for users who need to deal with data in the data dictionary. To put that another way, if you look inside the data dictionary, you should find information about how your database is structured and that information must be held in tables. It all sounds a little incestuous, because we end up with tables that define tables (including themselves), but the concept behind this rule is perfectly sound. As you become familiar with a particular RDBMS, you learn how to access the data which is stored in your tables. In learning that process, you also learn how to access the information about the database itself.

Comprehensive Data Sub-Language Rule

Rule 5: A relational system may support several languages and various modes of terminal use (for example, the fill-in-the-blanks mode). However, there must be at least one language whose statements are expressible, per some well-defined syntax, as character strings and that is comprehensive in supporting *all* of the following items:

> Data definition
> View definition
> Data manipulation (interactive and by program)
> Integrity constraints
> Authorization
> Transaction boundaries (begin, commit and rollback)

This rule may appear somewhat anachronistic. After all, we expect to drive most RDBMSs via a GUI nowadays. Do we really care if there is an underlying, unifying language?

The answer is 'Yes' if we expect that database to operate on anything other than a standalone PC. Once you expand a database to multi-user operation across a network, the communication between terminal and database engine is much more efficient if it can be expressed in simple character strings.

Whether Codd had this in mind when he formulated the rule is another matter; he may simply have been trying to ensure that users could always find a consistent way of interacting with their databases. However, the rule is still applicable today.

View Updating Rule

Rule 6: All views that are theoretically updatable are also updatable by the system.

On the face of it, this is a simple rule; it's short, concise and unambiguous. However, reading Codd's further expansion of Rule 6 rapidly disabuses you of that first naïve interpretation. He says *'Note that a view is theoretically updatable if there exists a time-independent algorithm for unambiguously determining a single series of changes to the base relations that will have as their effect precisely the requested changes in the view'*. Oh.

Perhaps some definitions might help to shed light on this obfuscation.

♦ *Relation*
Codd uses the term 'relation' to mean effectively a table of data.

♦ *Base relation/base table*
This is a table that exists within a database and excludes the more transient tables, such as answer tables. Answer tables are considered transitory since their values can change as the base tables are updated.

♦ *View*
  A view is a combination or subset of rows and/or columns from one or
  many base tables. Stored in a base table of customer information might
  be customer ID numbers, names, addresses, phone and fax numbers
  and a view of that data might show only the names and the fax numbers
  of all customers in Scotland. A view equates approximately to what we
  might call an answer to a query.

We can thus rewrite the expansion of Rule 6 as:

> Note that a query is theoretically updatable if there exists a time-independent al-
> gorithm for unambiguously determining a single series of changes to the underly-
> ing tables that will have as their effect precisely the requested changes in the
> answer table.

So, have my definitions helped to clarify the clarification? Not entirely,
no; but you have to agree that it's a further excellent grounding to help you
make headway with Codd's singularly abstruse use of English.

Another way of expressing Rule 6 might be as follows. You should be able,
not only to look at the data in an answer table, but also to edit and change
the data that you see there. However, there are restrictions. You should only
be allowed to edit this data if the updating action (be it modifying, inserting
or deleting information) makes sense and does not break any of the fundamental rules of the database structure.

As an example of an edit that doesn't make sense, consider this example.
Suppose that your base table is like Figure 21.3 and that the primary key is
SaleNo. You then query it to find the average value of a sale, with the result
shown in Figure 21.4.

SALES

SaleNo	EmployeeNo	Customer	Item	Supplier	Amount
1	1	Simpson	Sofa	Harrison	$235.67
2	1	Johnson	Chair	Harrison	$453.78
3	2	Smith	Stool	Ford	$82.78
4	2	Jones	Suite	Harrison	$3,421.00
5	3	Smith	Sofa	Harrison	$235.67
6	1	Simpson	Sofa	Harrison	$235.67
7	1	Jones	Bed	Ford	$453.00

Figure 21.3

ANSWER

AvgOfAmount
$731.08

Figure 21.4

Clearly the RDBMS cannot allow you to edit this value because the figure
it shows is derived from a number of different records.

As an example of an edit to an answer table which could cause loss of data
integrity, suppose that you create a query which shows the three fields from
the SALES table shown in Figure 21.5.

ANSWER

Customer	Item	Amount
Simpson	Sofa	$235.67
Johnson	Chair	$453.78
Smith	Stool	$82.78
Jones	Suite	$3,421.00
Smith	Sofa	$235.67
Simpson	Sofa	$235.67
Jones	Bed	$453.00

Figure 21.5

The act of adding records to this table must be forbidden because it is impossible to include a primary key value to the record that you add. Since all records must have a value for the primary key, allowing the addition of a record will compromise data integrity.

It can now be argued, however, that Rule 6 is of academic interest only because in 1988, a certain H. W. Buff published a paper entitled 'Why Codd's Rule No. 6 Must Be Reformulated'. As the title suggests, this paper proves that Rule 6 is fatally flawed. Buff's paper shows that no RDBMS can ever support this rule because 'there does not exist any algorithm which can decide, given any view, whether it is updatable or not'. What's more, he proved it.

In 'The Relational Model for Database Management Version 2', published in 1990, Codd acknowledges that Buff's paper is correct and modifies Rule 6 by defining an algorithm which will identify a good percentage of updatable views.

The bottom line is that we have to understand that the system cannot identify all views that can be safely updated. However, it is relatively easy for the system to partition answer tables into two groups:

♦ those which have been shown to be updatable
♦ the others

Clearly an effective RDBMS should allow us to update those which fall into the first category and exclude the update ability from answer tables which fall into the second.

Many PC-based RDBMSs take the easy way out and exclude all updates to answer tables. They therefore fail Rule 6.

High-Level Insert, Update and Delete

Rule 7: The capability of handling a base relation or a derived relation as a single operand applies not only to the retrieval of data but also to the insertion, update and deletion of data.

Remembering that Codd uses the term 'relation' to mean a table, we can interpret this rule as follows.

You expect the RDBMS to allow you to retrieve records with a single command, that is, it should let you query the database in the normal way. Rule 7 says that not only querying but also inserting, updating and deleting multiple records should be possible with a single command. In other words, if you want to delete all of the invoices which are older than five years, you don't have to locate each one and delete it individually. You should be able to eliminate them all with a single command.

The same applies to inserting and updating, so you should be able to issue one command which, for example, alters the discount rate from 5% to 10% on all items for which the stock level exceeds the weekly usage by a factor of 10.

This rule is important. For a start it significantly reduces the amount of code that you have to write in order to carry out complex processes. It also has important implications as soon as you start to use a system where the database engine is divorced from the front end. Why? Because the ability to perform multi-record changes to a table with a single command dramatic-ally reduces the communication between the front and back ends. When the link is over a WAN (Wide Area Network), this can speed up the whole process by an order of magnitude.

Physical Data Independence

> **Rule 8**: Application programs and terminal activities remain logically unim-paired whenever any changes are made in either storage representations or access methods.

Codd expands this rule by saying *'To handle this, the DBMS must support a clear, sharp boundary between the logical and semantic aspects on the one hand, and the physical and performance aspects of the base tables on the other; application pro-grams must deal with the logical aspects only.'*

In practice this means that the logical interaction that the user has with the database ('I want to find all of the orders which are overdue for pay-ment') should be divorced from the physical structure of the tables of data. Suppose that as a database expands, the database manager decides that an index is required on a particular table for performance reasons. This rule says that it should be possible for the index to be added without the users being aware that any change has been made. They (the users are the 'term-inal activities' referred to in the rule) and any application programs should be able to work without any alteration after the index is in place. The only difference they should see is a reduced response time.

Logical Data Independence

> **Rule 9**: Application programs and terminal activities remain logically unim-paired whenever information-preserving changes of any kind that theoretically permit unimpairment are made to the base tables.

If this one sounds rather like Rule 8, that's because it is; these rules are often considered as a pair. As an example of what this one means, suppose that you have a table of CUSTOMERS that for performance reasons you want to split into two, CUST_USA and CUST_REST. This allows you to search more rapidly through the customers in the USA, which is good, but what happens to all your existing programs and users which/who are used to interacting with an all-embracing table called CUSTOMERS? This rule says that if a DBMS is to be considered a relational DBMS, it has to allow both applications and users to go on dealing with CUSTOMERS as if it hadn't been split. In practice this can be done by creating a view (or query) which combines the two new tables into a single entity with the original name.

Note that complete conformity with this rule depends on compliance with Rule 6, the view updating rule. That is the one which says that all views which are theoretically updatable are also updatable by the system. If Rule 6 isn't obeyed, then although we can create a view called CUSTOMER from CUST_USA and CUST_REST, the users will be unable to interact with the data it contains in the same way as before.

Rules 8 and 9 are included in the rule set to provide a high degree of flexibility. Codd describes them in order to split the logical interaction with the database away from the physical and base structuring as much as possible. In turn this allows the database manager to make changes to the underlying structure without upsetting the way the user works and without requiring application programs to be rewritten. As Codd says:

> *The physical and logical independence rules permit data base designers for relational DBMS to make mistakes in their designs without the heavy penalties levied by nonrelational DBMS. This, in turn, means that it is much easier to get started with a relational DBMS because not nearly as much performance-oriented planning is needed prior to 'blast-off'.*

Integrity Independence Rule

> **Rule 10**: Integrity constraints specific to a particular relational data base must be definable in a relational data sub-language and storable in the catalog, not in the application programs.

A serious rule this one (of course, all rules are equally serious, some are just more 'equally serious' than others). It contains an important expansion:

> In addition to the two integrity rules (entity integrity and referential integrity) that apply to every relational database, there is a clear need to be able to specify additional integrity constraints reflecting either business policies or government policies.

After this rather oblique reference to referential and entity integrity as an integral part of relational databases, Codd then goes on to say:

> *To be more specific, the following two integrity rules apply to every relational database:*

> **Entity integrity**. *No component of a primary key is allowed to have a null value.*

> **Referential integrity**. *For each distinct nonnull foreign key value in a relational database, there must exist a matching primary key value from the same domain.*

Both referential and entity integrity are really important, not to say essential, parts of a relational database. Why Codd sees fit to introduce them as a mere addition to another rule is not at all clear. However, we have seen before that he has a tendency to include essential information as an expansion of a rule; another example is that no rule explicitly says that an RDBMS needs a data dictionary, though it is implicit in Rule 4.

Rule 10 says that referential and entity integrity rules must be capable of being stored in the system catalog (or data dictionary) rather than in the application programs. This is clearly essential. If such rules are stored only in the applications, it becomes easier for a user to accidentally (or maliciously) subvert that integrity. Almost all PC-based RDBMSs seem to ignore this rule. Some only allow you to impose referential and entity integrity through the application language. Others store each table as a separate file on disk and store the information in the header of the file. As far as I am aware, the only one in widespread use which maintains an effective data dictionary is Access.

However, this rule says more: it says that, in addition, an RDBMS needs to be able to store other integrity constraints and that we have to be able to store these in the catalog (data dictionary) and also to define them in the data sub-language. What might these 'other' constraints be? If you are storing someone's date of birth (DOB) and the date of their entry into school (DOE), it is clearly reasonable to set up a rule stating the DOE must be greater than DOB. In fact, you might decide that DOE has to be greater than DOB + 4 years. In either case, you want this rule to be applied in all cases, without argument. Rule 10 says that you must be able to define such rules in the usual control language that you use and that you must also be able to store the rule in the data dictionary.

One of the reviewers asked 'Doesn't this rule preclude the enforcement of constraints by forms?'. The answer is 'No'. Codd is ensuring, by including this rule, that we have the ability to enforce rules at the table level if we so wish. He isn't saying that we have to do so.

Distribution Independence

Rule 11: A relational DBMS has distribution independence.

This rule is vintage Codd; only six words and still opaque.
He expands the rule as follows:

By distribution independence I mean that the DBMS has a data sub-language that enables application programs and terminal activities to remain logically unimpaired:

♦ *when data distribution is first introduced (if the originally installed DBMS manages nondistributed data only);*

♦ *when data is redistributed (if the DBMS manages distributed data).*

One of the huge benefits of networking is that it allows multi-user access to a database; that is, the users can be distributed across the network. However, it is also possible to distribute the data across the same network. Thus you can have your EMPLOYEES table stored centrally at company headquarters and the CUSTOMER table held locally at branch level.

This rule says that even if the tables of data are moved around, your users shouldn't be aware of the change in location; neither should any applications that you have developed need to be rewritten. This has several consequences. For a start, you should be able to develop an application on a standalone PC and then migrate to a fully networked system employing distributed data without pain. It also means that you should be able to make changes easily to the distribution of the data. So, if the CEO suddenly decides that all data must be held centrally, that should be easy to implement.

Nonsubversion Rule

> **Rule 12**: If a relational system has a low-level (single-record-at-a-time) language, that low level cannot be used to subvert or bypass the integrity rules and constraints expressed in the higher level relational language (multiple-records-at-a-time).

To put it another way, a user must not be allowed to go directly to a table and add, delete or alter records with the low-level language if such a change would be at odds with the higher level rules (such as referential integrity) which have been applied to the tables and are stored in the data dictionary.

21.5 Summary

So, those are Ted Codd's original rules for defining an RDBMS. As I said at the start, there is a fine line to be drawn between accuracy and verbosity, and I have tried to tread it carefully. Nevertheless, it has taken a long time to cover all of the rules, so long that it may be difficult to see the 'take home message'. In addition the order in which the rules appear is perhaps less than optimal. So, below, I have presented a set of even less exact definitions in what I consider to be a more reasonable order. They may help you to get the general overall flavour.

♦ Data must be stored only in tables (Rule 1).
♦ Each table must have a primary key and given the table name, field name and primary key value, it must be possible to identify unequivocally any piece of data in the database (Rule 2).
♦ The database must have a data dictionary which stores the meta-data, that is the data which describes the database itself. The data in the data dictionary must be stored in the same manner as in the main database, that is in tables (Rule 4).
♦ Integrity rules, such as referential integrity, should be storable in the data dictionary (Rule 10).
♦ There must be a single language which allows the database to be manipulated (Rule 5).
♦ This language must allow multiple updates, inserts etc. to be performed with single commands (Rule 7).
♦ However, neither this language, nor any other, must be able to make changes to individual records which subvert the integrity rules stored in the data dictionary (Rule 12).
♦ Physical, logical and distribution changes to the database structure, such as the addition of an index, the splitting of a table, or the movement of a table onto another disk, should be transparent to the user (Rules 8, 9 and 11).
♦ Answer tables must be updatable whenever possible (Rule 6).
♦ Nulls must be treated consistently (Rule 3).

As a final exercise, you might want to ask yourself, as Codd suggested all those years ago 'Does my RDBMS really meet all of these rules?'. If it doesn't, then it isn't really a Relational DBMS at all (Rule 0).

22

Normalization

Most of the tables shown in this chapter are not included on the CD-ROM, since there is very little that you can do with them. Indeed, most of the tables in this chapter are demonstrations of how *not* to construct a table. However, the READINGS tables and queries which appear towards the end of the chapter are included in case you want to play around with the SQL statements.

22.1 Normalization

Part of the attraction of using an RDBMS is that you can manage large complex chunks of data. This can have the advantage of unifying the data handling within your organization. For example, it means that all your customer names and addresses are stored once only and everyone within the company can access up-to-date information. The disadvantage of building complex collections of tables is that you need to be highly organized – and to be careful to get the right data into the correct tables. If you get it wrong you may find that some queries are impossible to perform; you might find it impossible to check for a correlation between the hours that your salespeople spend on the road and their sales of brand X. Normalization is a process that makes it easier to design the table structures properly in the first place so that unaskable queries don't arise. In addition, normalization tends to minimize the duplication of data within a database. This has the advantage of both reducing the storage space required and speeding up queries.

As we examine the process of normalization you will find that we become concerned with quite pernickety detail, especially as we get up to the higher levels of normalization. You will find that we become obsessed with just which field is dependent, in exactly which way, upon another. However, it is essential that you bear in mind at all times that behind all of this detail is a very simple principle. We are trying to get the right information into the right tables. In turn this is because we want the database to work efficiently and without error. Don't fall into the trap of becoming obsessed with the minutiae and losing sight of the goals. Don't be misled into believing that database professionals really care one way or the other about 'functional dependency' (see below). We don't. Or at least we do, but only because, if we can control it, we can build better databases. We're really noble.

> Sadly, the other thing that some database developers love is to use the terminology to impress non-database people over coffee. 'Guess what I found this morning? A table in Simpson's databases with a non-key attribute transitively dependent on the primary key! Of course I had to give him a written warning.'

A brief (honestly, very brief) history may help to explain where all of these minutiae came from. It may also help us to keep a sense of perspective about what we are trying to achieve.

When people started to work with relational databases, they understood that it was probably a good idea to split the data up into different tables. The difficult question was, of course, 'Which data should go into which table?'. At first the answer seemed simple. You identify the real world objects that you are trying to model with your database (Employees, Orders, Customers, Products etc.) and give each one its own table. As I said in Chapter 12, this is still an excellent rule of thumb that is still valid today. It is so important, I'll repeat it in italics:

As a general rule, you should identify the real world objects that you are trying to model with your database (Employees, Orders, Customers, Products, etc.) and give each one its own table.

This works fine most of the time, but it is too imprecise under certain circumstances. When you apply this, and only this, rule you are likely to build databases that suffer from specific problems (which will be outlined in detail below). As a result of these problems, people began to look for ways to avoid them. More specifically, they looked for general rules that could be applied to a set of tables which, if followed exactly, would guarantee that the problems couldn't occur.

Essentially you can think of the levels of normalization which are described here as successive attempts to eliminate problems. The first level of normalization eliminates very basic problems, the second removes slightly more subtle ones, the third level copes with considerably more subtle ones and so on.

Normalization has three main aims:

1. To find and group together all of the properties that appertain to a particular object.
2. To remove redundant information. This is another way of saying that there is no point in storing a person's name, date of birth, address, spouse's name, number of children, etc. in multiple locations within one database.

3. To provide unique identification for individual records. You need to be sure that when you delete 'Mark Whitehorn' from the payroll that you are firing the correct individual.

In order to normalize data you need:

♦ An understanding of functional dependency.
♦ Common sense (don't leave home without it).
♦ An understanding of what the data 'means' (we can call this 'Requirement Definition'; see below).
♦ An understanding of what your company needs to do with the data.
♦ A knowledge of how normalization works (obviously).

Normalization is a process that is carried out in levels (first level 1, then level 2 and so on). However, to make a database perfectly workable under almost all conditions requires only going down to level three (or a little bit further... see below).

Before we start, we must make a brief diversion into the worlds of functional dependencies and requirement definition.

22.1.1 Functional Dependency

The world is full of functional dependencies; equations are a good example. If you know the length, width and height of a piece of wood, you can calculate its volume:

Volume = Length × Width × Height

We can say that the volume is functionally dependent on the length, width and height. In database terms we are more frequently concerned with the functional dependencies between fields. Consider the table shown in Figure 22.1, called ORDERS.

ORDERS

OrderNo*	ItemNo*	EmployeeNo	CustomerNo	ItemName	Quantity
121	3	4	1024	Nut	3
121	4	4	1024	Bolt	67
121	8	4	1024	Washer	3
122	3	9	176	Nut	9
122	8	9	176	Washer	9
123	3	4	234	Nut	345
123	8	4	234	Washer	345
124	4	9	321	Bolt	9

*Denotes a part of the primary key

Figure 22.1

Order Number 121 was processed by Employee Number 4. Since each record in this table is recording information about a part of an order, we can have several records for each order. (This is, incidentally, a badly designed table which my fingers itch to normalize, but we are using it for illustrative purposes so I'll leave it alone.) If I tell you that in this particular firm only one employee is ever credited with any given order, you can now be sure that whenever you see the value 121 in the OrderNo field, you will find the value 4 in the EmployeeNo field. There is no doubt, no uncertainty.

In this case, therefore, we can say that, in this table:

- EmployeeNo is *functionally dependent* on OrderNo.
- OrderNo *functionally determines* EmployeeNo.
- OrderNo is the *determinant*.

It is important to note that the relationship is one-way – we cannot say that OrderNo is functionally dependent on EmployeeNo. Why not? Well, if you look at the table and find the value 4 in EmployeeNo you cannot with certainty predict the value that will be found in OrderNo, since in this case it could be 121 or 123.

Now – a series of questions.

- Which fields are functionally dependent on the primary key (remembering that in this table the primary key is made up of two fields, OrderNo and ItemNo)?

  Answer: all of them, since the primary key uniquely identifies each record.

- Are any of the fields functionally dependent on *part* of the primary key?

  Answer: yes, ItemName.

- Does it matter that this field is dependent upon part of the primary key?

  Answer: Yes.

You will find that the process of normalization involves attempting to remove various forms of functional dependency and, in fact, functional dependency upon part of the primary key is a form that we try to eliminate.

However, it is worth stressing that there is nothing wrong with functional dependencies as such. Indeed databases are, by their very nature, full of functional dependencies.

In essence, normalization is all about preserving the functional dependencies that we want while not introducing ones that we don't want.

22.1.2 Requirement Definition

Consider the table in Figure 22.2. All of the records in this table contain unique values for the field City, so we might think that the company policy

STAFF

EmployeeNo	LastName	FirstName	City	Type	Pay
4	Whitehorn	Mark	Dundee	Sales Person	15000
5	Jones	Sally	Liverpool	Manager	20000
6	Williams	Henry	Hereford	Sales Person	15000
7	Johnson	Margaret	New York	Sales Person	15000
9	Smith	Fred	Seattle	Manager	20000
12	Smith	Sarah	Boston	Manager	20000
15	Johnson	Sally	Norwich	Sales Person	15000
17	Romanus	Eithi	Benson	Manager	20000

Figure 22.2

was that we assigned one employee (and only one) to each city. On the other hand, it might be chance that this small sample of eight records just happens to contain no duplicated cities. We simply cannot tell from the data, even if we are told that this table holds all of the current employees. However, we *need* to know what the rule is because as more records are added, the rule that we think we can see ('only one employee per city') may change. Why should this concern us? Well, suppose that it is a company rule that there will only ever be one employee per city. In that case, the value in Type is functionally dependent on the value in City. If the company intends, at a later date, to have both a manager and one or more salespersons in each city, then there is no such functional dependency.

In other words, the data doesn't tell us the whole story: we need to talk to the company and find out 'what the data means' in this case.

Again, this table implies that all salespeople are paid the same salary and that, while managers are better paid, they also, as a group, are all paid the same. But is this really a rule, or are there exceptions? It matters because it will have a profound effect upon the way you allocate the fields to different tables.

Some databases are well designed from the outset. If this is the case, then all of these questions will have been resolved before the tables were constructed and the information will be contained in some form of 'Requirement Definition' which, as the name suggests, formally describes the requirements that the database has to meet.

Sadly, not every single database that you will meet in your career as a database designer will have a formal requirement definition. Indeed, though it pains me to mention it, you may come across the odd requirement definition that contains one or more tiny flaws.

In these cases, you will have to return to the people for whom the database is being built (or modified) and seek elucidation.

However, the general point is crucial; determining the structure of the data within a database (in other words, deciding which tables you need and which data will go into which tables) is impossible without obtaining information from the people for whom it is being built. I will assume for the rest of this book that the data comes from a complete requirement definition, even though in many cases you may be working less formally than this.

22.1.3 First Normal Form (First Level of Normalization): 1NF

Most countries use some sort of location code (e.g. Zip code, Postcode). These can be incredibly useful in a database, since they make it easy to, for example, calculate the distribution of sales geographically. Sadly, each different country seems to have adopted its own, idiosyncratic system. This was fine in the 1960s; now, as more and more companies operate globally, it is a pain. It is not just that the length and type of the data varies, it is actually used in different ways. For example, some coding systems allow each city to be uniquely identified, while others do not. I have assumed, for the sake of the example below, that the company concerned has decided to implement its own coding system and assigned a unique code to each city.

First normal form is essentially just a description of a basic table. Remember that a 'Table' (as defined in Chapter 3) has to have a primary key (see Chapter 14), so this is not technically part of the definition of first normal form because it is assumed that any table we are considering for first normal form already has a primary key.

Given a table that has a primary key, we can say it is in first normal form if all of the data values are atomic values.

This requirement is actually an obvious one, but you wouldn't guess that from the definition. An atomic value is one that only has a single component. It means that the conglomeration of data shown in Figure 22.3 is not allowable in a normalized table. (Figure 22.3 shows a single table: Pay and CustomerNo are adjacent fields.

INFORMATION

EmployeeNo	LastName	FirstName	City	CityID	Type	Pay
4	Whitehorn	Mark	Dundee	DD	Sales Person	15000
9	Smith	Fred	Seattle	SE	Manager	20000

CustomerNo	OrderNo	ItemNo	ItemName	Quantity
1024	121	3	Nuts	3
		4	Bolts	67
		5	Washer	3
176	122	3	Nut	9
		8	Washer	9

Figure 22.3 *A single table: Pay and CustomerNo are adjacent fields.*

This table shows sample data; the structure of the table could be represented as in Figure 22.4.

The last three 'fields' contain non-atomic data. It isn't a major problem because modern RDBMSs make it very difficult for you to construct such an abomination anyway. In order to store the equivalent information we

INFORMATION
EmployeeNo
LastName
FirstName
City
CityID
Type
Pay
CustomerNo
OrderNo
ItemNo
ItemName
Quantity

Figure 22.4

can split the data into two tables (a process known as 'projection'), the structures of which look like Figure 22.5.

STAFF	ORDERS
EmployeeNo *	OrderNo *
LastName	ItemNo *
FirstName	EmployeeNo
City	CustomerNo
CityID	ItemName
Type	Quantity
Pay	

*Denotes a primary key

Figure 22.5

A sample of the data they could contain might look like Figures 22.6 and 22.7.

STAFF

EmployeeNo*	LastName	FirstName	City	CityID	Type	Pay
4	Whitehorn	Mark	Dundee	DD	Sales Person	15000
9	Smith	Fred	Seattle	SE	Manager	20000

Figure 22.6

ORDERS

OrderNo*	ItemNo*	EmployeeNo	CustomerNo	ItemName	Quantity
121	3	4	1024	Nut	3
121	4	4	1024	Bolt	67
121	8	4	1024	Washer	3
122	3	9	176	Nut	9
122	8	9	176	Washer	9

Figure 22.7

Given a little time and effort you can reconstruct all the data relating to one order. From a human perspective it may seem awkward at first to split the data into separate tables like this, but a computer can recombine it very rapidly when required. In addition, the advantages in terms of storage efficiency and the ease with which data can be altered and retrieved are enormous.

These tables meet the qualifications given above, so they are in first normal form.

However, there are still problems, which can be defined as 'modification anomalies'.

1. If we change the name of an item (e.g. 'Washer' to 'Locking Washer'), we have to change many records since this information is spread throughout the ORDERS table.

2. We cannot add a new item until we have sold one (an example of an 'insertion anomaly'). If we did so, the primary key of the ORDERS table would have to contain a null value that is not allowed in a primary key.

3. If we delete an order, we may remove the only reference to an item (an example of a 'deletion anomaly').

A more general way of expressing points 2 and 3 is to say that the 'items' are still too involved with the 'orders'. We'll solve these problems with the second level of normalization.

22.1.4 Second Normal Form (Second Level of Normalization): 2NF

To be in second normal form a table must:

1. be in first normal form
2. have all non-key fields fully functionally dependent on the primary key.

(A non-key field is one that does not form part of the primary key).

I have expressed point 2 in 'database speak' to give an idea of the language used and so that you can use it to impress people. It does, however, border on the opaque. It means that you should have to use all of the primary key in order to determine the value in each of the other fields. This is true for some of them. For example, you need to know both the OrderNo and the ItemNo to determine the quantity of items ordered. However, this is not true for them all. Another way of expressing this rule is to say that you should not be able to identify any part of the record uniquely by using only part of the primary key.

This is clearly possible in the ORDERS table of Figure 22.8. If you know the ItemNo, which is only part of the primary key, you can always work out what the ItemName will be for that record. Given an ItemNo of 3, the ItemName must be Nut. The same is true for OrderNo and EmployeeNo. OrderNo 121 is always associated with EmployeeNo 4.

ORDERS

OrderNo*	ItemNo*	EmployeeNo	CustomerNo	ItemName	Quantity
121	3	4	1024	Nut	3
121	4	4	1024	Bolt	67
121	8	4	1024	Washer	3
122	3	9	176	Nut	9
122	8	9	176	Washer	9

Table 22.8

We can 'cure' this problem by splitting up the data. This can be shown first as table and field names, as in Figure 22.9, and then as some sample data (Figures 22.10, 22.11 and 22.12).

This separation doesn't put ORDERSPECS into 2NF, because we can still determine the ItemName from the ItemNo (which is only part of the primary key of this table). So a further split is required (Figures 22.13, 22.14 and 22.15).

These tables (and hence the entire database) are now in 2NF.

STAFF	ORDERS	ORDERSPECS
EmployeeNo*	OrderNo*	OrderNo*
LastName	EmployeeNo	ItemNo*
FirstName	CustomerNo	ItemName
City		Quantity
CityID		
Type		
Pay		

Figure 22.9

STAFF

EmployeeNo*	LastName	FirstName	City	CityID	Type	Pay
4	Whitehorn	Mark	Dundee	DD	Sales Person	15000
9	Smith	Fred	Seattle	SE	Manager	20000

Figure 22.10

ORDERS

OrderNo*	EmployeeNo	CustomerNo
121	4	1024
122	9	176

Figure 22.11

ORDERSPECS

OrderNo*	ItemNo*	ItemName	Quantity
121	3	Nut	3
121	4	Bolt	67
121	8	Washer	3
122	3	Nut	9
122	8	Washer	9

Figure 22.12

It is important to stress at this point (lest we forget) that we are not going through this process simply to follow some arbitrary set of rules. The whole exercise is entirely practical; if you don't normalize a database while you are designing it then you are likely to run into problems once you start using the database seriously. Getting this database to 2NF has saved us from the modification anomalies that were outlined above.

One of the reviewers added: 'Perhaps say at this point how intuitive the result is. Of course we have tables for INVENTORY, STAFF and ORDERS and for the many-to-many relationship between INVENTORY and ORDER'.

STAFF	ORDERS	ORDERSPECS	INVENTORY
EmployeeNo*	OrderNo*	OrderNo*	ItemNo*
LastName	EmployeeNo	ItemNo*	ItemName
FirstName	CustomerNo	Quantity	
City			
CityID			
Type			
Pay			

Figure 22.13

ORDERSPECS

OrderNo*	ItemNo*	Quantity
121	3	3
121	4	67
121	8	3
122	3	9
122	8	9

Figure 22.14

INVENTORY

ItemNo*	ItemName
3	Nut
4	Bolt
8	Washer

Figure 22.15

However, there are still potential problems inherent in this structure. See if you can work out what they are. The actual number of problems you can find will depend upon the requirement definition, which I haven't given to you, but have a go anyway. I'll give you one problem to get you started: we cannot add a new type of employee (e.g. part time) without actually creating such an employee (since we cannot have a null value for EmployeeNo).

Answers
1. As stated above, we cannot add a new type of Employee in the table STAFF (e.g. part time) without actually creating such an employee (since we cannot have a null value for EmployeeNo).
2. We cannot add a new City to the database until we have someone working there.
3. If we change the pay for type Manager we have to update lots of records.
4. If we happen to delete all of the employees who are of type Summer Worker, we lose forever the information about what that type of worker is paid.
5. If we delete the only person working in Dundee we lose Dundee's CityID.

Should these sorts of problem worry us unduly? 'Yes', is the simple answer, and not just because of the potential difficulties. It can often be easier to obtain and keep data up to date if the database is well organized.

For example, your Health Authority (or whatever your local equivalent happens to be called) may already be producing and making available in electronic format a table of the doctors in its area, together with the addresses of their practices. The Authority will probably have given each doctor a unique code number and it may well have done the same for the practice. Suppose you are developing an auditing system that refers to some of the doctors in the Authority. If your database is badly structured, the information about doctors may be scattered across several tables. That will make it very difficult to you to make use of the Health Authority's table.

If, on the other hand, you go to the third level of normalization, you will find that you should be able to incorporate any tables of generic information, such as the Health Authority's DOCTOR table, without problem. And the huge advantage is that, as doctors come and go, someone else has the problem of updating that information. All you need to do is to obtain the relevant updated table every month and insert it.

So let's go for it.

22.1.5 Third Normal Form (Third Level of Normalization): 3NF

To be in third normal form, a table must:

1. be in second (and hence also first) normal form
2. have all non-key fields non-transitively dependent on the primary key.

Another great definition. It means that a non-key field (that is, a field which does not form part of the primary key) must always be solely dependent on the primary key and not on anything else, such as another non-key field. So, in the INVENTORY table above, ItemName is fine because it is solely dependent on ItemNo. However, in the STAFF table, CityID is dependent upon City, which is not the primary key of that table. Are there any others you can see?

In order to answer this question, we can look at the sample data and we also need to consult the requirement definition. For example, is Pay dependent upon Type? (That is, are all managers paid $20,000?) The sample data doesn't tell us, but let's assume that the requirement definition explicitly states that pay is solely dependent upon job type.

An easy trap to fall into is to identify FirstName as dependent on LastName. In one sense it is; as far as I am concerned, 'Mark' is always tied to 'Whitehorn'. But that isn't necessarily true for all records, as would be the case if my two brothers, Simon and Jamie, worked for the same company.

We can split up the tables again. Try it yourself as an exercise.

The structure is shown in Figure 22.16; the tables (Figures 22.17–22.22) are now in 3NF.

JOBTYPE	CITIES	STAFF	ORDERS	ORDERSPECS	INVENTORY
Type*	CityID*	EmployeeNo*	OrderNo*	OrderNo*	ItemNo*
Pay	City	LastName	EmployeeNo	ItemNo*	ItemName
		FirstName	CustomerNo	Quantity	
		CityID			
		Type			

Figure 22.16

JOBTYPE

Type*	Pay
Sales Person	15000
Manager	20000

Figure 22.17

CITIES

CityID*	City
DD	Dundee
SE	Seattle

Figure 22.18

STAFF

EmployeeNo*	LastName	FirstName	CityID	Type
4	Whitehorn	Mark	DD	Sales Person
9	Smith	Fred	SE	Manager

Figure 22.19

ORDERSPECS

OrderNo*	ItemNo*	Quantity
121	3	3
121	4	67
121	8	3
122	3	9
122	8	9

Figure 22.20

ORDERS

OrderNo*	EmployeeNo	CustomerNo
121	4	1024
122	9	176

Figure 22.21

INVENTORY

ItemNo*	ItemName
3	Nut
4	Bolt
8	Washer

Figure 22.22

So that is normalization to the third level. It isn't just a boring academic exercise; rather, it is an essential process you must follow during the design phase of a database to avoid problems at a later stage.

One reviewer added: 'Here again is a good point to stress:

♦ How intuitive this is. CITY is obviously an entity.
♦ The test for an object (e.g. TYPE) is 'Does it have properties (e.g. Pay)?'

22.1.6 Summary So Far

First Normal Form (1NF)
Mainly concerned with basic table structure. All fields must contain only atomic data.

Second Normal Form (2NF)
Concerned with the relationship between the keyed and non-key fields.
The primary key must be useful – and given a primary key composed of two or more fields, you must *not* be able to determine values in the rest of the table from any subset of the primary key.

Third Normal Form (3NF)
Concerned with the relationships between the non-key fields. Non-key fields must be dependent on the primary key. They must also be mutually independent (that is, one non-key field must not be dependent upon another non-key field).

22.1.7 Why We Aren't Going Any Further

There are four further levels of normalization:

♦ BCNF (Boyce–Codd normal form), which is a reinforcement of 3NF.
♦ Fourth normal form (MVD: Multi-Valued Dependencies)
♦ Fifth normal form (PJ/NF: Project-Join/Normal Form) also known as (Projection Join/Normal Form)
♦ DK/NF (Domain Key/Normal Form)

In other words, it is possible to construct tables which are in third normal form yet which still have modification anomalies, and there are four more ways of ensuring that those anomalies are removed. Normalization is all about making the database usable, so at first sight it seems only reasonable to tell you that you must normalize all databases to DK/NF and to show you how to do that. In theory, you should squeeze the structure 'til the pips squeak – until all the redundancy is gone.

However, this is supposed to be a practical book, and in practice very few people need to think about normalizing above third normal form. If this sounds unlikely, spend a couple of minutes trying to design a table that is in third normal form and yet still has modification anomalies.

Perhaps you can, but I find it quite difficult and I teach the subject! The point I'm trying to make is that tables which are in third normal form and which still have modification anomalies are very rare. In fact, they are usually counter-intuitive; in other words, people usually never even think of building them.

So after due consideration I think we'll stop here. If you are trying to get a database built and you are reading this chapter to ensure that you eliminate most of the problems that are realistically going to crop up in your database, you already know enough.

22.1.8 An Example

Of course, it is grossly unfair to ask you to try to think of a table that is in third normal form and yet has modification anomalies and then not show you one. If you couldn't come up with one, you now won't be able to sleep at night. So, just for amusement (and to illustrate why such tables are contrived), consider this.

Suppose that we need to store information about the items that we manufacture in a factory. Each item can be composed of one or more material, and each has to be subjected to one or more 'treatments' after assembly (Figure 22.23).

INVENTORY

ItemNo*	Material*	Treatment*
25	Steel	Warming
25	Rubber	Warming
27	Steel	Pressure test
27	Paper	Oil pre-soak
27	Steel	Oil pre-soak
27	Paper	Pressure test
35	Brass	Pressure test
35	Brass	Flow test
39	Steel	Heating
40	Steel	Heating

*denotes a field which forms part of the primary key

Figure 22.23

You can run through the definitions and you should find that the table is in third normal form. Nevertheless, it has modification anomalies. You will notice that item 27 has four records in this table. This is because it is made of two materials and has two treatments. We need at least two records to store this information (Figure 22.24).

INVENTORY

ItemNo*	Material*	Treatment*
27	Steel	Oil pre-soak
27	Paper	Pressure test

Figure 22.24

However, using only two records is misleading, since it implies that a relationship exists between the material and the treatment. In fact this is not true; item 27 is not being pressure tested because it is made of steel.

Tempting as it might be, it is also false to assume that we are oil pre-soaking the component because it contains paper. We may well have other paper components, such as user manuals, which it would be highly inappropriate to pre-soak in oil. We are pre-soaking this item in oil because it is a filter; in other words, there is no direct relationship between treatment and material.

In order to make it clear that there isn't a relationship between material and treatment, we need to duplicate the records as shown in the original table. This in turn leaves us with an update anomaly. If we want to add another treatment to, say Item 27, we will have to add two more records.

To resolve this problem we can split the table into two smaller tables (Figures 22.25 and 22.26).

ITEM-MATERIAL

ItemNo*	Material*
25	Steel
25	Rubber
27	Steel
27	Paper
35	Brass
39	Steel
40	Steel

Figure 22.25

ITEM-TREATMENT

ItemNo*	Treatment*
25	Warming
27	Pressure test
27	Oil pre-soak
35	Pressure test
35	Flow test
39	Heating
40	Heating

Figure 22.26

You see what I mean about contrived. I don't think that many people would have built the initial table in the first place!

22.1.9 Normalization Doesn't Automatically Remove All Redundancy

I said above that one of the aims of normalization was to remove redundant information, and it is. However, it is worth stressing that normalization doesn't *guarantee* to remove all redundancy; it guarantees to remove only that redundancy which can be removed by splitting a table into two (a process known as projection). Therefore it is possible to normalize a table and still have redundancy, and hence update anomalies, lurking in the tables.

To illustrate this, consider a table which stores information about the readings taken from electricity meters. Let's assume that each meter is numbered and the same meter is never read more than once on the same day. A sensible table structure might be that of Figure 22.27 with `MeterNo` and `Date` combining to form the primary key.

READINGS

MeterNo*	Date*	Reading
1	18 May 1991	20
1	11 Nov 1991	91
1	12 Apr 1992	175
1	21 May 1992	214
1	01 Jul 1992	230
1	21 Nov 1992	270
1	12 Dec 1992	290
1	01 Apr 1993	324
2	18 May 1991	619
2	17 Sep 1991	712
2	15 Mar 1992	814
2	21 May 1992	913
2	17 Sep 1992	1023
3	19 May 1991	20612
3	11 Nov 1991	21112
3	15 Mar 1992	21143
3	21 May 1992	21223
3	17 Sep 1992	21456
3	21 Mar 1993	22343

Figure 22.27

However, this table doesn't show, for example, how much electricity has been used between each reading. The obvious solution is to run a query to produce a table like Figure 22.28.

MeterNo	Date	CurrentReading	PreviousReading	UnitsUsed
1	11 Nov 1991	91	20	71
1	12 Apr 1992	175	91	84
1	21 May 1992	214	175	39
1	01 Jul 1992	230	214	16
1	21 Nov 1992	270	230	40
1	12 Dec 1992	290	270	20
1	01 Apr 1993	324	290	34
2	17 Sep 1991	712	619	93
2	15 Mar 1992	814	712	102
2	21 May 1992	913	814	99
2	17 Sep 1992	1023	913	110
3	11 Nov 1991	21112	20612	500
3	15 Mar 1992	21143	21112	31
3	21 May 1992	21223	21143	80
3	17 Sep 1992	21456	21223	233
3	21 Mar 1993	22343	21456	887

Figure 22.28

The problem is that this query can take a long time to run if there are a reasonable number of records in the table. For example, given 550 records, the following SQL statement took 55 seconds to run.

SOLUTION1

```
SELECT READINGS.MeterNo, READINGS.Date, READINGS.Reading,
Max(READINGS_1.Reading) AS MaxOfReading,
READINGS.Reading-Max(READINGS_1.Reading) AS UnitsUsed
FROM READINGS, READINGS AS READINGS_1
WHERE ((READINGS.MeterNo=[READINGS_1].[MeterNo]) AND
(READINGS.Reading[READINGS_1].[Reading]))
GROUP BY READINGS.MeterNo, READINGS.Date, READINGS.Reading;
```

See Chapter 25 for more information about SQL.

And that was on a Compaq ProLiant with four processors and 384 Mbyte of RAM.

The problem is that the query has to find, in effect, the record that corresponds to the *previous* reading for the specific meter. It is this notion of some type of interconnection between the records which makes the query tortuous.

One tempting solution is to store a reference to the previous reading in the base table, as in Figure 22.29.

READINGS2

ReadingNo	MeterNo	Date	Reading	PreviousReading
1	1	18 May 1991	20	
2	1	11 Nov 1991	91	1
3	1	12 Apr 1992	175	2
4	1	21 May 1992	214	3
5	1	01 Jul 1992	230	4
6	1	21 Nov 1992	270	5
7	1	12 Dec 1992	290	6
8	1	01 Apr 1993	324	7
9	2	18 May 1991	619	
10	2	17 Sep 1991	712	9
11	2	15 Mar 1992	814	10
12	2	21 May 1992	913	11
13	2	17 Sep 1992	1023	12
14	3	19 May 1991	20612	
15	3	11 Nov 1991	21112	14
16	3	15 Mar 1992	21143	15
17	3	21 May 1992	21223	16
18	3	17 Sep 1992	21456	17
19	3	21 Mar 1993	22343	18

Figure 22.29

Queries which run against this, for example:

SOLUTION2
```
SELECT DISTINCTROW READINGS2.MeterNo, READINGS2.Date,
READINGS2.Reading AS CurrentReading,
READINGS2_1.Reading AS PreviousReading,
READINGS2.Reading-READINGS2_1.Reading AS UnitsUsed
FROM READINGS2
INNER JOIN READINGS2 AS READINGS2_1
ON READINGS2.PreviousReading = READINGS2_1.ReadingNo
WHERE (((READINGS2.Reading-READINGS2_1.Reading) Is Not Null))
ORDER BY READINGS2.MeterNo, READINGS2.Date;
```

produce exactly the same answer table as shown above, but are very much faster to run when used with large sets of data (less than 2 seconds).

We could even use a table like that in Figure 22.30, whereupon the SQL:

SOLUTION3
```
SELECT DISTINCTROW READINGS3.MeterNo, READINGS3.Date,
READINGS3.CurrentReading,
READINGS3.PreviousReading, CurrentReading-PreviousReading AS
UnitsUsed
FROM READINGS3
WHERE (((CurrentReading-PreviousReading) Is Not Null));
```

becomes trivial and very rapid indeed.

READINGS3

MeterNo	Date	CurrentReading	PreviousReading
1	18 May 1991	20	
1	11 Nov 1991	91	20
1	12 Apr 1992	175	91
1	21 May 1992	214	175
1	01 Jul 1992	230	214
1	21 Nov 1992	270	230
1	12 Dec 1992	290	270
1	01 Apr 1993	324	290
2	18 May 1991	619	
2	17 Sep 1991	712	619
2	15 Mar 1992	814	712
2	21 May 1992	913	814
2	17 Sep 1992	1023	913
3	19 May 1991	20612	
3	11 Nov 1991	21112	20612
3	15 Mar 1992	21143	21112
3	21 May 1992	21223	21143
3	17 Sep 1992	21456	21223
3	21 Mar 1993	22343	21456

Figure 22.30

However – and this is the crucial point – the second and third base tables shown (READINGS2 and READING3) are very odd. Despite being normalized, both still suffer from update and delete anomalies. In addition, READINGS3 contains redundant data.

For example, suppose that we discover that Meter no 1 was also read on 01 Feb 1993 and yielded a reading of 300. We can add a record to READINGS2 as shown in Figure 22.31.

ReadingNo	MeterNo	Date	Reading	PreviousReading
1	1	18 May 1991	20	
2	1	11 Nov 1991	91	1
3	1	12 Apr 1992	175	2
4	1	21 May 1992	214	3
5	1	01 Jul 1992	230	4
6	1	21 Nov 1992	270	5
7	1	12 Dec 1992	290	6
8	1	01 Apr 1993	324	7
9	2	18 May 1991	619	
10	2	17 Sep 1991	712	9
11	2	15 Mar 1992	814	10
12	2	21 May 1992	913	11
13	2	17 Sep 1992	1023	12
14	3	19 May 1991	20612	
15	3	11 Nov 1991	21112	14
16	3	15 Mar 1992	21143	15
17	3	21 May 1992	21223	16
18	3	17 Sep 1992	21456	17
19	3	21 Mar 1993	22343	18
20	1	01 Feb 1993	300	7

Figure 22.31

The fact that the row is 'out of sequence' (at least, in terms of dates) is of no consequence whatsoever. However, the addition of this latest record has rendered the pointer in the record with ReadingNo = 8 incorrect. The value that it has in PreviousReading now points to the wrong record. So, unless we locate the errant record and correct it, the table now has an internal inconsistency. It should be reasonably apparent that deleting records introduces the same sort of problem.

This is a major problem. Simple updates and/or deletions to/of one record can cause anomalies in other records. In order to *ensure* internal data integrity, some or all of the table has to be checked for integrity after every update. This is clearly not impossible to do, but it makes extra work for the developer and may well slow the database down, particularly in a multi-user environment. In addition, even if the developer's work is perfect, later maintenance work on the database may unknowingly circumvent the checks and lead to a loss of integrity.

So, it is important to realize that normalization doesn't, on its own, remove all update and deletion anomalies or even all redundant data.

I became aware of this problem via the database column that I write for *Personal Computer World*. (In fact, readers of that magazine provided the solutions shown). I became intrigued by this idea of normalization being an imperfect tool, and when I had the privilege of interviewing Chris Date, I showed him the tables and asked him to discuss them. His answer is enlightening, not just about normalization but about the database design process as a whole.

Chris Date:

> Most of database design is still an art not a science; it's very subjective, precisely because it is not, mostly, very scientific. There is some science – normalization is a science – but 90% of it is gut feel.
>
> [When] we talk about normalization [we can ask ourselves] 'What is the effect of normalization?' Well, basically it's to reduce redundancy, but in order to consider that question carefully we have to have a careful definition of what redundancy is; but without getting into such a careful definition (because I don't think I could give you one) I will simply point out that normalization *per se* does not in general eliminate all redundancy.
>
> What normalization does is – normalization to the ultimate normal form – it gets you to a position that guarantees that you will not have any anomalies, update anomalies, that can be removed by taking projections [that is, by splitting the table up into sub-tables]. Here it is; it doesn't say it'll get rid of all anomalies, it just says get rid of anomalies that can be removed by taking projections. So yes, you can have redundancy and normalization doesn't help with this question. Normalization is the one tiny piece of science we have, but it is not enough – there are all kinds of other questions – is this [here he indicated READINGS2] a good design, a bad design? I don't know, because it is subjective – there is no science there. The only sort of working definition of redundancy you can have is if somehow you can make something smaller, then you have redundancy. My gut feel is that it's a bad design and I can't quantify or qualify that really.

22.1.10 Summary

Where does all of this leave the process of normalization? Is it really a useful process?

Absolutely. Failure to use normalized tables is likely to result in loss of data integrity. In addition, it may well leave you with overly large tables that will, in turn, dramatically slow down the queries that are run against them. Finally, it may result in a situation in which certain questions become impossible to ask of a database. Or rather, you are welcome to ask the question, but you will not be able to generate a correct answer. So, normalization is very important.

Does this mean that professional database developers spend hours poring over their tables, ferreting out functional dependencies?

No, but once you get used to building databases you should find that you don't either. Most developers, either consciously or unconsciously, apply the general rule of thumb described at the start of this chapter. In addition, as people get used to building tables, redundant data begins to stick out like a sore thumb and they split it out into separate tables as a matter of course. The combined effect is that good developers build tables that do not contain redundant data and do not have modification anomalies. Which is, after all, what normalization is all about.

23

The Data
Dictionary

23.1 The Data Dictionary

You design tables, you give the tables fields, you create joins between tables, you build queries etc. Have you ever stopped to think where that information is stored? Where does the database store the information about which tables have which fields, which tables are joined etc.?

In a relational database, this information, according to Codd (see Chapter 21) must be stored in a 'data dictionary'.

A 'data dictionary', also known as a 'system catalog', is a centralized store of information about the database. It contains information about the tables – their number, names, the fields they contain, data types, primary keys, indexes, the joins which have been established between those tables (foreign keys), referential integrity, cascade update, cascade delete etc. The information that is stored in the data dictionary is called the 'metadata'.

The next question is 'In what way should the data dictionary store the meta-data?'. In Codd's view, the answer is quite simple. Tables are where data is stored, so when we need to store data about the actual database itself, it has to be stored in tables. It sounds a little recursive, but it works well in practice.

The idea of storing all of this information in tables is to provide consistency. No matter what information you need from, or about, a database, you will find it in the same format, i.e. in tables.

Microsoft Access conforms to this model, though in normal use the data dictionary tables are hidden because they can be dangerous in inexperienced hands. However, it is interesting (and educational) to play with these tables, and it's perfectly safe to do so provided you make a copy of the entire database and put it somewhere safe first. If you don't take heed of this warning, you have only yourself to blame if your database goes up in a puff of pink smoke.

If you do wish to see these tables (in your copy database), click on Tools, Options, View and choose Show System Objects. (In Access 2.0 click on View, Options and under the category General, set the option 'Show system objects' to yes). The dictionary tables will then appear among those you're used to seeing in the normal list of tables. They all start with the letters MSys, which makes them easy to spot. There are quite a few of them; for instance, there are separate tables for relationships, queries and macros, and these can be opened and viewed in the normal way. Certain others, columns and indexes, for example, can only be viewed or modified if you change the security permissions to allow you to do so. Now I'm *not* suggesting that you do modify the structure, but...

To change permissions, first have a look at how the permissions are set for one of the tables you can access. Click on Tools, Security, User and Group Permissions (in Access 2.0 use Security, Permissions) and note the settings. Then do the same for a table that you can't access and make the settings identical.

One of the major functions of a true data dictionary is to enforce the constraints placed upon the database by the designer, such as referential integrity and cascade delete. In the early days of the PC, none of the 'relational' DBMSs offered a true data dictionary, but for two reasons this wasn't a major concern. Firstly, the early PCs were very slow and incapable of manipulating large, complex, multi-table sets of data. Instead, they tended to be used for fairly simple, single-table work (address lists, for example), so the deficiencies in the DBMS didn't show up as much as they might have done. Secondly, few PCs were running truly mission-critical systems, so if the data became a little 'damaged', who really cared? (Well, of course, the companies involved cared very much, but the software world which sold the DBMSs didn't seem overly concerned.)

So, the early PC-based RDBMSs passed responsibility for this level of control to the programmer. This meant that writing a totally secure database was perfectly possible in, say dBASE. The snag was that you had to be a good programmer; it took a great deal of effort and you had to be very familiar with the relational model. In addition, there was no centralized area where the relationships could be found and examined, so maintenance was difficult. If you suspected a join was being incorrectly supported, you had to hunt through, and understand, all of the relevant code to find the area which was compromising the data.

As PC-based RDBMSs have grown up and come of age, there is now a strong need for a data dictionary. Access does maintain a data dictionary and, as a result, doesn't inflict this extra workload on the developer.

24

More on Queries: Data Manipulation

Data manipulation is a vital part of the relational model. After all, there is little point in storing data correctly, safely and securely if that is all you ever do with it. Stored data has no value if you cannot question it and extract it in some way for humans to examine. So if you want to know more about databases, you will probably want to know about querying more than any other part.

In turn, you may want to know about SQL, which is covered in the next chapter. SQL is based upon the use of 'relational operators', which is what this chapter is all about.

You do *not* need to read *this* chapter in order to understand the one on SQL; indeed you can get through the whole of the rest of your life without reading this chapter. The only reason for reading it is that occasionally you will hear people in the database world referring to 'Projection', 'Union', etc. When you want to know what they are talking about, read this chapter. It won't change your life (unlike the one on SQL, which is full of genuinely useful information) but it will allow you to understand what other people are talking about.

24.1 Relational Operators

Most of us are familiar with the standard algebraic operators ($+$, $-$, $*$ and $/$) which signify addition, subtraction, multiplication and division. We use these operators almost without thinking to manipulate numerical values or variables that represent values.

Thus if we know that $A = 5$, $B = 6$ and $C = 10$, and that $D = A + (B \times (C/A))$ we can calculate that $D = 5 + (6 \times (10/5)) = 5 + (6 \times 2) = 5 + 12 = 17$.

In a database, we store the data in tables (also known as relations) and the relational model provides a set of operators (known, therefore, as relational operators) with which we can manipulate tables (that is to say, relations). The discerning, sensitive reader will have noticed that I am showing a slight tendency to slip into 'database speak' at this point. In fact, since the very term 'relational operators' includes the word 'relational', the temptation to write this chapter using the more correct terms – relation, tuple, attribute etc. (see Glossary) – was strong. I admit I was tempted. On balance I finally resisted, preferring consistency within the book. However, it is worth noting before we start that tables are relations and relations are sets of rows.

Also worth noting is that in general RDBMSs do not expect (or even allow) you to perform relational algebra directly upon tables of data. These operators are simply the building blocks from which operations like queries are built up by the RDBMS.

In order to demonstrate these operators we need a sample table or three (Figure 24.1).

EMPLOYEES

EmployeeNo	FirstName	LastName	DateOfBirth	DateEmployed
1	Bilda	Groves	12 Apr 1956	01 May 1989
2	John	Greeves	21 Mar 1967	01 Jan 1990
3	Sally	Smith	01 May 1967	01 Apr 1992

SALES

SaleNo	EmployeeNo	Customer	Item	Supplier	Amount
1	1	Simpson	Sofa	Harrison	$235.67
2	1	Johnson	Chair	Harrison	$453.78
3	2	Smith	Stool	Ford	$82.78
4	2	Jones	Suite	Harrison	$3,421.00
5	3	Smith	Sofa	Harrison	$235.67
6	1	Simpson	Sofa	Harrison	$235.67
7	1	Jones	Bed	Ford	$453.00

SALES2

SaleNo	EmployeeNo	Customer	Item	Supplier	Amount
3	2	Smith	Stool	Ford	$82.78
5	3	Smith	Sofa	Harrison	$235.67
213	3	Williams	Suite	Harrison	$3,421.00
216	2	McGreggor	Bed	Ford	$453.00
217	1	Williams	Sofa	Harrison	$235.67
218	3	Aitken	Sofa	Harrison	$235.67
225	2	Aitken	Chair	Harrison	$453.78

Figure 24.1 *The sample tables used to demonstrate the basic relational operators.*

In 1972 Ted Codd proposed a set of eight relational operators, as follows:

- Restrict (also known as 'Select', but not the same SELECT as found in SQL)
- Project
- Union
- Difference
- Intersection
- Product
- Join
- Divide

Other operators are possible, but these are by far the most commonly used. We'll look at each of them in turn.

Some of these relational operators (Restrict, Project, Union, Difference and Product) are primitive. That means that they are 'formally undefined'. Given these five we can define Intersection, Join and Divide.

24.1.1 Restrict (Select)

Restrict simply extracts records from a table. Thus if we perform a restriction on the table SALES where Customer = 'Simpson', the result would be that of Figure 24.2.

ANSWER

SaleNo	EmployeeNo	Customer	Item	Supplier	Amount
1	1	Simpson	Sofa	Harrison	$ 235.67
6	1	Simpson	Sofa	Harrison	$ 235.67

Figure 24.2

24.1.2 Project

Projection selects zero or more fields from a table and generates a new table that contains all of the records and only the selected fields. Thus if we project EMPLOYEES on FirstName and LastName the result is as shown in Figure 24.3.

ANSWER

FirstName	LastName
Bilda	Groves
John	Greeves
Sally	Smith

Figure 24.3

This seems straightforward; however, if we project SALES on EmployeeNo and Customer the result is the table in Figure 24.4.

Despite the fact that SALES has seven records, the answer table has only six. This is because one of them (Figure 24.5) would be duplicated in the answer table and tables are not permitted to contain duplicated records.

SALES

EmployeeNo	Customer
1	Johnson
1	Jones
1	Simpson
2	Jones
2	Smith
3	Smith

Figure 24.4

1	Simpson

Figure 24.5

If we projected SALES on SaleNo, EmployeeNo and Customer then the answer table will contain seven records (Figure 24.6), because in the original table the values in SalesNo are unique.

ANSWER

SaleNo	EmployeeNo	Customer
1	1	Simpson
2	1	Johnson
3	2	Smith
4	2	Jones
5	3	Smith
6	1	Simpson
7	1	Jones

Figure 24.6

24.1.3 Union

Union creates a new table by adding the records of one table to another. Clearly, for this to work well it is essential that the tables have the same structure. The union of tables SALES and EMPLOYEES is unimaginable because the two tables are clearly very different in structure. In order for tables to be 'union compatible', they must have the same number of fields and each of the field pairs has to draw its values from the same domains (see Chapter 26 on domains for more details). The tables SALES and SALES2 are union compatible and the result would be the table in Figure 24.7.

Note that two records (Figure 24.8) were shared by the two tables but have appeared only once each in the ANSWER table, because duplicate records are eliminated. Note also that the order in which records appear as the result of a union is unimportant.

24.1.4 Difference

The difference of two tables is a third table which contains the records which appear in the first but *not* in the second. The tables concerned must

ANSWER

SaleNo	EmployeeNo	Customer	Item	Supplier	Amount
1	1	Simpson	Sofa	Harrison	$ 235.67
2	1	Johnson	Chair	Harrison	$ 453.78
3	2	Smith	Stool	Ford	$ 82.78
4	2	Jones	Suite	Harrison	$3421.00
5	3	Smith	Sofa	Harrison	$235.67
6	1	Simpson	Sofa	Harrison	$ 235.67
7	1	Jones	Bed	Ford	$ 453.00
213	5	Williams	Suite	Harrison	$3421.00
216	2	McGreggor	Bed	Ford	$ 453.00
217	1	Williams	Sofa	Harrison	$ 235.67
218	4	Aitken	Sofa	Harrison	$ 235.67
225	4	Aitken	Chair	Harrison	$ 453.78

Figure 24.7

SaleNo	EmployeeNo	Customer	Item	Supplier	Amount
3	2	Smith	Stool	Ford	$ 82.78
5	3	Smith	Sofa	Harrison	$235.67

Figure 24.8

ANSWER

SaleNo	EmployeeNo	Customer	Item	Supplier	Amount
1	1	Simpson	Sofa	Harrison	$ 235.67
2	1	Johnson	Chair	Harrison	$ 453.78
4	2	Jones	Suite	Harrison	$3421.00
6	1	Simpson	Sofa	Harrison	$ 235.67
7	1	Jones	Bed	Ford	$ 453.00

Figure 24.9

ANSWER

SaleNo	EmployeeNo	Customer	Item	Supplier	Amount
213	3	Williams	Suite	Harrison	$3421.00
216	2	McGreggor	Bed	Ford	$ 453.00
217	1	Williams	Sofa	Harrison	$ 235.67
218	3	Aitken	Sofa	Harrison	$ 235.67
225	2	Aitken	Chair	Harrison	$ 453.78

Figure 24.10

be union compatible. Thus the difference of SALES and SALES2 is shown in Figure 24.9.

Note that, unlike Union, the order of the tables is vital. Thus the difference of SALES2 and SALES (Figure 24.10) is not the same.

However, the records that are 'missing' from the two ANSWER tables are the same (Figure 24.11). That is to say in both cases it is the records that are common to the two base tables involved in the difference operation which do not appear in the answer table.

SaleNo	EmployeeNo	Customer	Item	Supplier	Amount
3	2	Smith	Stool	Ford	$ 82.78
5	3	Smith	Sofa	Harrison	$235.67

Figure 24.11

24.1.5 Intersect

The intersection of two tables is a third table which contains the records which are common to both of them. Thus the intersection of SALES and SALES2 is as shown in Figure 24.12.

ANSWER

SaleNo	EmployeeNo	Customer	Item	Supplier	Amount
3	2	Smith	Stool	Ford	$ 82.78
5	3	Smith	Sofa	Harrison	$235.67

Figure 24.12

Unlike the difference operation, the order of the tables is unimportant and, of course, the two tables must be union compatible.

(If at this point you are wondering if Difference and Intersection do essentially the same operation on the data and just keep different bits at the end of it, you get three gold stars because it shows you've been paying attention. I'm impressed.)

24.1.6 Product

The product of two tables is a third which contains all of the records in the first one, added to each of the records in the second. Thus if the first table has three records and the second has seven, the product will have 21 records. The product of EMPLOYEES and SALES is shown in Figure 24.13.

This product operation has been applied quite correctly. However, the astute reader will note that this table contains seven rows which appear to be 'meaningful' and 14 which do not. This is because we are dealing with a raw operator that takes no account of the values in fields nor of any meaning that those values may imply or indicate.

In practice, the product operation usually needs to be modified by further operations in order to yield the answer we want.

24.1.7 Join

Join is a word that has several different meanings in the database world. In Chapter 25 on SQL you will find the word 'join' used in SQL itself, a use that is derived from this relational operator. In terms of operators, the term has a fairly specific meaning; it is an operator which behaves just like a mixture of the Product and Restrict operators. Suppose that you want to examine the sales that have been made by your employees. In order to do this, you need information from both the EMPLOYEES and SALES tables. (In fact, the table SALES2 contains information about more sales, and if we wanted to include this information we would first use the union operator. However,

ANSWER

EmployeeNo	FirstName	LastName	DateOfBirth	DateEmployed	SaleNo
1	Bilda	Groves	12 Apr 1956	01 May 1989	1
1	Bilda	Groves	12 Apr 1956	01 May 1989	2
1	Bilda	Groves	12 Apr 1956	01 May 1989	3
1	Bilda	Groves	12 Apr 1956	01 May 1989	4
1	Bilda	Groves	12 Apr 1956	01 May 1989	5
1	Bilda	Groves	12 Apr 1956	01 May 1989	6
1	Bilda	Groves	12 Apr 1956	01 May 1989	7
2	John	Greeves	21 Mar 1967	01 Jan 1990	1
2	John	Greeves	21 Mar 1967	01 Jan 1990	2
2	John	Greeves	21 Mar 1967	01 Jan 1990	3
2	John	Greeves	21 Mar 1967	01 Jan 1990	4
2	John	Greeves	21 Mar 1967	01 Jan 1990	5
2	John	Greeves	21 Mar 1967	01 Jan 1990	6
2	John	Greeves	21 Mar 1967	01 Jan 1990	7
3	Sally	Smith	01 May 1967	01 Apr 1992	1
3	Sally	Smith	01 May 1967	01 Apr 1992	2
3	Sally	Smith	01 May 1967	01 Apr 1992	3
3	Sally	Smith	01 May 1967	01 Apr 1992	4
3	Sally	Smith	01 May 1967	01 Apr 1992	5
3	Sally	Smith	01 May 1967	01 Apr 1992	6
3	Sally	Smith	01 May 1967	01 Apr 1992	7

EmployeeNo	Customer	Item	Supplier	Amount
1	Simpson	Sofa	Harrison	$ 235.67
1	Johnson	Chair	Harrison	$ 453.78
2	Smith	Stool	Ford	$ 82.78
2	Jones	Suite	Harrison	$3421.00
3	Smith	Sofa	Harrison	$235.67
1	Simpson	Sofa	Harrison	$ 235.67
1	Jones	Bed	Ford	$ 453.00
1	Simpson	Sofa	Harrison	$ 235.67
1	Johnson	Chair	Harrison	$ 453.78
2	Smith	Stool	Ford	$ 82.78
2	Jones	Suite	Harrison	$3421.00
3	Smith	Sofa	Harrison	$235.67
1	Simpson	Sofa	Harrison	$ 235.67
1	Jones	Bed	Ford	$ 453.00
1	Simpson	Sofa	Harrison	$ 235.67
1	Johnson	Chair	Harrison	$ 453.78
2	Smith	Stool	Ford	$ 82.78
2	Jones	Suite	Harrison	$3421.00
3	Smith	Sofa	Harrison	$235.67
1	Simpson	Sofa	Harrison	$ 235.67
1	Jones	Bed	Ford	$ 453.00

Table 24.13 *This is a single table:* SaleNo *and* EmployeeNo *are adjacent fields.*

for the sake of brevity, we will assume that we are only interested in the sales recorded in SALES.)

The first job is to perform a product on these tables. Next we need to perform a selection which removes the records where SALES.EmployeeNo is not equal to EMPLOYEES.EmployeeNo.

The result would be something like Figure 24.14.

ANSWER

EmployeeNo	FirstName	LastName	DateOfBirth	DateEmployed	SaleNo
1	Bilda	Groves	12 Apr 1956	01 May 1989	1
1	Bilda	Groves	12 Apr 1956	01 May 1989	2
1	Bilda	Groves	12 Apr 1956	01 May 1989	6
1	Bilda	Groves	12 Apr 1956	01 May 1989	7
2	John	Greeves	21 Mar 1967	01 Jan 1990	3
2	John	Greeves	21 Mar 1967	01 Jan 1990	4
3	Sally	Smith	01 May 1967	01 Apr 1992	5

EmployeeNo	Customer	Item	Supplier	Amount
1	Simpson	Sofa	Harrison	$ 235.67
1	Johnson	Chair	Harrison	$ 453.78
1	Simpson	Sofa	Harrison	$ 235.67
1	Jones	Bed	Ford	$ 453.00
2	Smith	Stool	Ford	$ 82.78
2	Jones	Suite	Harrison	$3421.00
3	Smith	Sofa	Harrison	$235.67

Figure 24.14 *This is a single table: SaleNo and EmployeeNo are adjacent fields.*

Notice that we have 'thrown away' one of the EmployeeNo columns because, after the Restrict, it contained the same data.

24.1.8 Divide

In order to demonstrate division, it will help if we cut down and alter the SALES table a little, just for this divide operator (Figure 24.15).

SALES

Customer	Item
Simpson	Sofa
Johnson	Bed
Smith	Stool
Jones	Sofa
Smith	Sofa
Simpson	Sofa
Jones	Bed

Figure 24.15

We will also invent a new table called ITEMS, which lists the names of one or more items (Figure 24.16).

Figure 24.16

Now, if we divide SALES by the copy of ITEMS shown in Figure 24.16 we get the answer table of Figure 24.17.

Figure 24.17

If we divide SALES by the copy of ITEMS shown in Figure 24.18 we get the answer table in Figure 24.19.

Figure 24.18

Figure 24.19

Finally, if we divide SALES by the copy of ITEMS shown in Figure 24.20 we get the answer table in Figure 24.21.

Figure 24.20

Figure 24.21

It should be possible to work out from this that the Divide operator is finding records in the SALES table which have values in its field Item which match the values in the table ITEMS. The more values that are supplied in the ITEMS table, the fewer records are likely to be returned in the answer table, because the match has to be for all of the data in the ITEMS table.

Note that the second table can have multiple fields.

24.2 Summary

The following is not rigorous, nor is it detailed; but if you have read and understood the previous section it should provide a quick reference to remind you what the operators are and what they do.

Two of the operators (**Restrict** and **Project**) operate on single tables.

♦ **Restriction** extracts records.
♦ **Projection** extracts fields.

Assuming that each operation is performed on a table with 20 records, the number of records in the answer table will be:

♦ **Restriction** – between 0 and 20
♦ **Projection** – between 1 and 20 (because duplicates are removed)

The remaining six operators (**Union, Difference, Intersect, Product, Join** and **Divide**) all perform operations on two tables.

♦ **Union** adds the records from two tables.
♦ **Difference** subtracts the records in one table from those in another.
♦ **Intersection** locates the records that are common to two tables.
♦ **Product** multiplies the records in the two tables.
♦ **Join** both multiplies and restricts the records in two tables.
♦ **Divide** extracts records and fields from one table on the basis of data in the second.

Assuming that each of the following operations is performed on a pair of tables with 20 and 10 records respectively, the number of records in the answer table will be:

♦ **Union** – between 20 and 30
♦ **Difference** – between 10 and 20 (assuming that we subtract the table with 10 records from that with 20)
♦ **Intersection** – between 0 and 10
♦ **Product** – exactly 200
♦ **Join** – between 0 and 200
♦ **Divide** between 0 and 2

This last figure (for Divide) may seem a little odd. However, as the number of records in the divisor table increases, the number of records in the answer table drops rapidly. A more realistic case to consider here might be one where we divide a table with 20 records by a table with two records. The number of records in the answer table in this case will be between 0 and 10.

25

SQL

The majority of the SQL statements shown in this chapter are in an Access file called CHAP25A.MDB. The SQL statements therein are as shown here; in other words, they are in essentially standard SQL. Since Access will understand standard SQL as well as its own dialect, the queries will run quite happily. However, if you view the queries using the Access GUI query builder, it may rewrite the statements in the Access SQL dialect.

Also note that the SQL statements shown are cross-referenced to the queries in CHAP25A.MDB file by name. This name is shown at the left-hand side of the page and should not be confused with the SQL statement itself, which appears directly below it.

More and more database querying is carried out with a GUI tool; Access has a great one and I think it's wonderful. Yet here I am, devoting an entire chapter to SQL – a nasty, reactionary text-based querying system. Why am I doing this to you?

Delightful as the current crop of querying tools are to use, and excellent as they are for relatively simple questions, they do not have the flexibility to permit you to formulate certain more complex types of question, and this is where SQL scores. It is endlessly adaptable, and knowing something about it is eminently worthwhile for those occasions when it's the only way of reaching the answer you desire. If that doesn't tempt you, remember that, in certain social circles, zero knowledge of SQL can seriously damage your street cred. On the other hand, being able to drop the odd 'Why don't you use a GROUP BY here?' can make you appear to be a database freak of the first water.

SQL stands for Structured Query Language, which is pronounced either as S-Q-L (as the three letters) or as Sequel. It appears that the former pronunciation is more common in the UK and the latter in the USA, but as the two are interchangeable it shouldn't be a cause of anxiety.

Despite many similarities to C, Pascal, BASIC *et al.*, SQL is not a programming language. It is a data access language or data sub-language, and as such is a very restricted language which deals only with how tables of data can be manipulated. It lacks many of the other features (such as the ability to write information to a particular place on the screen) which characterize a full programming language.

SQL is often referred to as a standard but when you actually start using it you find that, like most standards, it's not as standard as all that. The examples given here are in a generic form of SQL – you may well find discrepancies if you use another dialect. Having said that, the differences are not great and should not pose serious problems. For instance, although by default Access uses a slightly different dialect, it will usually accept this generic SQL quite happily. The sample queries included with this chapter are written in generic SQL and almost all will run in Access.

The sample tables shown in Figures 25.1 and Figure 25.2 are the main tables that are used in the examples.

EMPLOYEES

EmployeeNo	FirstName	LastName	DateOfBirth	DateEmployed	CarNo
1	Bilda	Groves	12 Apr 1956	01 May 1989	2
2	John	Greeves	21 Mar 1967	01 Jan 1990	
3	Sally	Smith	01 May 1967	01 Apr 1992	5
4	Fred	Jones	03 Apr 1986	01 May 1994	3

SALES

SaleNo	EmployeeNo	Customer	Item	Supplier	Amount
1	1	Simpson	Sofa	Harrison	$235.67
2	1	Johnson	Chair	Harrison	$453.78
3	2	Smith	Stool	Ford	$82.78
4	2	Jones	Suite	Harrison	$3,421.00
5	3	Smith	Sofa	Harrison	$235.67
6	1	Simpson	Sofa	Harrison	$235.67
7	1	Jones	Bed	Ford	$453.00

CARS

CarNo	Make	Model
1	Triumph	Spitfire
2	Bentley	Mk. VI
3	Triumph	Stag
4	Ford	GT 40
5	Shelby	Cobra
6	Ford	Mustang
7	Aston Martin	DB Mk III
8	Jaguar	D Type

Figure 25.1 *Sample tables.*

The name SQL itself is somewhat misleading, as it implies that this sub-language is concerned exclusively with querying. In fact, the language is sufficiently rich to allow the user to perform many other operations such as creating tables, but it remains true that the commonest usage of the

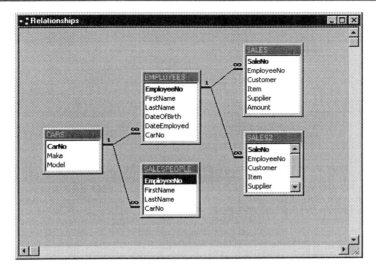

Figure 25.2 *The joins between the tables, including two extra tables which are introduced during the chapter.*

language is asking questions of a database. This part of the language comprises the Data Manipulation Language (DML) statements of SQL.

DML statements are, by convention, written in UPPER-CASE. The first ones we'll look at are SELECT, FROM, DISTINCT and WHERE.

25.1 SELECT and FROM

The first of those statements is SELECT. It is used to extract a collection of fields from a given table. FROM simply directs attention to the table in question. Thus the statement:

SELECT & FROM 1

```
SELECT SaleNo, Item, Amount
FROM SALES;
```

will yield Figure 25.3.

SaleNo	Item	Amount
1	Sofa	$235.67
2	Chair	$453.78
3	Stool	$82.78
4	Suite	$3,421.00
5	Sofa	$235.67
6	Sofa	$235.67
7	Bed	$453.00

Figure 25.3

SQL doesn't eliminate duplicates by default, so:

SELECT & FROM 2
```
    SELECT Item, Amount
    FROM SALES;
```

will yield Figure 25.4, which has duplicated records.

Item	Amount
Sofa	$235.67
Chair	$453.78
Stool	$82.78
Suite	$3,421.00
Sofa	$235.67
Sofa	$235.67
Bed	$453.00

Figure 25.4

25.1.1 DISTINCT

You can force SQL to remove the duplicates by using the statement DISTINCT, which dictates that all rows in the answer table must be unique. The query:

DISTINCT 1
```
    SELECT DISTINCT Item, Amount
    FROM SALES;
```

produces Figure 25.5.

Item	Amount
Bed	$453.00
Chair	$453.78
Sofa	$235.67
Stool	$82.78
Suite	$3,421.00

Figure 25.5

25.1.2 WHERE

SELECT lets you choose the fields with which to work and WHERE lets you choose the records.

WHERE 1
```
    SELECT Item, Amount
    FROM SALES
    WHERE Item = "Sofa";
```

produces Figure 25.6,

Item	Amount
Sofa	$235.67
Sofa	$235.67
Sofa	$235.67

Figure 25.6

while:

WHERE 2
```
SELECT Item, Amount
FROM SALES
WHERE Item = "Sofa" AND Customer = "Smith";
```

yields Figure 25.7.

Item	Amount
Sofa	$235.67

Figure 25.7

You will have noticed a general pattern emerging here (I hope) which is that simple SELECT commands follow a basic pattern:

```
SELECT field name(s)
FROM table name
WHERE condition(s)
```

All sorts of variations are already possible combining SELECT and WHERE statements; as you can see from the last example, WHERE clauses can contain conditions.

25.1.3 Conditions

We'll digress here to cover the range of conditions that are acceptable within a WHERE clause. Conditions typically consist of logical expressions which can be evaluated for truth; in other words, they are checked to discover whether they are true or false.

Thus if we use the SQL statement:

CONDITIONS 1
```
SELECT EmployeeNo, FirstName, LastName, DateOfBirth,
DateEmployed
FROM EMPLOYEES
WHERE EmployeeNo = 2;
```

then we can expect the RDBMS to examine every record in the EMPLOYEE table and place in the answer table only those records for which the condition:

```
WHERE EmployeeNo = 2
```

is true. As you'd hope, this is only true for one record (Figure 25.8).

EmployeeNo	FirstName	LastName	DateOfBirth	DateEmployed
2	John	Greeves	21 March 1967	01 January 1990

Figure 25.8

A condition is constructed from operators such as those shown in Table 25.1.

Table 25.1 *Operators used in SQL*

Symbol	Meaning	Example	Notes	Records returned from Employee table
=	Equal to	EmployeeNo = 2		1
>	Greater than	EmployeeNo > 2		2
<	Less than	EmployeeNo < 2		1
<>	Not equal to	EmployeeNo <> 2		3
=	Greater than or equal to	EmployeeNo >= 2		3
<=	Less than or equal to	EmployeeNo <= 2		2
IN	Equal to a value within a collection of values	EmployeeNo IN (2, 3, 4)		3
LIKE	Similar to	LastName LIKE 'Gr*'	Finds Greeves and Groves. Uses wildcards. Wildcards vary between SQL implementations	2
BETWEEN...AND	Within a range of values, including the two values which define the limits	EmployeeNo BETWEEN 2 AND 4	Equivalent to: EmployeeNo IN (2, 3, 4)	3
IS NULL	Field does not contain a value	DateEmployed IS NULL		0

The logical operators in Table 25.2 have a lower priority than those in Table 25.1 and are therefore processed after them, unless parentheses are used to alter precedence.

Table 25.2 *More operators used in SQL*

Symbol	Meaning	Example(s)	Notes	Records returned from Sales table
AND	Both expressions must be true in order for the entire expression to be judged true	SaleNo > 3 AND Customer = 'Smith'	AND is evaluated before OR	1
OR	If either or both expressions are true, the entire expression is judged to be true	SaleNo > 3 OR Customer = 'Smith'	AND is evaluated before OR	5
NOT	Inverts truth	SaleNo NOT IN (2, 3, 4)	(Just as well it isn't available for the real world!)	4

The following SQL statement asks for a table of the items and amounts from the SALES table for sale numbers greater than 6:

```
CONDITIONS 2
     SELECT Item, Amount
     FROM SALES
     WHERE SaleNo > 6;
```

with the result shown in Figure 25.9,

Item	Amount
Bed	$453.00

Figure 25.9

while this one only wants to see records relating to sofas for sale numbers greater than 6:

CONDITIONS 3
```
SELECT Item, Amount
FROM SALES
WHERE Item = 'Sofa' AND SaleNo > 6;
```

There are none.

This next statement asks for all records for sofas, suites and beds, regardless of sale number:

CONDITIONS 4
```
SELECT Item, Amount
FROM SALES
WHERE Item IN ('Sofa', 'Suite', 'Bed');
```

with the result shown in Figure 25.10,

Item	Amount
Sofa	$235.67
Suite	$3,421.00
Sofa	$235.67
Sofa	$235.67
Bed	$453.00

Figure 25.10

and this one adds a condition which specifies records for the same three pieces of furniture with sale numbers greater than 6:

CONDITIONS 5
```
SELECT Item, Amount
FROM SALES
WHERE Item IN ('Sofa', 'Suite', 'Bed') AND SaleNo > 6;
```

with the result shown in Figure 25.11.

Item	Amount
Bed	$453.00

Figure 25.11

It is worth noting in passing that the use of the operators AND, OR and NOT may seem counter-intuitive at first. For example, if we alter the operator AND to OR in the previous statement:

CONDITIONS 6

```
SELECT Item, Amount
FROM SALES
WHERE Item IN ('Sofa', 'Suite', 'Bed') OR SaleNo > 6;
```

would we expect more or fewer records in the answer table? The answer is more (Figure 25.12).

Item	Amount
Sofa	$235.67
Suite	$3,421.00
Sofa	$235.67
Sofa	$235.67
Bed	$453.00

Figure 25.12

Intuition might suggest that AND increases the number of records while OR restricts them, but, in fact, the converse is true. As a general rule, the more ANDs that you add to a condition, the fewer records appear in the answer table. Of course, this will depend upon the data. What is always true is that adding ORs to a condition must leave the number of records in the answer table the same or increase it. Adding ANDs must leave it the same or decrease it.

Conditions are nothing if not logical, and rendering a series of conditions into plain English is a good way of understanding what it will do in practice.

25.1.4 ORDER BY

I said earlier that a general pattern was emerging. We can expand it a little now by adding another clause called ORDER BY to the statement.

The basic pattern is now:

```
SELECT field name(s)
FROM table name
WHERE condition(s)
ORDER BY field name(s)
```

ORDER BY gives you control over the order in which records appear in the answer table generated by the query. You specify the field by which you want records ordered, as in the following statement:

ORDER BY 1

```
SELECT Item, Amount, SaleNo
FROM SALES
WHERE Item = "Sofa"
ORDER BY SaleNo;
```

with the result shown in Figure 25.13, where the records are ordered by the number of each sale, with the default being ascending order. Note that the

Item	Amount	SaleNo
Sofa	$235.67	1
Sofa	$235.67	5
Sofa	$235.67	6

Figure 25.13

field used to ORDER BY doesn't *have* to appear as one of those SELECTED, although that is typically the case.

One of the reviewers added: 'it does in a lot of SQL dialects however!'

If you feel you want to specify the sort order, the command is ASC, as shown below:

```
SELECT Item, Amount
FROM SALES
WHERE SaleNo > 2
ORDER BY Item ASC;
```

The result is shown in Figure 25.14.

Item	Amount
Bed	$453.00
Sofa	$235.67
Sofa	$235.67
Stool	$82.78
Suite	$3,421.00

Figure 25.14

This is a perfectly acceptable statement, but it's tautological, being the equivalent of:

ORDER BY 2
```
SELECT Item, Amount
FROM SALES
WHERE SaleNo > 2
ORDER BY Item;
```

since ASC is the default.

The next statement:

ORDER BY 3
```
SELECT Item, Amount
FROM SALES
WHERE SaleNo > 2
ORDER BY Item DESC;
```

will produce exactly the same data (Figure 25.15), but it will be sorted differently, since DESC, as you'll have gathered, sorts records in descending order.

Item	Amount
Suite	$3,421.00
Stool	$82.78
Sofa	$235.67
Sofa	$235.67
Bed	$453.00

Figure 25.15

You can use sorts in both directions, as below:

```
ORDER BY 4
     SELECT Item, Customer, SaleNo, Amount
     FROM SALES
     WHERE SaleNo > 0
     ORDER BY Customer ASC, Amount DESC;
```

This will sort the customer records in ascending order, with the amounts each customer has spent shown in descending order, as in Figure 25.16.

Item	Customer	SaleNo	Amount
Chair	Johnson	2	$453.78
Suite	Jones	4	$3,421.00
Bed	Jones	7	$453.00
Sofa	Simpson	6	$235.67
Sofa	Simpson	1	$235.67
Sofa	Smith	5	$235.67
Stool	Smith	3	$82.78

Figure 25.16

If you don't specify an order in the answer table, the records will be returned in any order that the RDBMS thinks is a good idea at the time. (Bill added 'hopefully chosen for performance or usability reasons!') In fact, you might find when you run the SQL statements in the sample Access database, those which don't contain ORDER BY will show the records in a different order from that shown in this book. Remember that if the order of the records in the answer table is important to you, you must use an ORDER BY clause.

25.1.5 Wildcards

Wildcards are used in SQL much as they are used elsewhere for occasions when you want a range of data that fits a certain pattern. The variation below is not uncommon:

WILD CARDS 1
```
    SELECT *
    FROM SALES
    WHERE SaleNo > 1;
```

with the result shown in Figure 25.17.

SaleNo	EmployeeNo	Customer	Item	Supplier	Amount
2	1	Johnson	Chair	Harrison	$453.78
3	2	Smith	Stool	Ford	$82.78
4	2	Jones	Suite	Harrison	$3,421.00
5	3	Smith	Sofa	Harrison	$235.67
6	1	Simpson	Sofa	Harrison	$235.67
7	1	Jones	Bed	Ford	$453.00

Figure 25.17

In this case, the * symbol is used as a wildcard, meaning 'all fields'. It's a shorthand form of:

WILD CARDS 2
```
    SELECT SaleNo, EmployeeNo, Customer, Item, Supplier, Amount
    FROM SALES
    WHERE SaleNo > 1;
```

which yields the same answer table.

25.1.6 Sub-queries

We'll take another diversion, this time into the realm of sub-queries. You already know that the WHERE clause makes use of conditions, such as:

```
    WHERE SaleNo > 1
```

This use of conditions can be expanded into sub-queries to add further refinement to queries. Consider this example:

SUB-QUERIES 1
```
    SELECT Customer
    FROM SALES
    WHERE EmployeeNo IN
      (SELECT EmployeeNo
      FROM EMPLOYEES
      WHERE DateEmployed > 5/5/1989);
```

which produces the table in Figure 25.18.

Customer
Smith
Jones
Smith

Figure 25.18

The statement inside parentheses is known as a sub-query, and it would work perfectly happily as a query all on its own. (Incidentally, this is a good case to illustrate how dialects of SQL differ. Access requires that the date be wrapped up in # symbols, so in Access the last line reads:

```
WHERE DateEmployed > #5/5/1989#);
```

Any operation performed on a table or tables results in another table, one containing the answer. This is termed 'closure' and it is an invariable rule (see Chapter 15). The sub-query above produces, as you would expect from the foregoing, an answer table which is shown in Figure 25.19.

EmployeeNo
2
3
4

Figure 25.19

By looking at the answer table generated by the sub-query, we can see that the original statement can be simplified to:

SUB-QUERIES 2
```
SELECT Customer
FROM SALES
WHERE EmployeeNo IN (2,3,4);
```

The records from the SALES table for which this is true are shown in Figure 25.20.

SaleNo	EmployeeNo	Customer	Item	Supplier	Amount
3	2	Smith	Stool	Ford	$82.78
4	2	Jones	Suite	Harrison	$3,421.00
5	3	Smith	Sofa	Harrison	$235.67

Figure 25.20

So the query actually yields Figure 25.21.

Customer
Smith
Jones
Smith

Figure 25.21

Referring back to the start of the chapter, note that we could eliminate the duplicate records by adding the word Distinct to the first line of the SQL command.

By now, I hope, it is apparent that this SQL statement translates into English as 'Give me the names of all of the customers who have been dealt with by any employee who was employed after 05 May 1989'.

25.1.7 Built-in Functions

SQL includes several simple statistical functions (Table 25.3).

Table 25.3 *Statistical functions*

Function	
SUM	Total
COUNT	The number of occurrences
AVG	Average
MIN	Minimum
MAX	Maximum

Thus it is possible (though not normal practice) to write SQL statements such as:

BUILT-IN FUNCTIONS 1

```
SELECT SUM(Amount)
FROM SALES;
```

Some systems will actually accept this. Access, for example, generates a 'dummy' field name (Expr1000) and yields the table in Figure 25.22.

Expr1000
$5,117.57

Figure 25.22

However, it is more common to explicitly name the field in which the output should be placed. For example:

```
SELECT SUM(Amount) "Sum of Amount"
FROM SALES;
```

or:

BUILT-IN FUNCTIONS 2

```
SELECT SUM(Amount) AS SumOfAmount
FROM SALES;
```

or even:

BUILT-IN FUNCTIONS 3

```
SELECT DISTINCTROW SUM(SALES.Amount) AS SumOfAmount
FROM SALES;
```

which is how it appears in the Access dialect of SQL.

All three of the above yield a table like that in Figure 25.23.

SumOfAmount
$5,117.57

Figure 25.23

The AS followed by a field name simply tells the SQL statement to put the data into a field of that name in the answer table.

It is permissible to mix two or more functions, for example:

BUILT-IN FUNCTIONS 4
```
    SELECT SUM(Amount) AS SumOfAmount,
    COUNT(Amount) AS CountOfAmount,
    AVG(Amount) AS AvgOfAmount,
    MIN(Amount) AS MinOfAmount,
    MAX(Amount) AS MaxOfAmount
    FROM SALES;
```

which yields Figure 25.24.

SumOfAmount	CountOfAmount	AvgOfAmount	MinOfAmount	MaxOfAmount
$5,117.57	7	$731.08	$82.78	$3,421.00

Figure 25.24

One of the reviewers added: 'in many SQL dialects one writes either:

```
    COUNT(DISTINCT FieldName)
```

or

```
    COUNT(*)
```

not

```
    COUNT(FieldName)'
```

It's also perfectly permissible to mix fields like this:

BUILT-IN FUNCTIONS 5
```
    SELECT COUNT(Customer) AS CountOfCustomer,
    AVG(Amount) AS AvgOfAmount
    FROM SALES;
```

giving Figure 25.25.

CountOfCustomer	AvgOfAmount
7	$731.08

Figure 25.25

These functions will even operate correctly on fields which contain no data. If we amend the base table, for the sake of this example only, to be as shown in Figure 25.26 (this table is in the sample MDB file as ALTEREDSALES), then the SQL statement:

BUILT-IN FUNCTIONS 6

```
SELECT COUNT(Customer) AS CountOfCustomer,
AVG(Amount) AS AvgOfAmount
FROM ALTEREDSALES;
```

SaleNo	EmployeeNo	Customer	Item	Supplier	Amount
1	1	Simpson	Sofa	Harrison	$235.67
2	1	Johnson	Chair	Harrison	$453.78
3	2		Stool	Ford	$82.78
4	2	Jones	Suite	Harrison	
5	3	Smith	Sofa	Harrison	$235.67
6	1		Sofa	Harrison	$235.67
7	1	Jones	Bed	Ford	$453.00

Figure 25.26

(essentially identical to BUILT-IN FUNCTIONS 5) will give Figure 25.27.

CountOfCustomer	AvgOfAmount
5	$282.76

Figure 25.27

The COUNT function finds only five values; AVG sums the values that it finds and divides the result by 6 (the number of values in that particular field) rather than 7 (the number of records).

However, these functions are designed to yield only a single figure each. Thus an SQL statement like:

BUILT-IN FUNCTIONS 7

```
SELECT Customer,
AVG(SALES.Amount) AS AvgOfAmount
FROM SALES;
```

is illegal because:

```
SELECT Customer
```

can (and in this case would) have an output consisting of multiple records, while the second part:

```
SELECT AVG(SALES.Amount) AS AvgOfAmount
```

can only have an output of a single record.

Several SQL implementations provide more than the basic functions. For example, Access also provides those in Table 25.4.

Table 25.4 *More statistical functions*

Function	
StDev	Standard deviation
Var	Variance

It is just this kind of deviation from the standard that demonstrates that SQL is still a fairly 'fluid' language.

25.1.8 GROUP BY – Collecting Information

GROUP BY seems to be more difficult to understand than some other constructions. Bill agrees; during proofreading he added:

> GROUP BY seems to confuse everyone. It would be nice to describe what it is trying to accomplish. Something like 'Splitting your records into groups and creating one "summary" record in the answer table for each group'.

Which is a good way to think about it.

So far, our generic SELECT statement looks like this:

```
SELECT field name(s)
FROM table name
WHERE condition(s)
ORDER BY field name(s)
```

We can expand it with:

```
SELECT field name(s)
FROM table name
WHERE condition(s)
GROUP BY Field name(s)
ORDER BY field name(s)
```

Above, we looked at the command ORDER BY, which provides a way of presenting information in ascending or descending order. Further control over your answer data is given by GROUP BY. The syntax is:

```
GROUP BY Field name(s)
```

To illustrate its usefulness, we'll consider the simple statement below:

GROUP BY 1

```
SELECT AVG(Amount) AS AvgOfAmount
FROM SALES;
```

which gives Figure 25.28.

AvgOfAmount
$731.08

Figure 25.28

This averages the values found in the Amount field for all records in the SALES table. Suppose you want to examine the records which refer to customer 'Simpson'? You'd use WHERE, as follows:

GROUP BY 2
```
SELECT AVG(Amount) AS AvgOfAmount
FROM SALES
WHERE Customer = "Simpson";
```

giving Figure 25.9.

AvgOfAmount
$235.67

Figure 25.29

Now suppose you want to do this for each customer. An inelegant brute force solution would be to run the query multiple times, once for each customer. A particularly clever solution is to get the SQL statement to group the records together by the name of the customer and then apply the AVG function to the values in the groups.

We can visualize the process like this. We go from the table of Figure 25.30 to that of Figure 25.31, and thence to Figure 25.32, which is a full but compact summary of the required information.

SaleNo	EmployeeNo	Customer	Item	Supplier	Amount
1	1	Simpson	Sofa	Harrison	$235.67
2	1	Johnson	Chair	Harrison	$453.78
3	2	Smith	Stool	Ford	$82.78
4	2	Jones	Suite	Harrison	$3,421.00
5	3	Smith	Sofa	Harrison	$235.67
6	1	Simpson	Sofa	Harrison	$235.67
7	1	Jones	Bed	Ford	$453.00

Figure 25.30

SaleNo	EmployeeNo	Customer	Item	Supplier	Amount
2	1	Johnson	Chair	Harrison	$453.78
7	1	Jones	Bed	Ford	$453.00
4	2	Jones	Suite	Harrison	$3,421.00
6	1	Simpson	Sofa	Harrison	$235.67
1	1	Simpson	Sofa	Harrison	$235.67
5	3	Smith	Sofa	Harrison	$235.67
3	2	Smith	Stool	Ford	$82.78

Figure 25.31

Customer	AvgOfAmount
Johnson	$453.78
Jones	$1,937.00
Simpson	$235.67
Smith	$159.23

Figure 25.32

The SQL statement required to perform this magic is:

GROUP BY 3

```
SELECT Customer, AVG(Amount) AS AvgOfAmount
FROM SALES
GROUP BY Customer
Order BY Customer;
```

Impressive, isn't it?

The GROUP BY clause can be used more simply than this. For example:

GROUP BY 4

```
SELECT Customer
FROM SALES
GROUP BY Customer;
```

produces Figure 25.33.

Customer
Johnson
Jones
Simpson
Smith

Figure 25.33

At first it appears that this is the same as:

GROUP BY 5

```
SELECT DISTINCT Customer
FROM SALES;
```

which yields exactly the same answer table, but adding another field demonstrates the difference. Thus:

GROUP BY 6

```
SELECT DISTINCT Customer, Amount
FROM SALES;
```

produces Figure 25.34,

Customer	Amount
Johnson	$453.78
Jones	$453.00
Jones	$3,421.00
Simpson	$235.67
Smith	$82.78
Smith	$235.67

Figure 25.34

whereas:

GROUP BY 7

```
SELECT Customer, Amount
FROM SALES
GROUP BY Customer;
```

fails to run. Why is this?

Essentially it is for the same reasons that were raised when discussing the conflict that can arise when using functions.

The command:

GROUP BY 8

```
SELECT Customer
FROM SALES
GROUP BY Customer;
```

says 'Sort the records in the SALES table so that identical values in the Customer field are together. Then 'crush together' the records with identical Customer values so that they *appear* to be one record'.

Thus:

```
SELECT Customer, Amount
FROM SALES
GROUP BY Customer;
```

fails because there is a conflict (real in this particular case, potential in other cases) between the number of records that should be output. (Although grouping by Customer, Amount would work.)

```
SELECT Customer
FROM SALES
GROUP BY Customer;
```

will output four records, as in Figure 25.35, while:

Customer
Johnson
Jones
Simpson
Smith

Figure 25.35

GROUP BY 9

```
SELECT Amount
FROM SALES;
```

will output seven records, as in Figure 25.36.

Amount
$235.67
$453.78
$82.78
$3,421.00
$235.67
$235.67
$453.00

Figure 25.36

Combining these two incompatible requests is impossible, and SQL engines will refuse the statement.

As you can see from the above, there is no obligation to combine GROUP BY with one or more of the functions. However, it is commonly done because often we only want to group records in order to be able to perform some type of manipulation on selections of records.

It is perfectly possible to GROUP BY more than one field. Thus:

```
GROUP BY 10
    SELECT Customer, Supplier, AVG(Amount) AS AvgOfAmount
    FROM SALES
    GROUP BY Customer, Supplier;
```

produces more groups than the SQL statement above which grouped by one field because it is grouping those records which share the same value in Customer and Supplier. The answer table is shown in Figure 25.37, which raises another interesting question. How can you tell how many records are actually contributing to each group?

Customer	Supplier	AvgOfAmount
Johnson	Harrison	$453.78
Jones	Ford	$453.00
Jones	Harrison	$3,421.00
Simpson	Harrison	$235.67
Smith	Ford	$82.78
Smith	Harrison	$235.67

Figure 25.37

One answer (although by no means the only one) is:

```
GROUP BY 11
    SELECT Count(*) AS NumberInGroup,
    Customer, Supplier, AVG(Amount) AS AvgOfAmount
    FROM SALES
    GROUP BY Customer, Supplier;
```

The only addition is the Count(*) AS NumberInGroup bit, which simply says that the number of records in each group should be counted. The result is shown in Figure 25.38.

NumberInGroup	Customer	Supplier	AvgOfAmount
1	Johnson	Harrison	$453.78
1	Jones	Ford	$453.00
1	Jones	Harrison	$3,421.00
2	Simpson	Harrison	$235.67
1	Smith	Ford	$82.78
1	Smith	Harrison	$235.67

Figure 25.38

We could equally well use:

```
GROUP BY 12
    SELECT Count(Customer) AS NumberInGroup, Customer, Supplier,
    AVG(Amount) AS AvgOfAmount
    FROM SALES
    GROUP BY Customer, Supplier;
```

which returns the same answer table.

GROUP BY is an incredibly powerful tool and it can be made even more so with the addition of HAVING.

25.1.9 GROUP BY...HAVING – Collecting Specific Information

Whereas the GROUP BY clause puts records into logical groupings, the HAVING clause allows you to select the groups that you want to see, based on values which appertain to that group. Consider the example given above:

```
GB&H 1
    SELECT Customer, Supplier, AVG(Amount) AS AvgOfAmount
    FROM SALES
    GROUP BY Customer, Supplier;
```

which gives Figure 25.39.

Customer	Supplier	AvgOfAmount
Johnson	Harrison	$453.78
Jones	Ford	$453.00
Jones	Harrison	$3,421.00
Simpson	Harrison	$235.67
Smith	Ford	$82.78
Smith	Harrison	$235.67

Figure 25.39

Suppose, now the records are grouped in this way, that we are only interested in the groups where the average amount is $250 or more?

The foolish solution is:

```
GB&H 2
    SELECT Customer, Supplier, AVG(Amount) AS AvgOfAmount
    FROM SALES
    GROUP BY Customer, Supplier
    ORDER BY AVG(Amount);
```

which gives Figure 25.40. Although this renders the desired values easy to find, it still leaves the job of actually locating them to the user.

Note that I have slipped in an ORDER BY into that last statement. Bill said 'Whoa! ORDERing groups seems like a whole new concept! Maybe comment somewhere that "operations" on groups are similar to those on records'. He is, as usual, quite right.

Customer	Supplier	AvgOfAmount
Smith	Ford	$82.78
Smith	Harrison	$235.67
Simpson	Harrison	$235.67
Jones	Ford	$453.00
Johnson	Harrison	$453.78
Jones	Harrison	$3,421.00

Figure 25.40

A much better solution is:

GB&H 3

```
SELECT Customer, Supplier, AVG(Amount) AS AvgOfAmount
FROM SALES
GROUP BY Customer, Supplier
HAVING AVG(Amount) >= 250;
```

which gives Figure 25.41.

Customer	Supplier	AvgOfAmount
Johnson	Harrison	$453.78
Jones	Ford	$453.00
Jones	Harrison	$3,421.00

Figure 25.41

One reviewer added:

Might be worth saying 'HAVING is simply a WHERE done after GROUPing'.

You can, of course, still order the groups:

GB&H 4

```
SELECT Customer, Supplier, AVG(Amount) AS AvgOfAmount
FROM SALES
GROUP BY Customer, Supplier
HAVING AVG(Amount) >= 250
ORDER BY AVG(Amount);
```

which gives Figure 25.42.

Customer	Supplier	AvgOfAmount
Jones	Ford	$453.00
Johnson	Harrison	$453.78
Jones	Harrison	$3,421.00

Figure 25.42

25.1.10 Working with Multiple Tables

So far we have looked at using the SELECT statement with a single table. Clearly, since the relational model encourages us to split complex data into separate tables, we will often find it necessary to recover data from two or more tables. In order to do this, we have to use the SELECT statement to draw data from both tables and the WHERE clause to form the joins.

Before we do, let's try querying the tables without using the WHERE clause.

MULTI-TABLE 1

```
SELECT SALES.Customer, EMPLOYEES.LastName, SALES.EmployeeNo,
EMPLOYEES.EmployeeNo
FROM SALES, EMPLOYEES;
```

This gives Figure 25.43.

Customer	LastName	SALES.EmployeeNo	EMPLOYEES.EmployeeNo
Simpson	Groves	1	1
Johnson	Groves	1	1
Smith	Groves	2	1
Jones	Groves	2	1
Smith	Groves	3	1
Simpson	Groves	1	1
Jones	Groves	1	1
Simpson	Greeves	1	2
Johnson	Greeves	1	2
Smith	Greeves	2	2
Jones	Greeves	2	2
Smith	Greeves	3	2
Simpson	Greeves	1	2
Jones	Greeves	1	2
Simpson	Jones	1	4
Johnson	Jones	1	4
Smith	Jones	2	4
Jones	Jones	2	4
Smith	Jones	3	4
Simpson	Jones	1	4
Jones	Jones	1	4
Simpson	Smith	1	3
Johnson	Smith	1	3
Smith	Smith	2	3
Jones	Smith	2	3
Smith	Smith	3	3
Simpson	Smith	1	3
Jones	Smith	1	3

Figure 25.43

Note that this SQL statement includes for the first time the table names when fields are being specified. Up to this point our SELECT statements have referred to single tables. Since field names within a single table must be unique, the field name alone allowed us to identify the fields unambiguously. However, field names can (and often are) shared by different tables.

For example, both SALES and EMPLOYEES have a field called EmployeeNo. Therefore the only way to identify a precise field uniquely is to use the table name as well. SQL syntax typically has the table name first in upper-case, followed by a dot, followed by the field name in lower-case.

SQL allows you to substitute temporary synonyms for table names:

MULTI-TABLE 2
```
SELECT S.Customer, S.Amount, E.FirstName, E.LastName,
S.EmployeeNo, E.EmployeeNo
FROM SALES S, EMPLOYEES E;
(FROM SALES AS S, EMPLOYEES AS E; is also acceptable.)
```

which can shorten statements considerably, but also tends to makes them less readable. Note that although the synonyms are not defined until the FROM clause, they can still be used in the SELECT clause, which tells you something about the way in which the SQL statement is read by the RDBMS.

To return to the multiple table query, if we add a WHERE clause like this:

MULTI-TABLE 3
```
SELECT S.Customer, S.Amount, E.FirstName, E.LastName,
S.EmployeeNo, E.EmployeeNo
FROM SALES S, EMPLOYEES E
WHERE S.EmployeeNo = E.EmployeeNo;
```

we get Figure 25.44.

Customer	Amount	FirstName	LastName	S.EmployeeNo	E.EmployeeNo
Simpson	$235.67	Bilda	Groves	1	1
Johnson	$453.78	Bilda	Groves	1	1
Smith	$82.78	John	Greeves	2	2
Jones	$3,421.00	John	Greeves	2	2
Smith	$235.67	Sally	Smith	3	3
Simpson	$235.67	Bilda	Groves	1	1
Jones	$453.00	Bilda	Groves	1	1

Figure 25.44

Referring to the base tables shows that this is a much more useful answer table than the previous one. Essentially this one is letting us look at the data in the SALES table, but instead of seeing the numbers which represent the employees we can see their names.

Without a WHERE clause, the answer table contains every record in the SALES table matched against every record in the EMPLOYEE table, giving $4 \times 7 = 28$ records. The WHERE clause ensures that we see in the answer table only those records in which the EmployeeNo in SALES matches the EmployeeNo in EMPLOYEES. This is reasonable, since we are using the value in SALES.EmployeeNo to indicate which employee made the sale.

In practice, you don't have to have the EmployeeNo fields visible in the answer table, and typically they would be excluded, appearing only in the WHERE clause.

MULTI-TABLE 4

```
SELECT S.Customer, S.Amount, E.FirstName, E.LastName
FROM SALES AS S, EMPLOYEES AS E
WHERE S.EmployeeNo = E.EmployeeNo;
```

which gives Figure 25.45.

Customer	Amount	FirstName	LastName
Simpson	$235.67	Bilda	Groves
Johnson	$453.78	Bilda	Groves
Smith	$82.78	John	Greeves
Jones	$3,421.00	John	Greeves
Smith	$235.67	Sally	Smith
Simpson	$235.67	Bilda	Groves
Jones	$453.00	Bilda	Groves

Figure 25.45

It is possible to join more than two tables by adding to the WHERE clause. For example:

MULTI-TABLE 5

```
SELECT SALES.Customer, EMPLOYEES.FirstName, CARS.Make,
CARS.Model
FROM CARS, EMPLOYEES, SALES
WHERE EMPLOYEES.EmployeeNo = SALES.EmployeeNo
AND EMPLOYEES.CarNo = CARS.CarNo;
```

which gives Figure 25.46.

Customer	FirstName	Make	Model
Simpson	Bilda	Bentley	Mk. VI
Johnson	Bilda	Bentley	Mk. VI
Simpson	Bilda	Bentley	Mk. VI
Jones	Bilda	Bentley	Mk. VI
Smith	Sally	Shelby	Cobra

Figure 25.46

Note that this query is finding the car driven by the salesperson who dealt with a given customer, so it isn't supposed to present particularly meaningful information.

The most recent standard for SQL (SQL-92) includes a new way of expressing joins such that:

MULTI-TABLE 6
```
SELECT SALES.Customer, EMPLOYEES.LastName, SALES.Amount
FROM SALES, EMPLOYEES
WHERE SALES.EmployeeNo = EMPLOYEES.EmployeeNo;
```

which gives Figure 25.47,

Customer	LastName	Amount
Simpson	Groves	$235.67
Johnson	Groves	$453.78
Simpson	Groves	$235.67
Jones	Groves	$453.00
Smith	Greeves	$82.78
Jones	Greeves	$3,421.00
Smith	Smith	$235.67

Figure 25.47

can be replaced by:

MULTI-TABLE 7
```
SELECT SALES.Customer, EMPLOYEES.LastName, SALES.Amount
FROM SALES INNER JOIN EMPLOYEES
ON EMPLOYEES.EmployeeNo = SALES.EmployeeNo;
```

This produces exactly the same answer table and is generally considered to be more readable. However, it does raise another question. 'What is this INNER business?'.

25.1.11 Inner (Natural) Joins

Suppose that your boss says 'Give me a list of all the cars and the salesperson to whom each is allocated'.

You are immediately tempted to use the SQL statement:

INNER JOIN 1
```
SELECT CARS.Make, CARS.Model, EMPLOYEES.FirstName,
EMPLOYEES.LastName
FROM CARS INNER JOIN EMPLOYEES
ON CARS.CarNo = EMPLOYEES.CarNo;
```

but this will give the answer table in Figure 25.48, which doesn't list all of the cars because, for instance, that delectable D-type Jaguar hasn't been allocated to anyone.

Make	Model	FirstName	LastName
Bentley	Mk. VI	Bilda	Groves
Triumph	Stag	Fred	Jones
Shelby	Cobra	Sally	Smith

Figure 25.48

In fact, your boss has phrased the question badly, since her original question assumes that every car *is* allocated to an employee, and this is not the case. However, voicing your opinion about her inexact use of English is likely to be a CLM (Career-Limiting Move). It's better to keep quiet and find a query which will list all of the cars and also shows which cars have been allocated to which lucky employees.

But before that, we'll have a look at what's wrong with the query shown above. By default, a join combines the two tables via fields that have identical values; this is known as a 'Natural' or 'Inner' join. However, if one or both of the fields contain exclusive values (I am using the term 'exclusive' to mean that the values are found in one table but not the other) then the join ignores the records that are associated with these values. Thus the table CARS has a delightful Aston Martin, CarNo = 7, but since there is no corresponding value in EMPLOYEES.CarNo, this fine automobile never appears in the answer table.

So, instead of a natural join, what you need to use here is an unnatural join. OK, I admit it, that was just to see if you were awake. It is really known as an 'outer' join.

25.1.12 Outer Joins

There are two distinct flavours of outer join – left and right.

The following SQL statement:

OUTER JOIN 1

```
SELECT CARS.Make, CARS.Model, EMPLOYEES.FirstName,
EMPLOYEES.LastName
FROM CARS LEFT JOIN EMPLOYEES
ON CARS.CarNo = EMPLOYEES.CarNo;
```

yields Figure 25.49.

Make	Model	FirstName	LastName
Triumph	Spitfire		
Bentley	Mk. VI	Bilda	Groves
Triumph	Stag	Fred	Jones
Ford	GT 40		
Shelby	Cobra	Sally	Smith
Ford	Mustang		
Aston Martin	DB Mk III		
Jaguar	D Type		

Figure 25.49

Essentially the substitution of LEFT JOIN for INNER JOIN has made all the difference. It ensures that every record from the first table appears in the answer table.

The other flavour of an outer join is RIGHT, which simply ensures that every record in the table on the right-hand side of the join is included in the answer table, so:

OUTER JOIN 2

```
SELECT CARS.Make, CARS.Model, EMPLOYEES.FirstName,
EMPLOYEES.LastName
FROM CARS RIGHT JOIN EMPLOYEES
ON CARS.CarNo = EMPLOYEES.CarNo;
```

yields Figure 25.50.

Make	Model	FirstName	LastName
		John	Greeves
Bentley	Mk. VI	Bilda	Groves
Triumph	Stag	Fred	Jones
Shelby	Cobra	Sally	Smith

Figure 25.50

It ought to go without saying (which is another way of saying 'it is important to note') that:

OUTER JOIN 3

```
SELECT CARS.Make, CARS.Model, EMPLOYEES.FirstName,
EMPLOYEES.LastName
FROM EMPLOYEES LEFT JOIN CARS
ON CARS.CarNo = EMPLOYEES.CarNo;
```

produces the same answer table. In other words, the LEFT and RIGHT simply refer to the tables as named in the SQL statement. So:

```
FROM EMPLOYEES LEFT JOIN CARS
```

and

```
FROM CARS RIGHT JOIN EMPLOYEES
```

will include all the employees and some of the cars;

```
FROM CARS LEFT JOIN EMPLOYEES
```

and

```
FROM EMPLOYEES RIGHT JOIN CARS
```

will include all the cars and some of the employees.

So, you can have all of the cars some of the time and indeed all of the people some of the time. But what you really want to know is, can we have all of the cars and all of the people all of the time? The answer, not surprisingly, is 'Yes'. In order to do so, we can make use of UNION.

25.1.13 UNION

UNION returns all of the records from two queries and displays them, *minus any duplicates*, in a single table. Thus:

UNION 1

```
SELECT CARS.Make, CARS.Model, EMPLOYEES.FirstName,
EMPLOYEES.LastName
FROM CARS RIGHT JOIN EMPLOYEES
ON CARS.CarNo = EMPLOYEES.CarNo
UNION
SELECT CARS.Make, CARS.Model, EMPLOYEES.FirstName,
EMPLOYEES.LastName
FROM CARS LEFT JOIN EMPLOYEES
ON CARS.CarNo = EMPLOYEES.CarNo;
```

produces Figure 25.51.

Make	Model	FirstName	LastName
		John	Greeves
Aston Martin	DB Mk III		
Bentley	Mk. VI	Bilda	Groves
Ford	GT 40		
Ford	Mustang		
Jaguar	D Type		
Shelby	Cobra	Sally	Smith
Triumph	Spitfire		
Triumph	Stag	Fred	Jones

Figure 25.51

Clearly the two answer tables that are produced by the separate SELECT statements must be compatible in order for the UNION to combine them sensibly. So:

UNION 2

```
SELECT CARS.CarNo, CARS.Model, EMPLOYEES.FirstName,
EMPLOYEES.LastName
FROM CARS RIGHT JOIN EMPLOYEES
ON CARS.CarNo = EMPLOYEES.CarNo
UNION
SELECT CARS.Make, CARS.Model, EMPLOYEES.FirstName,
EMPLOYEES.LastName
FROM CARS LEFT JOIN EMPLOYEES
ON CARS.CarNo = EMPLOYEES.CarNo;
```

attempts to put text and numeric data into the same field and should fail. (In practice, some RDBMSs will allow this and convert the resulting field to the lowest common denominator, such as text.)

However, the result (Figure 25.52) may not be particularly meaningful.

CarNo	Model	FirstName	LastName
		John	Greeves
2	Mk. VI	Bilda	Groves
3	Stag	Fred	Jones
5	Cobra	Sally	Smith
Aston Martin	DB Mk III		
Bentley	Mk. VI	Bilda	Groves
Ford	GT 40		
Ford	Mustang		
Jaguar	D Type		
Shelby	Cobra	Sally	Smith
Triumph	Spitfire		
Triumph	Stag	Fred	Jones

Figure 25.52

The first example I gave for UNION (combining a LEFT and RIGHT join) serves as an excellent example of the use of UNION, but it certainly isn't the only way in which it can be used. Suppose that you have another table of salespeople who, for whatever reason, are stored in a separate table (Figure 25.53) from the other employees.

SALESPEOPLE

EmployeeNo	FirstName	LastName	CarNo
1	Fred	Williams	1
2	Sarah	Watson	4
3	James	Hatlitch	6
4	Simon	Webaston	
5	Sally	Harcourt	
6	Martin	Boxer	
7	Trevor	Wright	7

Figure 25.53

You want to throw a party for all the employees and to include those salespeople with company cars (because they have volunteered to drive the employees home afterwards).

You can use:

UNION 3

```
SELECT FirstName, LastName
FROM EMPLOYEES
UNION SELECT FirstName, LastName
FROM SALESPEOPLE
WHERE SALESPEOPLE.CarNo Is Not Null;
```

to yield Figure 25.54.

FirstName	LastName
Bilda	Groves
Fred	Jones
Fred	Williams
James	Hatlitch
John	Greeves
Sally	Smith
Sarah	Watson
Trevor	Wright

Figure 25.54

You can also use UNION to produce a list of all employees and sales people who have company cars:

UNION 4

```
SELECT SALESPEOPLE.FirstName, SALESPEOPLE.LastName, CARS.Make,
CARS.Model
FROM
(CARS INNER JOIN SALESPEOPLE
ON CARS.CarNo = SALESPEOPLE.CarNo)
```

```
UNION
SELECT EMPLOYEES.FirstName, EMPLOYEES.LastName, CARS.Make,
CARS.Model
FROM
(CARS INNER JOIN EMPLOYEES
ON CARS.CarNo = EMPLOYEES.CarNo);
```

which gives Figure 25.55.

FirstName	LastName	Make	Model
Bilda	Groves	Bentley	Mk. VI
Fred	Jones	Triumph	Stag
Fred	Williams	Triumph	Spitfire
James	Hatlitch	Ford	Mustang
Sally	Smith	Shelby	Cobra
Sarah	Watson	Ford	GT 40
Trevor	Wright	Aston Martin	DB Mk III

Figure 25.55

25.1.14 SELECT Summary

You are just about to encounter a table which has a field called 'Foo'. 'Foo' is a word used in computing as 'a sample name for absolutely anything'. In other words, in this context it means that the content of this field, and the content of any other fields which might be in this table, don't matter; they could be anything. 'Foo' is one of a collection of these terms (others are 'bar', 'baz', 'qux' and 'fred') which are wonderfully known as the metasyntactic variables. This information is of no use to you whatsoever, except as a long and involved way of saying, don't worry about the contents of the field called Foo in the next example table.

We have looked at the SELECT statement and its clauses. What I haven't covered, but is worth stressing, is that a familiarity with SQL enables you to use it with imagination, and that is when it becomes an incredibly powerful tool. For example, suppose you import a table of data like that in Figure 25.56 into a database and then try to make the field InvoiceNo into a primary key.

InvoiceNo	Foo
1	King
2	Baby Blue
3	Royal
2	Crested
5	Humbolt
2	Jackass

Figure 25.56

This should fail, because the field contains duplicate values. In this tiny table it is easy to find them, but what if it had 50,000 records? The answer is that with a little imagination, a query will find the errant records for us.

SELECT SUMMARY 1

```
SELECT InvoiceNo, Count(InvoiceNo) AS NoOfDuplications
FROM INVOICES
GROUP BY InvoiceNo
HAVING Count(InvoiceNo)>1;
```

which gives Figure 25.57.

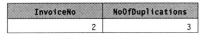

InvoiceNo	NoOfDuplications
2	3

Figure 25.57

SELECT is undoubtedly the most commonly used SQL statement, but we shouldn't forget the other members of the Data Manipulation Language (DML): INSERT, UPDATE and DELETE.

25.2 INSERT

A brief note about the sample Access database that is provided. It is tempting to open each query as an SQL view, read it and then look at the answer table by pressing the 'Datasheet View' button. This works for most of the examples provided, but not the INSERT queries. Press the 'Run' button instead.

It is also worth bearing in mind that these queries will update the base tables, so you should be working on a copy of the database. In addition, remember that the tables have primary keys, so if you run the same INSERT query twice without deleting the additional record, the query will fail to run the second time.

If all that wasn't enough, note also that I have encountered what appears to be a 'software anomaly' in using these queries in Access 2.0. The first example SQL INSERT statement will only run two or three times. Thereafter, even if the new record is dutifully deleted from the table into which the INSERT is made, the query will generate an error message. This is despite the fact that the query *hasn't* been edited, or even been opened for editing. Once this error message appears, the only way to get the query to run again is to delete the existing query, open a new one and type the SQL statement again. This behavior is not apparent in Access 97.

INSERT is used to add rows to a table. Thus the statement:

```
INSERT INTO SALES
VALUES (8, 1, "Jones", "Sofa", "Harrison", 235.67);
```

This is not the only allowable construction. Indeed, Access will run this syntactical construction, but if you save the query, Access converts it to:

INSERT 1

```
INSERT INTO SALES
SELECT 8, 1, "Jones", "Sofa", "Harrison", 235.67;
```

Both constructions will add the record shown in Figure 25.58 to the SALES table.

SaleNo	EmployeeNo	Customer	Item	Supplier	Amount
8	1	Jones	Sofa	Harrison	$235.67

Figure 25.58

Simple, isn't it? Note that in these first versions we haven't specified the field names explicitly, so we have to provide a value for each one in the correct order.

A slightly more verbose form is possible:

INSERT 2

```
INSERT INTO SALES ( SaleNo, EmployeeNo, Customer, Item,
Supplier, Amount )
SELECT 8, 1, "Jones", "Sofa", "Harrison", 235.67;
```

which has exactly the same result. We can also add to specific fields:

INSERT 3

```
INSERT INTO SALES ( SaleNo, EmployeeNo, Customer, Amount )
SELECT 9, 1, "Jones", 235.67;
```

which adds a single record (Figure 25.59).

SaleNo	EmployeeNo	Customer	Item	Supplier	Amount
1	1	Simpson	Sofa	Harrison	$235.67
2	1	Johnson	Chair	Harrison	$453.78
3	2	Smith	Stool	Ford	$82.78
4	2	Jones	Suite	Harrison	$3,421.00
5	3	Smith	Sofa	Harrison	$235.67
6	1	Simpson	Sofa	Harrison	$235.67
7	1	Jones	Bed	Ford	$453.00
8	1	Jones	Sofa	Harrison	$235.67
9	1	Jones			$235.67

Figure 25.59

But don't forget closure. Any operation that we perform on a table (or tables) in a relational database must have, as its result, another table. So, suppose we write an INSERT statement like this:

```
INSERT INTO SALES
VALUES
    (SELECT *
    FROM SALES2
    WHERE SaleNo > 200);
```

The table SALES2 looks like Figure 25.60, and this SQL statement will add the five records for which SaleNo is greater than 200 to the SALES table.

SALES2

SaleNo	EmployeeNo	Customer	Item	Supplier	Amount
3	2	Smith	Stool	Ford	$ 82.78
5	3	Smith	Sofa	Harrison	$235.67
213	3	Williams	Suite	Harrison	$3421.00
216	2	McGreggor	Bed	Ford	$ 453.00
217	1	Williams	Sofa	Harrison	$ 235.67
218	3	Aitken	Sofa	Harrison	$ 235.67
225	2	Aitken	Chair	Harrison	$ 453.78

Figure 25.60

Closure is important here because the statement within the parentheses:

```
(SELECT *
FROM SALES2
WHERE SaleNo > 200);
```

generates a table in its own right which is then INSERTed into SALES.

As has been mentioned before, SQL is not always as standard as it should be. As another example, the syntax for this statement in Access is:

INSERT 5
```
INSERT INTO SALES
SELECT *
FROM SALES2
WHERE SaleNo > 200;
```

25.3 UPDATE

The UPDATE command is wonderfully powerful and allows you to alter the values in fields.

The general format of the command is:

```
UPDATE tablename
SET FieldName(s) = value
WHERE FieldName = value
```

although the WHERE condition is optional. Thus:

UPDATE 1
```
UPDATE SALES
SET Customer ="Smith";
```

will change Figure 25.61 to Figure 25.62.

SaleNo	EmployeeNo	Customer	Item	Supplier	Amount
1	1	Simpson	Sofa	Harrison	$235.67
2	1	Johnson	Chair	Harrison	$453.78
3	2	Smith	Stool	Ford	$82.78
4	2	Jones	Suite	Harrison	$3,421.00
5	3	Smith	Sofa	Harrison	$235.67
6	1	Simpson	Sofa	Harrison	$235.67
7	1	Jones	Bed	Ford	$453.00

Figure 25.61

SaleNo	EmployeeNo	Customer	Item	Supplier	Amount
1	1	Smith	Sofa	Harrison	$235.67
2	1	Smith	Chair	Harrison	$453.78
3	2	Smith	Stool	Ford	$82.78
4	2	Smith	Suite	Harrison	$3,421.00
5	3	Smith	Sofa	Harrison	$235.67
6	1	Smith	Sofa	Harrison	$235.67
7	1	Smith	Bed	Ford	$453.00

Figure 25.62

As you might imagine, this command can be a little devastating in the wrong hands.

The WHERE command generally limits its scope. So:

UPDATE 2

```
UPDATE SALES
SET Customer ="Smith"
WHERE Customer = "Simpson";
```

will act on the same initial table to produce Figure 25.63.

SaleNo	EmployeeNo	Customer	Item	Supplier	Amount
1	1	Smith	Sofa	Harrison	$235.67
2	1	Johnson	Chair	Harrison	$453.78
3	2	Smith	Stool	Ford	$82.78
4	2	Jones	Suite	Harrison	$3,421.00
5	3	Smith	Sofa	Harrison	$235.67
6	1	Smith	Sofa	Harrison	$235.67
7	1	Jones	Bed	Ford	$453.00

Figure 25.63

It is quite possible to use different fields in the SET and WHERE clauses. Thus:

UPDATE 3

```
UPDATE SALES
SET Customer ="Smith"
WHERE SaleNo < 5;
```

produces Figure 25.64.

SaleNo	EmployeeNo	Customer	Item	Supplier	Amount
1	1	Smith	Sofa	Harrison	$235.67
2	1	Smith	Chair	Harrison	$453.78
3	2	Smith	Stool	Ford	$82.78
4	2	Smith	Suite	Harrison	$3,421.00
5	3	Smith	Sofa	Harrison	$235.67
6	1	Simpson	Sofa	Harrison	$235.67
7	1	Jones	Bed	Ford	$453.00

Figure 25.64

Other variations are possible, and indeed common. For example:

UPDATE 4
```
UPDATE SALES
SET AMOUNT = AMOUNT * 1.1;
```

will increase all the values in SALES.Amount by 10%, as in Figure 25.65.

SaleNo	EmployeeNo	Customer	Item	Supplier	Amount
1	1	Simpson	Sofa	Harrison	$259.24
2	1	Johnson	Chair	Harrison	$499.16
3	2	Smith	Stool	Ford	$91.06
4	2	Jones	Suite	Harrison	$3,763.10
5	3	Smith	Sofa	Harrison	$259.24
6	1	Simpson	Sofa	Harrison	$259.24
7	1	Jones	Bed	Ford	$498.30

Figure 25.65

This sort of variant is particularly useful if profits are slumping.

25.4 DELETE

The DELETE command allows you to delete specific records from specific tables.

The general format of the command is:

```
DELETE FieldName(s)
FROM tablename
WHERE FieldName = value
```

The FieldName(s) section of the query can be misleading, since it implies that the DELETE command will simply remove individual fields from records. This is not the case; the DELETE command removes any and all **records** which match the WHERE condition. Rather frighteningly, the WHERE condition itself is optional. Thus:

DELETE 1
```
DELETE *
FROM SALES;
```

is a particularly powerful (not to say dangerous) statement. The output table looks like Figure 25.66.

SaleNo	EmployeeNo	Customer	Item	Supplier	Amount

Figure 25.66

To be more specific, this command deletes the entire contents of the SALES table. Be aware of the consequences of any injudicious use of this command.

More commonly (and less alarmingly) the command is used more like this:

DELETE 2
```
DELETE *
FROM SALES
WHERE EmployeeNo = 2;
```

which deletes two records and produces Figure 25.67.

SaleNo	EmployeeNo	Customer	Item	Supplier	Amount
1	1	Simpson	Sofa	Harrison	£235.67
2	1	Johnson	Chair	Harrison	£453.78
5	3	Smith	Sofa	Harrison	£235.67
6	1	Simpson	Sofa	Harrison	£235.67
7	1	Jones	Bed	Ford	£453.00

Figure 25.67

Of course, closure comes into its own, and we can write statements like:

DELETE 3
```
DELETE *
FROM EMPLOYEES
WHERE EmployeeNo IN
(SELECT EmployeeNo
FROM SALES
GROUP BY EmployeeNo
HAVING COUNT (*) < 2);
```

which is neither friendly nor amiable, though effective in database terms. (It deletes all employees from the EMPLOYEES table who have made fewer than two sales. The SALES table is unaffected, but one of our employees disappears from EMPLOYEES.)

Bear in mind that this statement will try to remove employees who have performed badly, although the data dictionary may in fact prevent this deletion in order to preserve data integrity. This will depend upon whether cascade delete has been set between the two tables. In the sample database, the query will complete.

One of the reviewers wrote 'What happens if you put field names into the delete statement?'

```
DELETE Customer
FROM SALES
WHERE EmployeeNo = 2;
```

It is a good question, and the answer is that this will have exactly the same effect as:

```
DELETE *
FROM SALES
WHERE EmployeeNo = 2;
```

In other words, the DELETE statement works only on entire records; specifying fields has no effect.

25.5 A Question (and a Free SQL Diagnostic Tool)

The two following SQL statements are perfectly legal and both will run. One of them will find all of the records where the SaleNo is greater than 200 and order the answer table by EmployeeNo and SaleNo. The other won't, and is essentially useless. The burning question is 'Which is the useful one?'.

Is it:

Q1

```
SELECT *
FROM SALES2
WHERE SaleNo>200
ORDER BY EmployeeNo, SaleNo;
```

or

Q2

```
SELECT *
FROM SALES2
WHERE SaleNo>200
ORDER BY EmployeeNo AND SaleNo;
```

The only difference, to save you wasting time comparing them, is in the ORDER BY statement.

Answer

Q1 is sensible and returns Figure 25.68.

Q2 returns Figure 25.69 because it has a very odd construction:

```
ORDER BY EmployeeNo AND SaleNo
```

SaleNo	EmployeeNo	Customer	Item	Supplier	Amount
217	1	Williams	Sofa	Harrison	$235.67
216	2	McGreggor	Bed	Ford	$453.00
225	2	Aitken	Chair	Harrison	$453.78
213	3	Williams	Suite	Harrison	$3,421.00
218	3	Aitken	Sofa	Harrison	$235.67

Figure 25.68

SaleNo	EmployeeNo	Customer	Item	Supplier	Amount
225	2	Aitken	Chair	Harrison	$453.78
218	3	Aitken	Sofa	Harrison	$235.67
217	1	Williams	Sofa	Harrison	$235.67
216	2	McGreggor	Bed	Ford	$453.00
213	3	Williams	Suite	Harrison	$3,421.00

Figure 25.69

Despite appearances, this does *not* say, 'order the records by EmployeeNo and then by SaleNo'. Instead it says, 'evaluate the expression EmployeeNo AND SaleNo for truth (the answer will come back as –1 (True) or 0 (False)) and then stack the records based on this value'. You can prove this to yourself by adding the expressions which are being evaluated to the list of information that you want to see.

Thus:

```
SELECT SaleNo>200 AS 'SaleNo>200',
EmployeeNo AND SaleNo AS 'Emp AND Sale',
EmployeeNo, SaleNo, Customer
FROM SALES2
WHERE SaleNo>200
ORDER BY EmployeeNo AND SaleNo;
```

produces Figure 25.70.

'SaleNo200'	'Emp AND Sale'	EmployeeNo	SaleNo	Customer
-1	-1	3	213	Williams
-1	-1	2	216	McGreggor
-1	-1	1	217	Williams
-1	-1	3	218	Aitken
-1	-1	2	225	Aitken

Figure 25.70

In all of the records the expression EmployeeNo AND SaleNo happens to evaluate to –1, so the sorting has no effect.

I take the trouble to show you this, not because I think you are likely to make this particular mistake, but if you are human you will make some mistakes somewhere along the line. If and when you come across an intractable SQL statement that runs but doesn't give you the answer you expect, then you can use SQL's own ability to show you the results of expressions as a diagnostic tool.

Incidentally, Access will run the last SQL statement exactly as shown, but when the query is saved the SQL syntax is converted to:

Q3
```
SELECT SaleNo>200 AS ['SaleNo>200'],
EmployeeNo AND SaleNo AS ['Emp AND Sale'],
EmployeeNo, SaleNo, Customer
FROM SALES2
WHERE SaleNo>200
ORDER BY EmployeeNo AND SaleNo;
```

which is therefore how it appears in the sample database.

25.6 Distinctly Exact (or Exactly DISTINCT)

This chapter is all about SQL, and I have tried to keep it as generic as possible so it makes very few references to the dialect found in Access. However, now that we have finished this look at generic SQL, one feature of the Access dialect is probably worth mentioning. For the rest of this chapter, you should use CHAP25B.MDB. In Access, the generic DISTINCT is replaced by DISTINCTROW. By that I meant that if you build a query in Access using the GUI, then by default it will generate an SQL statement which starts:

```
SELECT DISTINCTROW...
```

In many cases this will return the same record set as an SQL statement which starts:

```
SELECT...
```

or even:

```
SELECT DISTINCT...
```

The differences between SELECT and SELECT DISTINCT are explained above and now seems like a good time to look at the precise meaning of SELECT DISTINCTROW.

In order to demonstrate this we need a couple of tables (Figure 25.71).

Note that we have two clients called Sophie and that Puffin has yet to place an order with our company.

Both:

SELECT1TABLEONLY
```
SELECT Name
FROM CLIENTS;
```

and

SELECTDISTINCTROW1TABLEONLY
```
SELECT DISTINCTROW Name
FROM CLIENTS;
```

return seven records, as in Figure 25.72.

CLIENTS

ClientID	Name	Location
1	Sophie	Truckee
2	Andy	Truckee
3	Ross	Truckee
4	Sophie	Half Moon Bay
5	Steve	Truckee
6	Penguin	Dundee
7	Puffin	Auchmithie

ORDERS

OrderNo	ClientID	Item
1	1	Bagels
2	4	Cigars
3	4	Salami
4	4	Bagels
5	3	Plain biscuits
6	3	Plain biscuits
7	6	Sardines
8	1	Bagels
9	1	Smoked salmon
10	5	Large cigars
11	2	Sushi

Figure 25.71

Name
Sophie
Andy
Ross
Sophie
Steve
Penguin
Puffin

Figure 25.72

However:

SELECTDISTINCT1TABLEONLY
```
SELECT DISTINCT Name
FROM CLIENTS;
```

returns Figure 25.73.

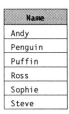

Name
Andy
Penguin
Puffin
Ross
Sophie
Steve

Figure 25.73

DISTINCT (as explained above) forces SQL to remove the duplicates in the answer table.

In this case (and in all cases where a single table is queried) there is no difference between SELECT and SELECT DISTINCTROW.

However, if we bring two tables into the query, the two forms can be distinguished.

SELECTBOTHTABLES

```
SELECT Name
FROM CLIENTS INNER JOIN ORDERS
ON CLIENTS.ClientID = ORDERS.ClientID;
```

returns Figure 25.74, which has one record for each order in the ORDERS table, because the join between the tables has essentially generated 11 records, of which we have asked to see only the name of the customer.

Name
Sophie
Sophie
Sophie
Sophie
Ross
Ross
Penguin
Sophie
Sophie
Steve
Andy

Figure 25.74

SELECTDISTINCTBOTHTABLES

```
SELECT DISTINCT Name
FROM CLIENTS INNER JOIN ORDERS
ON CLIENTS.ClientID = ORDERS.ClientID;
```

by contrast returns only five records (Figure 25.75).

Name
Andy
Penguin
Ross
Sophie
Steve

Figure 25.75

The SELECT statement on its own returns 11 records; then the DISTINCT part removes the duplicates.

The 'problem' with this answer table is that it implies that there are only five people placing orders, whereas we know there are six, because there are two people called Sophie. If we expand the SQL statement to include the location field:

```
MODIFIEDVERSIONSELECTDISTINCTBOTHTABLES
      SELECT DISTINCT Name, Location
      FROM CLIENTS INNER JOIN ORDERS ON CLIENTS.ClientID =
      ORDERS.ClientID;
```

then we get Figure 25.76.

Name	Location
Andy	Truckee
Penguin	Dundee
Ross	Truckee
Sophie	Half Moon Bay
Sophie	Truckee
Steve	Truckee

Figure 25.76

DISTINCT is very literal; it returns unique records in the answer table, whether or not they come from unique records in the original table.

I used the term 'problem' above, but of course this is only a problem if you don't know what DISTINCT is supposed to do. In fact, DISTINCT is doing exactly what it was designed to do.

My guess is that Microsoft felt that naïve users of a database might not appreciate this level of subtlety. If they saw a single name in an answer table, they would expect that it represented a single person. So the default in Access was set to DISTINCTROW, which, as you will by now have guessed, produces in this case a separate record in the answer table for each unique customer who has placed an order (as determined by being a different row in the source table).

Thus:

```
SELECTDISTINCTROWBOTHTABLES
      SELECT DISTINCTROW Name
      FROM CLIENTS INNER JOIN ORDERS
      ON CLIENTS.ClientID = ORDERS.ClientID;
```

returns Figure 25.77.

Name
Sophie
Andy
Ross
Sophie
Steve
Penguin

Figure 25.77

These tables and queries are all on the disk as DISTINCT.MDB.

I'll leave you with a brainteaser. If you include the primary key value from CUSTOMERS in all of these queries, does the difference between SELECT DISTINCT and SELECT DISTINCTROW disappear?

As they say in all the best textbooks, explain your answer!

25.7 Summary

SQL is extremely powerful and, if you spend any time at all with databases, it well repays the effort required to learn it. One of the best ways to learn it is to practice using it, which is why the sample database has more than 70 example queries.

26

Domains

The concept of a domain is a crucial part of the relational model, which is strange because it is ignored by almost every RDBMS I can call to mind.

A domain is a pool of values from which the values found in a given field in a particular table can be drawn. For example, suppose that we are defining a table to hold information about Employees. We decide that we will store the number of their parents who are living, so we declare a field to have the name ParentNo and we make it of type Integer. We decide to include only those parents who are related by direct involvement (thus eliminating problems with uncertain numbers of step-parents) and decide that there are only three possible values for this field, namely 0, 1 and 2. So, the domain for this field is defined as a subset of integers, namely 0, 1 and 2.

Domains don't have to contain numeric values. Consider a field called City in which are stored, quite reasonably, the names of cities. There are a finite number of cities in the world, so the domain for the field contains a finite number of values, such as 'London', 'Seattle', or 'Dundee'.

The domain for a field type called Day might well contain the values 'Monday', 'Tuesday', 'Wednesday', 'Thursday', 'Friday', 'Saturday' and 'Sunday'.

Domains come into their own when we start to join tables. The bad news is that very few RDBMSs fully support domains; instead they simply ignore them. In order to understand why they shouldn't ignore such a fundamental (and fundamentally useful) part of relational theory, consider the following example (Figure 26.1).

EMPLOYEES

EmployeeNo*	FirstName	LastName	DateOfBirth	DateEmployed
1	Bilda	Groves	12 Apr 1956	01 May 1989
2	John	Greeves	21 Mar 1967	01 Jan 1990
3	Sally	Smith	01 May 1967	01 Apr 1992

SALES

EmployeeNo	Customer	SaleNo*	Item	Supplier	Amount
1	Simpson	1	Sofa	Harrison	$ 235.67
1	Johnson	2	Chair	Harrison	$ 453.78
1	Simpson	6	Sofa	Harrison	$ 235.67
1	Jones	7	Bed	Ford	$ 453.00
2	Smith	3	Stool	Ford	$ 82.78
2	Jones	4	Suite	Harrison	$3421.00
3	Smith	5	Sofa	Harrison	$235.67

Figure 26.1

Let's assume that EMPLOYEES.EmployeeNo, SALES.EmployeeNo and SALES.SaleNo are of type Integer.

If you join the two tables using the two EmployeeNo fields, then all will be well. If, however, you make, say a one-to-many join between EMPLOYEES.EmployeeNo and SALES.SaleNo then the result will be meaningless.

The typical PC-based RDBMSs of today will happily allow you to make joins between two fields as long as those fields are of the same data type; in this case all three fields are of type Integer, so both meaningless and meaningful joins can be made. However, suppose that we declare two domains, as in Table 26.1.

Table 26.1

Name of domain	Permitted values
Emp	Integer between 1 and 2000 inclusive
Sales	Integer between 1 and 100000 inclusive

We then declare both of the EmployeeNo fields to be of type Integer and declare that both will draw their values from the domain called Emp. We further declare SaleNo to be of type Integer and also that it will draw its values from the domain Sales. Thereafter the RDBMS should only allow us to make joins between fields which are of the same data type and which draw their values from the same domain.

Domains are simply another safety mechanism; they prevent later users of the database from unfortunate errors. Since almost all RDBMSs fail to support them, they remain a theoretical consideration, which is a shame.

27

Indexing –
Speeding Up
Your Database

Humans can manipulate lists efficiently, as long as they are sorted alphabetically. For example, suppose that I gave you a list of 8,000 customers, all sorted alphabetically by last name, and then asked you to tell me how many people with the surname Robb existed in the table. It is unlikely that you would start at the top, examine every record from 1 to 8,000, counting the Robbs on the way. Instead you would scan through the list until you came to the last names that began with R. You would then scan more slowly until you found a 'Robb'. You would then scan back until you had found the first Robb and then count until you had found the last. Assuming that you were sure that the list was really in alphabetical order, you wouldn't bother looking anywhere else.

An RDBMS can do the same trick; given a sorted list (either alphabetically or numerically) it can find data much more rapidly. So far, so good. But consider a list, or table, with five fields (as in Figure 27.1). It can only ever be sorted by one field at a time.

If you need to find all of the Sallys, you can re-sort it by first name, as in Figure 27.2.

But then if I ask you to find the Robbs, you either re-sort the list, or check every single record.

RDBMSs have the same problem. If the records in a table are arranged on the disk in order of, say, last name, they cannot, by definition, also be arranged by first name. In addition, as soon as more records are added, the entire sorting process on last name has to be redone. (In practice, certain mechanisms for organizing database files on disk mean that the data can be

235

CUSTOMERS

CustomerNo	Title	FirstName	LastName	Town
6	Ms.	Norah	Cooper	Seattle
8	Mrs.	Grace	Falconer	London
2	Miss	Sally	Henderson	Dundee
7	Ms.	Helen	Lynch	Boston
3	Prof.	Harry	McColgan	Seattle
9	Mrs.	Mary	Robb	Dundee
1	Mr.	Brian	Thompson	Boston
4	Dr.	Sandra	Wellington	Boston
5	Mr.	Joseph	Whyte	London

Figure 27.1 *A sample table, sorted by* LastName.

CUSTOMERS

CustomerNo	Title	FirstName	LastName	Town
1	Mr.	Brian	Thompson	Boston
8	Mrs.	Grace	Falconer	London
3	Prof.	Harry	McColgan	Seattle
7	Ms.	Helen	Lynch	Boston
5	Mr.	Joseph	Whyte	London
9	Mrs.	Mary	Robb	Dundee
6	Ms.	Norah	Cooper	Seattle
2	Miss	Sally	Henderson	Dundee
4	Dr.	Sandra	Wellington	Boston

Figure 27.2 *The same table sorted by* FirstName.

kept *essentially* sorted on disk while still allowing it to be edited and updated. However, all of these systems have their limitations, and the fundamental problem still remains.)

In the light of this problem, indexing was born. Any RDBMS worth its salt must allow you to mark one or more fields as indexed. This is usually done during table design and, once you have done that, the RDBMS should construct and maintain the indexes transparently. An index is, in effect, a list of numerical values which gives the order of the records when they are sorted on a particular field. For example, the table in Figure 27.3 is sorted by CustomerNo.

One very small list (Figure 27.4) contains all of the information necessary to rearrange the records in alphabetical order by LastName. It tells us that the first customer in such a sorted list would be CustomerNo 6 (Norah Cooper) followed by CustomerNo 8 (Grace Falconer) and so on.

Figure 27.5 can be used to sort the same table by FirstName.

CUSTOMERS

CustomerNo	Title	FirstName	LastName	Town
1	Mr.	Brian	Thompson	Boston
2	Miss	Sally	Henderson	Dundee
3	Prof.	Harry	McColgan	Seattle
4	Dr.	Sandra	Wellington	Boston
5	Mr.	Joseph	Whyte	London
6	Ms.	Norah	Cooper	Seattle
7	Ms.	Helen	Lynch	Boston
8	Mrs.	Grace	Falconer	London
9	Mrs.	Mary	Robb	Dundee

Figure 27.3

Order By LastName	CustomerNo
1	6
2	8
3	2
4	7
5	3
6	9
7	1
8	4
9	5

Figure 27.4

Order By FirstName	CustomerNo
1	1
2	8
3	3
4	7
5	5
6	9
7	6
8	2
9	4

Figure 27.5

Although I have shown these indexes looking like tables, this isn't meant to imply that an RDBMS will generate extra tables in a database if you start using indexes. Indeed, the 'lists' that the RDBMS keeps are usually structured in a more complex way than I have shown here. They are structured in a more complex way in order to make them faster to search; but that added complexity doesn't alter the essential functionality that I am describing here.

Suppose you regularly query the above table looking for every customer who lives in Seattle. Given 8,000 records, such a query might take, say, 15 seconds on a given machine. If you tell the RDBMS to apply and keep an index on the Town field, the search time will come down to a couple of seconds. The larger the table, the greater the gain.

Now consider the situation if we add another table to the database (Figure 27.6).

ORDERS

OrderNo	CustomerNo	EmployeeNo
1	2	1
2	1	4
3	3	1
4	4	2
5	2	3
6	4	2
7	2	2

Figure 27.6

Suppose that CUSTOMERS.CustomerNo is a primary key and ORDERS.CustomerNo is a foreign key of that primary key.

Clearly, many of the queries that we run against these two tables will involve finding the orders that correspond to particular customers. Every such query means that the RDBMS has to perform a search on ORDERS.CustomerNo that is a foreign key. While primary keys are automatically indexed, the same is not true for foreign keys, despite the fact that they are often searched.

Many queries involve the RDBMS in searching foreign keys, so it is usually worth indexing them unless you have a good reason not to do so.

In some recent speed testing of RDBMSs, I did some queries on tables both with and without indexes on the foreign keys. One particular query on non-indexed tables had to be aborted after 18 hours (I needed the machine for something else). The same query (with the same RDBMS) was completed in under a minute with indexed tables.

All of which begs an interesting question. If indexes are such a good idea, why not simply index every field in every database? Despite their efficiency, indexes do take *some* processing power to maintain. This maintenance occurs whenever records are added to the table or updated. Every time a new record is added, or a foreign key value in an existing record is edited, some or all of the indexes have to be modified as well. Given a huge table and multiple indexes this can produce a significant delay before the RDBMS will allow the next record to be edited or added.

This means that indexes shouldn't be used indiscriminately, but there is nothing to stop you from using them intelligently, as long as you are aware of their pros and cons.

- ◆ *Pros*

  They speed up querying. This makes an impressive difference, even with small tables, and a dramatic difference with large ones.

- ◆ *Cons*

  They slow down data entry and editing. This won't be noticeable with small tables, but can be a problem with large ones.

So, what do I mean by 'intelligent use of indexes'? Suppose that you look after a massive database of orders. It just so happens that this table is updated with all the previous month's orders on the first day of every month. For the whole of the rest of the month, the table is frequently queried but never updated. What would you do? Well, I'd index all of the foreign keys and any of the fields which were ever queried, without worrying about how many indexes I was applying.

For the whole of the month, all of the users of the database would be able to query it and they would get answers back as rapidly as possible. On the morning of the first day of the month, I would remove all of the indexes. As the new orders were added, the users wouldn't see any speed penalty because the RDBMS wouldn't be constantly rebuilding the indexes after every edit.

You will be way ahead of me by this point. Once all of the new orders were added, I would reapply the indexes, the RDBMS would build them all once and for the rest of the month the queries would run like greased lightning.

28

What Does Null Mean?

A given field in a given record can contain data, or not. If you don't enter a value into a field in a particular record, you might think that the field was simply empty, but life isn't that simple. Instead the field is said to contain a null value. If, for example, a field is supposed to contain the phone number of a friend but you don't know the phone number, you don't enter any data. The field is then said to contain a null value.

At the most basic level, a null value simply denotes missing information. I was talking to a friend on the phone once about a database problem when our conversation was suddenly replaced by an electronic tone for about 3 seconds. At least, I had heard a tone which blotted out everything else, but I had no idea what my friend had heard. 'Did you hear a tone then?', I asked. 'No', replied my friend, 'I just heard a null'. She hadn't received any data during those three seconds – she had received an absence of data.

The odd thing about nulls is that we tend to refer to nulls positively. We don't say 'The field is empty'; we say, 'The field contains a null', meaning that it contains nothing.

Nulls can cause unending problems in databases at two distinct levels.

Firstly, at a theoretical level, what exactly is meant by a null has been causing problems for years. Date, in *An Introduction to Database Systems*, devotes more than 20 pages to the problems of trying to represent missing information in a database. He comes to the conclusion that, despite the fact that vendors provide support for nulls in their products, we should ignore this and not use nulls at all.

Secondly, in the real world most RDBMSs do support nulls and, of course, people make use of nulls in their applications. This causes problems, and the problems are all the more difficult to tie down because of the different ways in which vendors support nulls!

To try to give a flavour of the problems that they can cause, consider the following.

Imagine a hospital blood bank that receives un-typed blood from various sources (hopefully human). Each bottle has a unique identifier that is entered in a table called BLOODBANK (Figure 28.1), along with the physical location of the bottle in the store. There is also a field for the Type that is filled in once the blood in each bottle has been tested in the laboratory. Values such as A+ and O– are entered as appropriate, and a null means that the laboratory report on that bottle has not yet arrived.

BLOODBANK

Identifier	Type
32WWE	A+
45555	B+
456FF	O–
45FFG	AB+
4FGGG	
55EE4	B–
676FG	A+
FDD5F	AB+
FFFF4	
FGF66	B–
FGGGG	A+
GFGHG	A+

Figure 28.1

The hospital also receives patients and each has his or her details entered into another table, called PATIENTS (Figure 28.2), along with a unique patient number. All patients have their blood group determined as soon as possible after admission and this too goes into the table. If the blood group field for a patient shows a null value, it means that, for whatever reason, the information is not yet available from the lab.

PATIENTS

PatientNo	FirstName	LastName	Type
1	Bilda	Groves	O–
2	John	Greeves	A+
3	Sally	Smith	
4	Fred	Jones	AB–

Figure 28.2

If patient 2 is in need of a transfusion, you would query the database to find which bottles in the store contained blood of the correct type. John is type A+, so the query finds several matching entries (Figure 28.3) in the BLOODBANK table.

What about patient number 3? She hasn't been typed as yet, so what should happen if we query the database to find blood for her?

The answer should be that no records are returned; that is, no blood is identified as suitable for this patient. Access handles this 'correctly', but not all RDBMSs do so. Paradox, for example, matches the null values in

FindBloodForPatientNo2

FirstName	LastName	PatientNo	Type	Identifier
John	Greeves	2	A+	32WWE
John	Greeves	2	A+	GFGHG
John	Greeves	2	A+	676FG
John	Greeves	2	A+	FGGGG

Figure 28.3

PATIENTS.Type and BLOODBANK.Type, suggesting that Sally Smith could be given the blood in 4FGGG or FFFF4. Would you be prepared to put untyped blood into a patient? If you were that patient, would you be happy with this arrangement?

Ignoring the arguments about *whether* RDBMS should support nulls, in my view when they do they should never treat null values as equal. I know it is tempting, because of the way we use the word 'Null'. Expressions like 'Oh, there is a null value in that field' implies that the field actually contains something. But remember that a null isn't a type of entry like a one or a zero; it is the absence of an entry.

Take another example. Suppose that we are trying to match, not patients to blood, but hotel guests to rooms. If a room is occupied, then the guest number is inserted into a field (ROOMS.GuestNo); otherwise it is left as a null value. Surely in this case the use of a null value is OK?

No, nulls are being misused here. A null value means that you don't *know* the state of the real-world object represented by the data in the field. Assuming that the hotel is run correctly, we know which rooms are unoccupied, so a null value, which implies uncertainty, is inappropriate.

Instead of a null, we might insert an agreed value in here (perhaps a zero) to indicate an unoccupied room. However, this causes its own problems.

In my less rigorous moments, I have been known to argue that it doesn't matter too much how a particular RDBMS treats nulls, as long as that treatment is always consistent and as long as you are sure you know the rules by which it operates. However, the bottom line is that I still have a strong preference for ones that don't match on nulls. (Bill added 'That is what the "is null" operator is for!'.)

The take-home message is that a null doesn't mean 'the default value', nor does it mean 'we don't care what value goes in here'. It means 'We don't *know* what value goes in here'. The difference, particularly in the blood bank example, is vital and could be fatal. But...

...there is a big 'but' lurking here. I have only just begun to scratch the surface of the problems that nulls bring. For each argument that I have raised here, someone, somewhere, has a counter-argument. I would not for a moment suggest that in a trite thousand or so words I have done anything except alert you to the fact that there are problems associated with using nulls. Be careful out there.

29

Primary Keys – Scope and Truly Global Ones

In the database column that I write for *Personal Computer World*, I was discussing primary keys a while ago and offered the opinion that, for a small car restoration business, the registration number of the cars in the workshop would make a good primary key. A reader questioned this opinion, and the point is interesting because it illustrates the scope which a primary key must cover.

He wrote:

> Car registration numbers are very poor primary keys because they can easily change and therefore do not uniquely identify a vehicle. The chassis or VIN (Vehicle Identification Number) is far more suitable although not as easily obtained. People often argue that the registration number is good enough in the 'real world' but would probably not like to buy a written-off and repaired car just because it had a new reg.

In absolute terms the writer was perfectly correct. However, much as I hate to be contentious, I am also one of those people who thinks registration numbers are (sometimes) good enough for the real world. Which brings us neatly to a point which has a wider relevance than car registration numbers; indeed it is an important principle about primary keys in general.

The identifier that you choose as your primary key doesn't have to be unique in global terms, it just has to be unique within the context of the database in which it is used. In other words, a database exists to model a subset of the real world; as long as the identifier you choose remains unique within that subset, it is a suitable candidate for a primary key.

For example, if I was building a database which recorded every car in the country, I would without question use the VIN as the unique identifier, because it is the one property of a vehicle that cannot (legally) be changed. So, there's no argument in this case.

However, consider a garage which services and repairs cars. Suppose that the owner of the garage uses a database to track the work done on the customers' cars and that the sole function of this database is to ensure that each customer is billed correctly. Within the world of this particular database, the registration number uniquely identifies the car, so it is an excellent primary key. Even if the car happens to be legally re-registered during its time in the garage, the garage proprietor can simply change the registration number in the database, because the new number will still be unique.

Now, let's make it more complex. Suppose that the garage tracks the service and repair history of its customers' cars for several years. The chances are that one of the cars will eventually be legally re-registered and this will make the tracking of the car's service history problematical. So, in this case should the garage owner use the VIN or the registration number? My practical experience of garages suggest it would be a disaster to use anything other than the registration number.

Typically, mechanics fill out worksheets which identify the number of hours they have worked on each car, and they identify the cars by registration number. Why use the registration number? For the simple reason that it is plastered on the front and back of the car in big letters, so it's convenient. This leaves us with a stark choice.

We can elect to use the registration number:

♦ Advantage – easy to find and use
♦ Disadvantage – it may change with time

We can use the VIN number:

♦ Advantage – unlikely to change with time
♦ Disadvantage – inaccessible and tortuously long

We (the designers of databases) have to balance two opposing factors. Using the chassis/VIN as the primary key protects against problems as cars are re-registered; using the registration number will cause fewer errors due to finger trouble. Our job is to choose the lesser of two evils; in this case, I would unhesitatingly choose the registration number.

While I have absolutely no experimental evidence to back this up, I have little doubt that insisting that mechanics use the VIN to identify vehicles would introduce more errors into the database than we would reasonably expect to occur from changed registration numbers. In choosing the registration number we also avoid the wrath of the mechanics, who will hate using the VIN. Indeed, human nature being what it is, if we force them to use the VIN they might well introduce errors just to spite us.

I also suspect that a garage that welded cars together in a haphazard and illegal manner wouldn't cavil at altering its own database records in the dead of night.

Before we leave the subject, it is worth noting that genuinely global primary keys are very difficult to find. For example, even assuming that every person was honest, chassis/VINs are imperfect. Early in the history of cars, there was little standardization, and several manufacturers (such as Bentley) used very simple sequences of numbers; a Bentley with chassis number 3 (and hence in modern parlance, VIN 3) still exists, for example. Other manufacturers will have done the same, so we are likely to have multiple cars with VIN 3. This means that in practice, to get a global primary key we would have to use a key combining the manufacturer's name and the chassis/VIN. But for certain old and valuable cars that have undergone extensive modification, crash damage and subsequent rebuilding, it has been known for two perfectly complete cars from the same manufacturer to vie for the same chassis/VIN!

Glossary

This glossary doesn't attempt to define all of the terms used in the book, since I hope that I have defined them as they arise. However, the database world seems to operate on two very different levels. On an everyday level people use words like 'table' to describe the nuts and bolts of a database. At a more rigorous level (specifically in textbooks) people use words like 'relation'.

In practice there are differences between the meanings of these words. Thus a table is not precisely the same thing as a relation. Having said that, it is so nearly the same thing that in practical terms it makes no difference.

You may have problems because some people insist on using the more formal terms in conversation. If they used these more formal terms for reasons of precision I wouldn't mind, but as far as I can see almost inevitably they are used for reasons of obfuscation. (Bill added 'Or elitism, a very common malady'.) In my experience, the people who use terms like 'relation' in conversation rarely understand the subtle difference anyway.

However, you still have a problem if people use terms like 'tuple' and you haven't got the faintest idea what they are talking about.

So, here is a quick bluffer's guide to the database terminology that is not explicitly covered in this book.

Textbook speak	*Normal speak*
Relation	Table
Tuple	Record or Row
Attribute	Field or Column
Cardinality	Number of Records or Rows
Degree	Number of Fields or Columns
Arity (same as Degree)	Number of Fields or Columns
View	Query/Answer Table

Index